SONGS OF AUSTRALIAN WORKING LIFE

To Professor Bruno Nettl,
post-Canberra 1995,
from
Thérèse Radic.
May you waltz on my way again soon.

SONGS OF AUSTRALIAN WORKING LIFE

Compiled by Thérèse Radic

GREENHOUSE
PUBLICATIONS

First published in 1989 by
Greenhouse Publications Pty Ltd
122–126 Ormond Road
Elwood Victoria 3184 Australia

© Thérèse Radic 1989

Designed by Sandra Nobes
Typeset by Trade Graphics Pty. Ltd., Melbourne
Printed in Singapore by Kyodo Shing-Loong

National Library of Australia
Cataloguing-in-publication data:

Songs of Australian Working Life.

ISBN 0 86436 123 8.

1. Work-songs — Australia. 2. Songs, English — Australia. 3. Labor and laboring classes — Australia — Songs and music. I. Radic, Thérèse, 1935–

784.6'8331

All rights reserved. No part of this publication may be reproduced, stored in a retrieval system or transmitted, in any form or by any means, electronic, mechanical, photocopying, recording or otherwise, without the prior permission of the publisher.

Cover illustration 'The Free Selector' from the *Illustrated Australian News* 10/6/1882 reproduced by permission of the La Trobe Collection, State Library of Victoria

Photograph of Therese Radic by Lin Bender

FOREWORD

The labour movement in Australia has had a long and rich tradition of cultural activities, in particular in the area of songs and music. This tradition continues today. It is difficult to imagine Australia's culture without this important and central contribution.

This collection of songs represents a major publication which carefully records this contribution. The ACTU is pleased to have been associated with the project which has led to the collection and publication of this often neglected body of material.

It is pleasing to see it come to fruition in such a high-quality form.

Simon Crean
President
ACTU

Contents

Explanatory Note (x)
Preface (xi)

1. **'Banished from my Native Shore'** 1
   Moreton Bay 1
   The Catalpa 2
   Ben Hall 3
   In a Ramshackle Hut 5
   The Wild Colonial Boy 6
   The Mild Colonial Boy 7

2. **'Shearing Time'** 8
   Click go the Shears 8
   The Springtime it Brings on the Shearing 10
   The Banks of the Condamine (Two Versions) 11
   Flash Jack From Gundagai 13
   Lazy Harry's 14
   All For Me Grog or Across the Western Plains 16
   Australia's Happy Land or Come and Join the Union 18

3. **'We Travel a Lot of Country'** 20
   Travelling Down the Castlereagh 20
   The Flash Stockman 22
   Ladies of Brisbane or Augathella Station 24
   The Maranoa Drover or The Sandy Maranoa 25
   Where the Brumbies Come to Water 27
   The Queensland Drover or The Overlander 28
   The Dying Stockman 29

4. **'I Was a Cane Cutter'** 30
   Cane Killed Abel 30
   The Cane Cutters' Lament 31
   The Cane Gang 32

5. **'And I Whistle Through the Bush'** 33
   My Traps Are All A-Jangle or The Rabbit Trapper's Song 33
   The Buyer On Our Run 34
   Bullocky-O 36
   The Great Northern Line 37
   The Cockies of Bungaree 39
   The Conservationist 40

6. **'A-Digging I Will Go'** 42
   Look Out Below 42
   The Miner 43
   The Chinamen 44
   Man of the Earth 46
   Give Us Our Twopence Back 48

7. **'Here Comes a Union Boy'** 50
   The Union Boy 50
   The Ballad of 1891 51
   After the Strike 52
   Struggle in the West 54
   Hogan's Flat 56

8. **'Freedom in the Land'** 57
   Freedom's on the Wallaby 57
   The Ballad of Eureka 58
   Shores of Botany Bay 59
   To Dr Mannix 61

9. **'The Ship's Under Way'** 62
   Last Work We Go Home 62
   Queensland Whaler 63
   Cock of the Morning or Sailor Home from the Sea 65
   We Built Some Great Ships 66
   Ship Repairing Men 67
   The Anti-Fouling Roll 69

10. **'Oh Hear the Railway Whistle'** 70
    The Launceston and Deloraine Railway 70
    Billy Sheehan 72
    The Granville Rail Disaster 74
    The Poison Train 75

11. **'The Pinch of Want'** 77
    The Hungry Mile 77
    Waltzing Matilda (Two versions) 78
    The Sandy Hollow Line 81
    Soup 83
    Battler's Ballad 84
    Weevils in the Flour 87

12. 'Champions All' 88
Mandrake 88
Les Darcy 90
Keep Your Tail Up, Kangaroo 91
Up There Cazaly 93
The TAB Punters' Song 95

13. 'I'm Tall Dark and Lean'
The Land Where the Crow Flies Backwards 97
Prison's Nothing Special 99
Victor Podham's Rusty Hut 101
Gurindji Blues 103

14. 'Nothing Is As I Would Wish It To Be' 105
The Housewife's Lament 105
The Old Man and His Wife 107
Wallaby Stew 108
Gentle Annie 109
The Rebel Girl 110
Bread and Roses 112
Wife to a Cockie Farmer 113
Hush Little Baby 114
Don't Be Too Polite Girls 115

15. 'The Job is Hard' 117
The Pineapple Trimmers 117
The Boning Room Ladies 118
The Basic Wage Dream 119
A First Class Boiler Maker 120
Isa 121
Song of the Sheetmetal Worker 123
Peter the Cabby 124
Journeyin' 126
Pickin' Up Spuds 127
The Southern Cross Is Calling Me 129
The Westgate Bridge Disaster 131

16. 'Nothing Else To Do' 133
The Weekend Warrior 133

17. ' Now Digger was a Soldier' 135
Freiheit 135
I'm Going Back Again to Yarrawonga 136
Go to the War, Toiler 138
The Peatbog Soldiers 139
Kevin Conway 140
Fixin' to Die Rag 141
Canakkale Icinde At Gallipoli 143

18. 'The Banners of Union' 144
El Pueblo unido 144
Bella Ciao 146
Sebben che siamo donne 147
Ballad of the Sunworshippers 149
Bir Mayis 151
Bellogiannis Lives 153
Australian Steelworks 155

19. 'When the Earth is Owned by Labour' 157
The Commonwealth of Toil 157
Today Black is the Sky 159
The Marseillaise 162
The Internationale 164
The Red Flag 166
Solidarity Forever 168

Guitar Chords 170
Provenance 171
Select Bibliography 191
Index of First Lines 194

ACKNOWLEDGEMENTS

The author and publisher thank the following people and organisations for permission to reproduce their works.

Allans Music (Aust) Pty Ltd for the words and music of *Waltzing Matilda* (Marie Cowan version)
J. Albert & Son, 9 Rangers Road, Neutral Bay 2089 NSW for the words and music of *I'm going back again to Yarrawonga*. Used by permission. All rights reserved.
Peter Hamilton for the words and music of *Gentle Annie* and quote from 'Traditional Singers and Musicians of Victoria. Used by permission. All rights reserved.
Hugh Anderson for permission to reproduce *The Chinamen* from 'Charles Thatcher's Gold Diggers' Songbook' published by Red Rooster Press. Used by permission.
Don Henderson for the words and music of *A first class boiler maker, The Pineapple Trimmers, The Basic Wage Dream* and *Isa*. First published by Horwitz Grahame in 'I Can Sing' (1970).
Phyl Lobl for the words and music of *Man of the earth* and the music for *Give us our twopence back.'*
Richard Keam for the words and music of *Wife to a cocky farmer*.
Glen Tomasetti for the words and music of *Don't be too polite, girls*.
Clem Parkinson for the words and music of *Kevin Conway*.
Linda McLean for permission to reproduce *The Shores of Botany Bay* and *The Sandy Hollow Line* by Duke (H.P.) Tritton.
Ted Edgan for the words and music of *Gurindji Blues* and *The Drover's Boy*.
Kostas Tsourdalakis for the words and music of *Today black is the sky*.
Peter Parkhill for the notation and translation of *Today black is the sky*.
Ken Mansell for the words and music of *The Westgate Bridge Disaster*.
Col Webb for the words and music of *Pickin' up spuds*.
Joe Paolacci for the words and music of *The Southern Cross is calling me*.

Michael Leyden for the music of *Weevils in the flour*.
Dorothy Hewitt for the words to *Weevils in the flour* and *Cock of the morning*
Bill Berry for the music of *Cock of the morning* and *Antifouling Roll*.
Tom Bridges for the words and music of *The Granville Rail Disaster*.
John Dengate for the words and music of *Song of the sheet metal worker* and words to *It's a long way to Cunnamulla*.

And for permission to reproduce photographs on the following pages:
The *Age* pp 4 9 15 23 26 35 64 79 156
La Trobe Collection, State Library of Victoria p 38
John Werrett p 41
V-Line — State Transport Authority p 73
National Library of Australia p 68
from Andrew Reeves' *Another day Another dollar* (Sue McCulloch Melbourne 1988) p 163
from the University of Melbourne Archives, the United Carters and Drivers Union, Eight Hours Procession, 23 April 1906 p 169

From the collection of the South Australian Trades and Labour Council — Support march for the SEQEB June 1985 p 53

■   ■   ■

For their generous support during the research and publication processes essential for the production of this book, I would like to thank:

Jean McClean MLC, Gillian Harrison, Margarita Vasileva, Chris Westwood, Errol O'Neill, Glen Tomasetti, Georgina Binns, Prue N Dorf, Peter O'Shea, Hugh Anderson, Mimi Colligan, Chicka Dixon, Gary Foley, Felix Meagher, Warren Fahey, Dr Jane O'Brien, George and Dr Kay Dreyfus, John Ross, Garrie Hutchinson, Dr Harold Love, Dr Denis Davidson, Dr Percy Jones, Dr Richard Letts and members of the (then) Music Board's Staff, Wendy Lowenstein, Phyl Lobl, Dr Alicia Moyle, Professor Aubrey Pitt, Frank van Straten, Stephen and Len Radic, Sally Milner, Sue Mackinnon, Michelle Johnston.

I am deeply appreciative of the skills and the patience of Graeme Smith, a musicologist specialising in popular music, who acted as research assistant for this book and for its predecessor, *A Treasury of Favourite Australian Songs* (Currey O'Neil 1983, re-issued Viking O'Neil 1988)

Thérèse Radic
Melbourne 1989

EXPLANATORY NOTE

Where the words for the first verse of a song do not fit the melody as used for the other verses the added notes are indicated in brackets e.g.

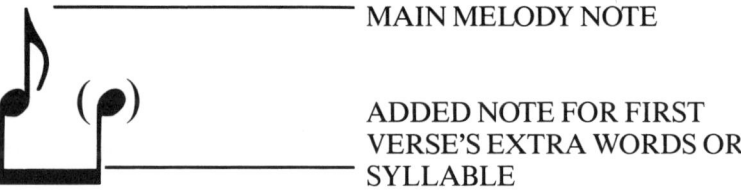

MAIN MELODY NOTE

ADDED NOTE FOR FIRST VERSE'S EXTRA WORDS OR SYLLABLE

PREFACE

The songs in this book celebrate the life and times of those men and women who gave practical shape to the ambitions of our nation builders. They are the songs of Australian workers, songs with music sometimes hundreds of years old, sometimes created only yesterday, songs whose words are based on popular verse forms from European oral traditions far older than the Australian events they describe.

They are songs collected together to demonstrate the vitality of the genre and to map the bare outlines of an evolving and expanding part of musical culture which has received little attention from either Australian historians or musicologists. It is a personal collection. It makes no attempt at representational balance, whether musical, historical, occupational or ethnic. It could hardly be otherwise, given the present pioneering nature of research into the uses of music by the Australian worker.

The majority of the songs have their remote origins in Anglo-Saxon and Celtic folk traditions, but there are also songs by Aboriginal singers using familiar American sources, as well as songs from ethnic communities whose musical idioms are still strange to us.

The collection begins with the songs of convicts sentenced to hard labour and ends with songs by migrants who chose hard labour here as the only way to dig themselves and their families out of economic disasters elsewhere. In between are the songs of shearers and swaggies, drovers and stockmen, bushrangers and rebels, cane cutters, rabbiters, bullockies and teamsters, cockies, miners, unionists, wharfies and dockers, sailors and whalers, soldiers and sportsmen, housewives, factory operatives, metalworkers, and meatworkers, cabbies, navvies, and out of work battlers. They speak, often bitterly and as often with humour, of hard labour and hard times, of poverty and sorrow, of exile and exploitation, of monotony and loneliness, dirt, drink and compulsive gambling, violence and cruelty, of injustice and of ways to remedy it, of the crucial roles of friendship and loyalty, of the need for unity of purpose and political action for the common good, and of the continual struggle to live with dignity and honour.

The earlier songs in the collection are survivors from an oral tradition in a state of eclipse at the time of the folk revival in the late 1950s. For a brief time, a small number of untrained collectors went into the field armed with nothing more than early model tape recorders and, it has been said elsewhere, inspired by politically left wing ideals of cultural nationalism.

They were preceeded, in the 1930s by A.L. Lloyd, the English musicologist and, in the late 40s, by the Rev. Dr Percy Jones, a Melbourne Catholic priest and later vice-director of the Faculty of Music at the University of Melbourne. The revival collectors included John Meredith and Bill and Alan Scott in New South Wales, Ron Edwards in Queensland, and Norm and Pat O'Connor with Mary Jean Officer in Victoria, together with the activists of the Sydney Bush Music Club and the folkmusic clubs of Victoria and Queensland. Their recordings were translated into simple transcriptions and published, first in club journals, then in book form, in the late 1960s and 70s. These were followed by the development of ideas about the historical and social significance of the songs through written commentaries by writer-collectors: Edgar Waters, John Manifold, Wendy Lowenstein and the prolific Hugh Anderson among others. Warren Fahey has disseminated much of the music through broadcasting of material from his own more technically sophisticated re-recordings of the first collectors' major folk singers and instrumentalists, and under his commercial label, Larrikin Records.

The later songs are by composers and writers who have built on the Australian folk tradition but who have also added elements from more recent popular song forms or from folk and popular music traditions, more recently revived among migrant practitioners from other cultures.

But the collection also contains songs not directly related to Australia. These are the battle hymns of the world-wide labour and protest movements, familiar to workers everywhere and adopted by the union movement in Australia. To these have been added more recent freedom songs, now in the process of being grafted on to our tradition through younger voices from older lands.

At the back of the book there are notes giving what is currently known of the origins of both words and music: who first collected them, published them, composed them. Any new information and any new songs would be warmly welcomed.

In looking for material for this book I have been impressed by the size and rapid growth of the repertoire, by the persistence of the genre over time, and by its ability to survive the political factions and intellectual fashions which adopt it. The emotional strength of the texts and the diversity and worth of the musical sources have earned my respect, as have the people who created them.

Thérèse Radic
Melbourne
1989

Banished from my Native Shore
MORETON BAY

One Sunday morning as I went walking, by Brisbane Waters I chanced to stray;
I heard a prisoner his fate bewailing, as on the sunny river bank he lay:
'I am a native of Erin's island, and banished now from my native shore;
They tore me from my aged parents and from the maiden whom I do adore.

'I've been a prisoner at Port Macquarie, at Norfolk Island and Emu Plains,
At Castle Hill and at cursed Toongabbie, at all those settlements I've worked in chains;
But of all places of condemnation and penal stations of New South Wales,
To Moreton Bay I have found no equal; excessive tyranny each day prevails.

'For three long years I was beastly treated, and heavy irons on my legs I wore;
My back with flogging is lacerated and often painted with my crimson gore.
And many a man from downright starvation lies mouldering now underneath the clay;
And Captain Logan he had us mangled at the triangles of Moreton Bay.

'Like the Egyptians and ancient Hebrews we were oppressed under Logan's yoke,
Till a native black lying there in ambush did give our tyrant his mortal stroke,
My fellow prisoners, be exhilerated that all such monsters such a death may find!
And when from bondage we are liberated our former suffering shall fade from mind.'

The Catalpa

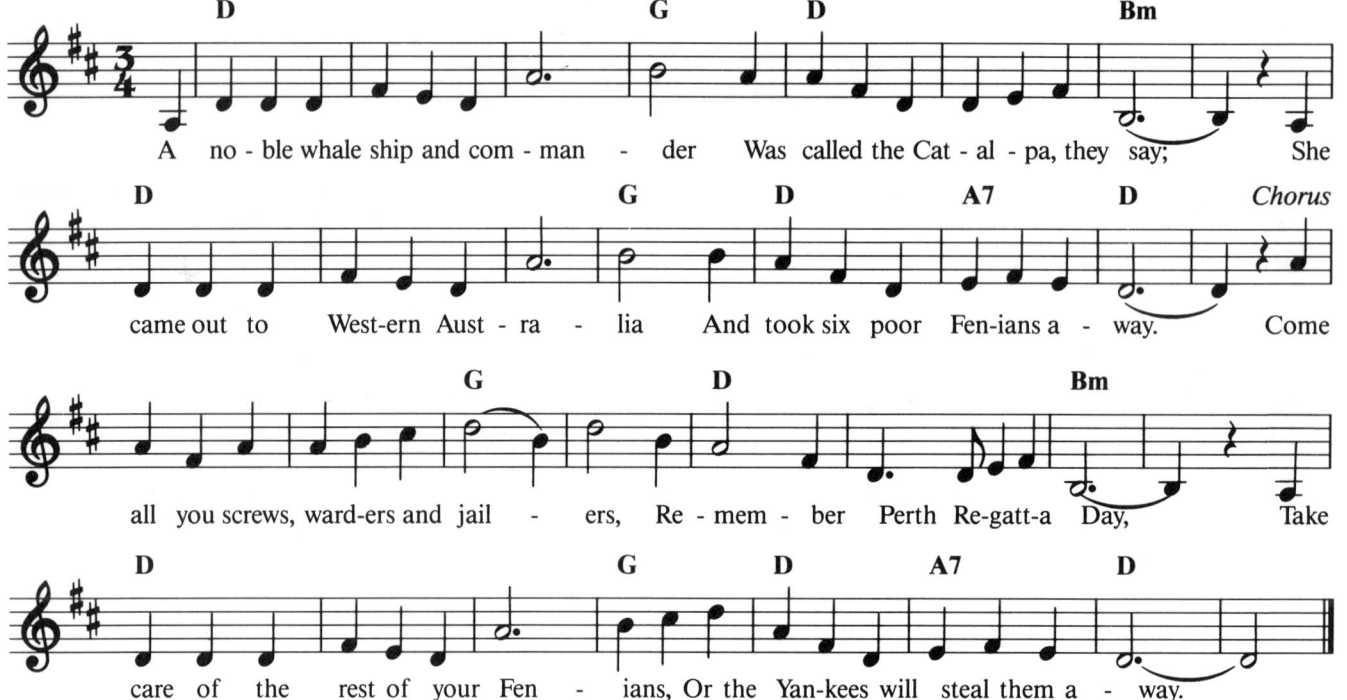

A noble whale ship and commander
Was called the Catalpa, they say;
She came out to Western Australia
And took six poor Fenians away.

Chorus:
Come all you screws, warders and jailers,
Remember Perth Regatta Day,
Take care of the rest of your Fenians,
Or the Yankees will steal them away.

For seven long years they had served here,
And seven long more had to stay,
For defending their country, Old Ireland,
For that they were banished away.

You kept them in Western Australia
Till their hair had begun to turn grey,
When a Yank from the States of America
Came out here and stole them away.

Now all the Perth boats were a-racing,
And making short tacks for the spot,
But the Yankee tacked into Fremantle
And took the best prize of the lot.

The Georgette, armed with bold warriors,
Went out the poor Yanks to arrest,
But she hoisted her star-spangled banner,
Saying, 'You will not board me, I guess'.

So remember those Fenians colonial,
And sing these few verses with skill,
And remember the Yankee that stole them
And the home that they left on the hill.

And now they're safe in America,
And there will be able to cry,
'Hoist up the green flag and shamrock,
Hurrah! for Old Ireland we'll die!'

BEN HALL

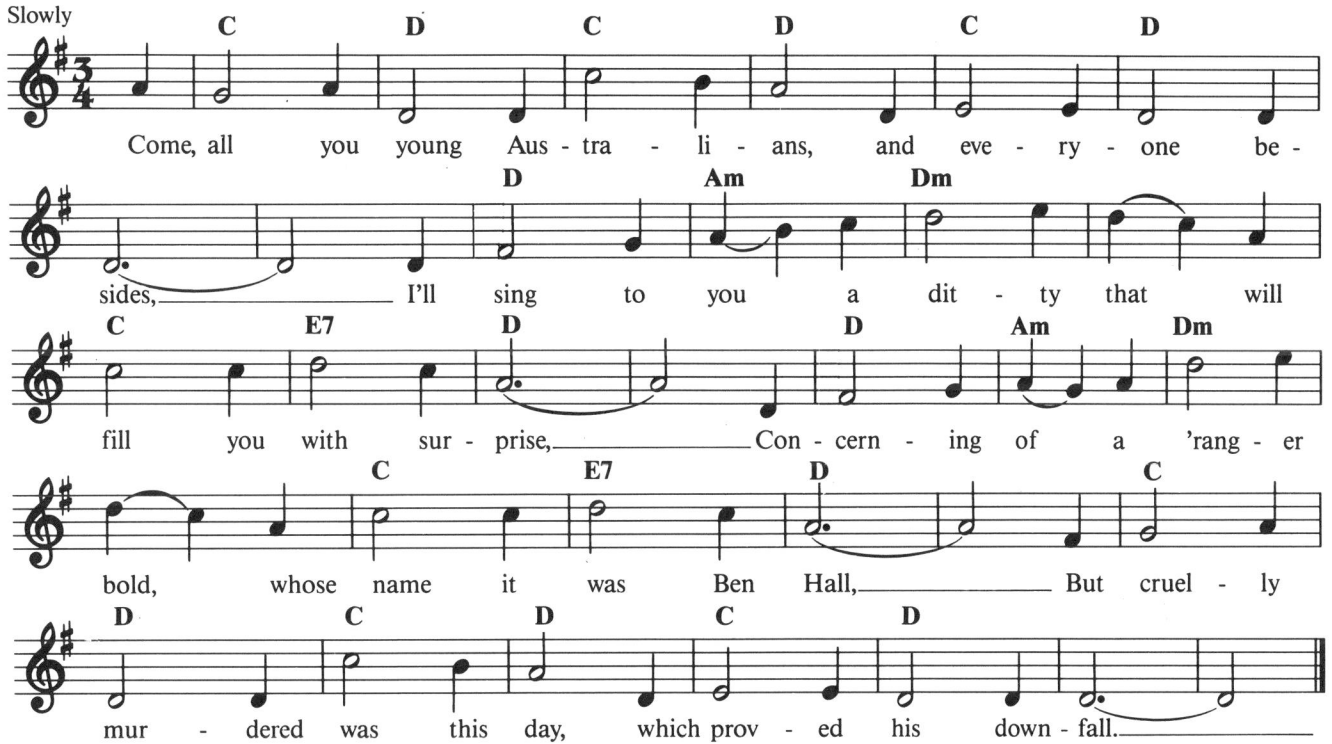

Come, all you young Australians, and everyone besides,
I'll sing to you a ditty that will fill you with surprise,
Concerning of a 'ranger bold, whose name it was Ben Hall,
But cruelly murdered was this day, which proved his downfall.

An outcast from society, he was forced to take the road,
All through his false and treacherous wife, who sold off his abode.
He was hunted like a native dog from bush to hill and dale,
Till he turned upon his enemies and they could not find his trail.

All out with his companions, men's blood he scorned to shed,
He oft-times stayed their lifted hands, with vengeance on their heads.
No petty, mean or pilfering act he ever stooped to do,
But robbed the rich and hearty man, and scorned to rob the poor.

One night as he in ambush lay all on the Lachlan Plain,
When, thinking everything secure, to ease himself had lain,
When to his consternation and to his great surprise,
And without one moment's warning, a bullet past him flies.

And it was soon succeeded by a volley sharp and loud,
With twelve revolving rifles all pointed at his head.
'Where are you, Gilbert? Where is Dunn?' he loudly did call.
It was all in vain, they were not there to witness his downfall.

They riddled all his body as if they were afraid,
But in his dying moment he breathed curses on their heads.
That cowardly hearted Condel, the sergeant of the police,
He crept and fired with fiendish glee till death did him release.

Although he had a lion's heart, more braver than the brave,
Those cowards shot him like a dog – no word of challenge gave.
Though many friends had poor Ben Hall, his enemies were few,
Like the emblems of his native land, his days were numbered too.

It's through Australia's sunny clime Ben Hall will roam no more.
His name is spread both near and far to every distant shore.
For generations after his parents will to their children call,
And rehearse to them the daring deeds committed by Ben Hall.

In A Ramshackle Hut

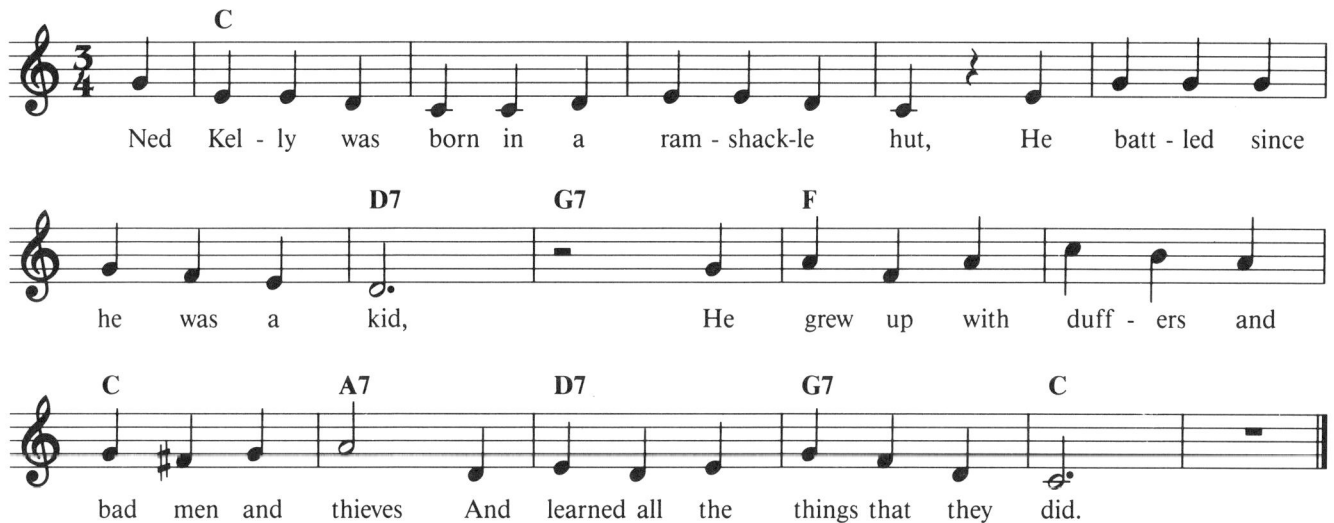

Ned Kelly was born in ramshackle hut,
He battled since he was a kid,
He grew up with duffers and bad men and thieves
And learned all the things that they did.

Ned Kelly would ride from the back-country hills,
He'd ride into town like a lord,
He'd steal all the squatters' fine horses, and then–
He would take them back for the reward.

At sixteen young Ned was a wild, reckless lad,
Helped hold up a coach without fear,
But he was arrested, remanded, and then,
They put him in gaol for a year.

When he came out, he was bitter and hard,
Far worse than he ever had been,
He robbed and he plundered, became a wild boy,
The wildest Australia had seen.

He shot down the troopers who came on his track,
And laughed at the price on his head,
Ten thousand pounds for the whole of the gang,
And two thousand pounds just for Ned.

The bank at Jerilderie next took his eye,
This job brought him lots of renown,
He wasn't contented to stick up the bank,
But he held up the whole flaming town.

Down at Glenrowan they held up the pub,
They were having a drink and a song,
The troopers rode up and surrounded the place,
The Kellys had waited too long.

Ned came out shooting, a gun in each hand,
And wearing his armour of steel,
He was fifteen times wounded before he fell down,
Never more would he plunder and steal.

They took him to Melbourne, and nursed him to health,
The judge said, 'You're guilty!' to Ned,
A rope from a rafter, the sun in the east,
And the famous Ned Kelly was dead.

Some say he's a hero who gave to the poor,
While others 'A killer!' they say,
It just goes to show the old saying is true,
The saying that 'Crime does not pay'.

Yet when I look round at some people I know,
And the prices of things that I buy,
I say to myself, 'Well, perhaps after all,
Poor Ned wasn't such a bad guy.'

THE WILD COLONIAL BOY

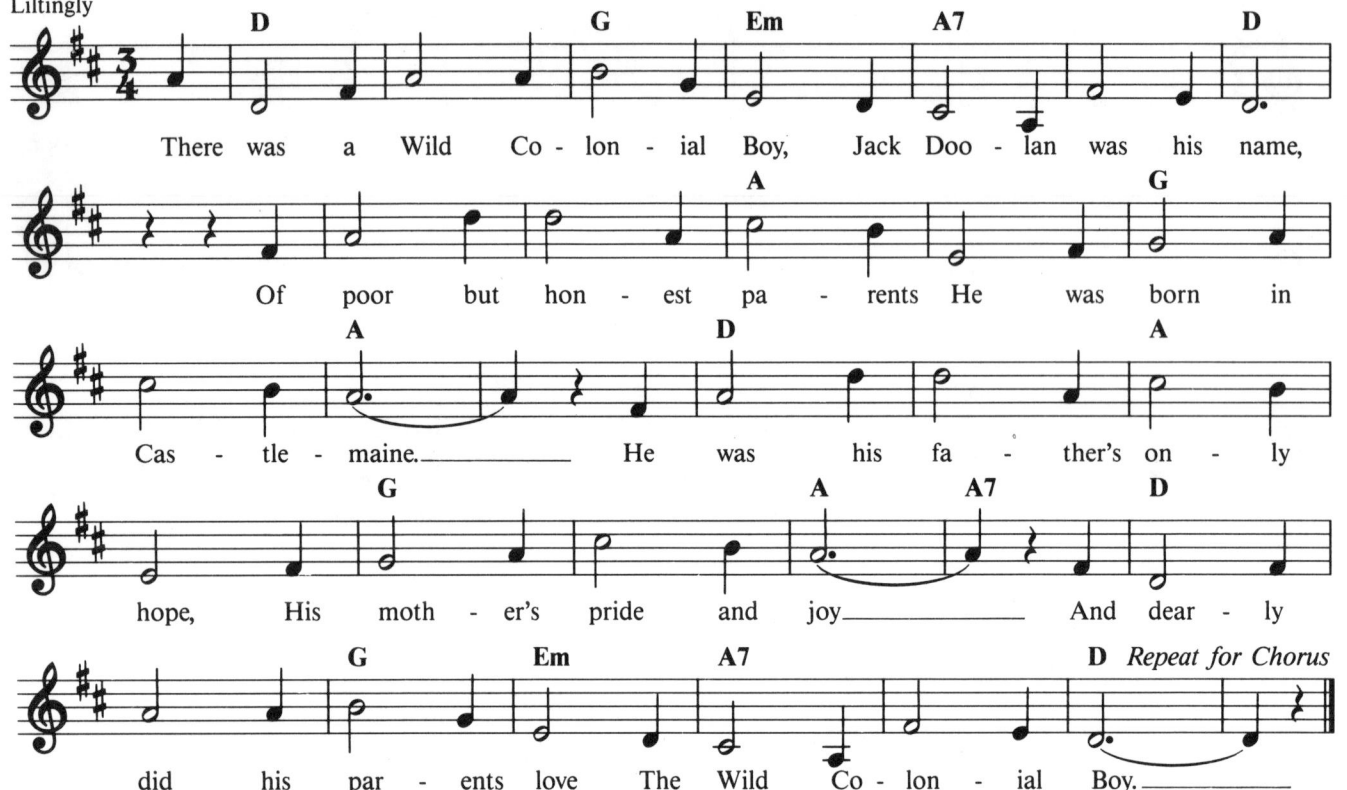

There was a Wild Colonial Boy,
Jack Doolan was his name,
Of poor but honest parents
He was born in Castlemaine.
He was his father's only hope,
His mothers' pride and joy
And dearly did his parents love
The Wild Colonial Boy.

Chorus:
So come away me hearties
We'll roam the mountains high,
Together we will plunder
And together we will die.
We'll scour along the valleys
And we'll gallop o'er the plains,
And scorn to live in slavery,
Bound down by iron chains.

At the age of sixteen years
He left his native home,
And to Australia's sunny shores,
A bushranger did roam.
They put him in the iron gang
In the government employ,
But never an iron on earth could hold
The Wild Colonial Boy.

In sixty-one this daring youth
Commenced his wild career,
With a heart that knew no danger
And no foeman did he fear.
He stuck up the Beechworth mail coach
And robbed Judge MacEvoy
Who, trembling cold, gave up his gold
To the Wild Colonial Boy.

He bade the judge good morning
And he told him to beware,
That he'd never rob a needy man
Or one who acted square,
But a judge who'd rob a mother
Of her one and only joy
Sure, he must be a worse outlaw than
The Wild Colonial Boy.

One day as Jack was riding
The mountainside along,
A-listening to the little birds,
Their happy laughing song.
Three mounted troopers came along,
Kelly, Davis and Fitzroy
With a warrant for the capture of
The Wild Colonial Boy.

'Surrender now! Jack Doolan,
For you see it's three to one;
Surrender in the Queen's own name,
You are a highwayman.'
Jack drew a pistol from his belt
And waved it like toy,
'I'll fight, but not surrender,' cried
The Wild Colonial Boy.

He fired at trooper Kelly
And brought him to the ground,
And in return from Davis
Received a mortal wound,
All shattered through the jaws he lay
Still firing at Fitzroy.
And that's the way they captured him,
The Wild Colonial Boy.

THE MILD COLONIAL BOY

There was a mild colonial boy, by name of R.J. Hawke
You'd think that he was Jesus Christ to hear the bastard talk
He is the system's only hope, the bosses pride and joy;
The darling of the media is this Mild Colonial Boy

He's never faced election by the worker's rank and file
Yet every night on telly, we're condemned to watch his dial.
He'll scowl and raise an eyebrow, 'tis nothing but a ploy
A useless bloody tame-cat is the Mild Colonial Boy.

He growls and drops expletives in a manner rather fierce.
He's just about as radical as good old Eric Pierce.
He claims to be a socialist, he's not the real McCoy,
A Labor opportunist is the Mild Colonial Boy.

He loves to meet with Fraser, and they have such cosy chats.
He's loaded with ambition, and he wears too many hats.
An action that is militant is certain to annoy
That gruff abrasive cream-puff called the Mild Colonial Boy.

And if he gets to parliament, we know he'll never stop
Till he's the biggest windbag in that well known talking shop
He'll shower them with bulldust, for he's seldom ever coy,
And that's the last we'll hear of him, the Mild Colonial Boy.

Shearing Time
Click Go The Shears

Out on the board the old shearer stands,
Grasping his shears in his thin bony hands;
Fixed is his gaze on a bare-bellied yoe,
Glory if he gets her, won't he make the ringer go.

Chorus:
Click go the shears boys, click, click, click,
Wide is his blow and his hands move quick,
The ringer looks around and is beaten by a blow,
And curses the old snagger with the bare-bellied yoe.

In the middle of the floor in his cane bottomed chair
Sits the boss of the board with his eyes everywhere,
Notes well each fleece as it comes to the screen,
Paying strict attention that it's taken off clean.

The colonial experience man, he is there of course,
With his shiny leggin's on, just got off his horse,
Gazes all around him like a real connoisseur,
Scented soap and brilliantine and smelling like a whore.

The tar-boy is there waiting in demand
With his blackened tar-pot, in his tarry hand,
Spies one old sheep with a cut upon it's back,
Here's what he's waiting for it's 'Tar here, Jack!'

Now the shearing is all over, we've all got our cheques,
So roll up your swags and it's off down the track,
The first pub we come to it's there we'll have a spree
And everyone that comes along it's 'Have a drink with me'.

There we leave him standing shouting for all hands,
Whilst all around him every 'shouter' stands,
His eye is on the keg which now is lowering fast,
He works hard, he drinks hard, and goes to hell at last!

The Springtime It Brings On The Shearing

Words derived from E.J. Overbury's 'The Wallaby Track'.

The springtime it brings on the shearing,
And it's then you will see them in droves,
To the west-country stations all steering,
A-seeking a job off the coves.

Chorus:
With my raggedy old swag on my shoulder
And a billy quart-pot in my hand,
I tell you we'll 'stonish the new chums,
When they see how we travel the land.

From Boonabri up to the border,
Then it's over to Bourke; there and back.
On the hills and the plains you will see them,
The men on the Wallaby Track.

And after the shearing is over
And the wool season's all at an end,
It is then you will see the flash shearers
Making johnny-cakes round in the bend.

THE BANKS OF THE CONDAMINE

Man:
O hark the dogs are barking, love, I can no longer stay;
The men are all gone mustering, and it is nearly day.
And I must be off by morning light before the sun does shine,
To meet the Roma shearers on the banks of the Condamine.

Girl:
O Willy, dearest Willy, O let me go with you!
I'll cut off all my auburn fringe, and be a shearer too;
I'll cook and count your tally, love, while ringer- o you shine,
And I'll wash your greasy moleskins on the banks of the Condamine.

Man:
O Nancy, dearest Nancy, with me you cannot go!
The squatters have given orders, love, no woman should do so.
And your delicate constitution is not equal unto mine,
To withstand the constant tigering on the banks of the Condamine.

Girl:
O Willy, dearest Willy, then stay at home with me;
We'll take up a selection, and a farmer's wife I'll be.
I'll help you husk the corn, love, and cook your meals so fine
You'll forget the ram-stag mutton on the banks of the Condamine.

Man:
O Nancy, dearest Nancy, pray do not hold me back!
Down there the boys are waiting, and I must be on the track.
So here's a goodbye kiss, love; back home I will incline
When we've shore the last of the jumbucks on the banks of the Condamine.

The Banks Of The Condamine

Alternative version

'Hark, hark, the dogs are barking.
My love, I must away,
For the lads they're all horse-breaking;
No longer can I stay.
I'm bound for the camp, my love;
'Tis many a weary mile
To join those jolly horse-breakers
On the banks of the Condamine.'

Oh Willie, dearest Willie,
Don't leave me here behind
To curse and rue the day that
You ever learnt to ride;
For parting with my own true love's
Like parting with my life.
Why don't you be a selector
And I will be your wife?

'I'll cut off all my yellow locks
And go along with you,
Put on a pair of moleskins
And be a rider too;
I'll cook and boil your billy while
At riding you doth shine,
And I'll wash your dirty moleskins
On the banks of the Condamine.'

'Oh, Nancy, dearest Nancy,
With me you cannot go,
For the boss has just gave orders–
No females there, you know.
Your delicate constitution's
Not equal unto mine;
Then you could not ride an outlaw
On the banks of the Condamine.'

Flash Jack From Gundagai

Words from Banjo Paterson's 'Old Bush Songs'.

I've shore at Burrabogie, and I've shore at Toganmain,
I've shore at big Willandra and on the old Coleraine,
But before the shearin' was over I've wished myself back again
Shearin' for old Tom Patterson, on the One Tree Plain.

Chorus:
All among the wool, boys, all among the wool,
Keep your blades full boys, keep your blades full.
I can do a respectable tally myself whenever I like to try,
And they know me round the backblocks as Flash Jack from Gundagai.

I've shore at big Willandra and I've shore at Tilberoo,
And once I drew my blades, my boys, upon the famed Barcoo,
At Cowan Downs and Trida, as far as Moulamein,
But I always was glad to get back again to the One Tree Plain.

I've pinked 'em with the Wolseleys and I've rushed with B-bows, too,
And shaved 'em in the grease, my boys, with the grass seed showing through.
But I never slummed my pen, my lads, whate'er it might contain,
While shearin' for old Tom Patterson, on the One Tree Plain.

I've been whalin' up the Lachlan, and I've dossed on Cooper's Creek,
And once I rung Cudjingie shed, and blued it in a week.
But when Gabriel blows his trumpet, lads, I'll catch the morning train,
And I'll push for old Tom Patterson's on the One Tree Plain.

LAZY HARRY'S

Words from Banjo Paterson's 'Old Bush Songs'.

This next tune is the more popular one.

We started down from Reio (Roto) when the sheds had all cut out,
We'd whips and whips of rhino that we'd want to knock about,
So we shouldered our Matildas and we headed out for town,
With a three spot cheque between us that wanted knocking down.

We crossed the Murrumbidgee near the Yanko in a week,
We passed through old Narrandera and we camped on Burnett Creek,
We never stopped at Wagga, for we'd Sydney in our eye,
But we camped at Lazy Harry's on the road to Gundagai.

I've met a lot of girls me boys, and drunk a lot of beer,
I've met some funny customers that left me kind of queer,
But for beer to knock you sideways and for girls that'd make you sigh,
You must camp at Lazy Harry's on the road to Gundagai.

We slings off our Matildas and we walked into the bar,
And called for rum and rasberry and a shilling each cigar,
And the girl that served the prenzo, she winked at Bill and I,
So we camped at Lazy Harry's on the road to Gundagai.

In three weeks our spree was over and our cheques were all knocked down,
So we shouldered our Matildas and headed out of town,
And the girls they stood a nobbler as we sadly said goodbye,
And we tramped from Lazy Harry's on the road to Gundagai.

Across The Western Plains
or All For Me Grog

At an easy, contemplative pace

Well I am a ramblin' lad, and me story it is sad,
If ever I get to Lachlan I should wonder,
For I spent all me brass in the bottom of the glass,
And across the western plains I must wander.

Chorus:
And it's all for me grog, me jolly, jolly grog,
It's all for me beer and tobacco,
For I spent all me tin in a shanty drinking gin,
Now across the western plains I must wander.

Well I'm stiff, stony broke and I've parted from me moke,
And the sky is lookin' black as flamin' thunder;
The shanty boss is blue 'cause I haven't got a sou,
That's the way they treat you when you're down and under.

I'm crook in the head and I haven't been to bed,
 Since first I touched this shanty with me plunder.
I see centipedes and snakes, and I'm full of aches and shakes,
And I think it's time to push for way out yonder.

I'll take to the Old Man Plain, and criss-cross him once again,
Until me eyes the track no longer see, boys;
And me beer and whisky brain search for sleep, but all in vain,
And I feel as if I've had the Darling Pea, boys.

So it's hang yer jolly grog, yer hocussed shanty grog,
The beer that is loaded with tobacco;
Graftin' humour I am in, and I'll stick the peg right in
And settle down once more to some hard yakka.

Australia's Happy Land
or Come And Join The Union

The shearing's nearly over, but with many, much I fear,
The price they tried to cut down has cost them very dear.
So give your kind attention, and I'll tell you in my song
Of squatters and those shearer boys, the way they jog along.
The life is one of luxury, it's truly something grand
To be a roving shearer in Australia's Happy Land.

In February, eighty-six, I left Burke with a sigh,
I saddled up my neddies and bade the girls good-bye,
My friends and I together, for Nocoleche bound,
To meet those Paroo squatters, and fight them for the pound.
They used the 'Town and Country' to break up our gallant band,
But we sent the cry of victory through Australia's Happy Land.

It's now some sixteen years ago, I had a friendly glass,
The 'City arms' being patronized by the hard-working class.
I say its years are past and gone, yet proud am I to see,
That vendor of cheap Carlton, Lord of Tinapagee –
Audacious the expressions does his ignorance think grand,
'I'll starve you to submission in Australia's Happy Land.'

The fight ended – then to shearing, but soon we had to stop;
The flood it spread like lightning from Wanarring to Dunlop.
You might think they'd lend a neddy for to run your horses in
But on Noc, there's no assistance, you may sink or you may swim.
With your bridle strap around you, it was truly something grand,
To swim through the flood-waters of Australia's Happy Land.

Our horses got, we started, the country all a lake,
It was hard to find a dry spot to cook your johnny-cake.
With clothes wet through and blankets, to sleep in quite a treat,
I really can't imagine how a man could have the cheek –
Did Trollope have to foot it through the Paroo's heavy sand,
With his 'one continuous picnic' in Australia's Happy Land?

To bring down the price of shearing, did you skite you had the knack,
Grass seeds are bad round Paddington, 'What! not cut out yet, Mac?'
It wants but a beginning, to sign I know they'll dart,
With crawlers two and a jackaroo, you made a noble start.
Did men come out from Dunlop, did they make you understand,
Did you really say a pound you'd pay in Australia's Happy Land?

The price of wool is very low, the rents are very high,
'Another rub our runs to scrub', that's been the squatter's cry.
But come and join our union, adopt no crying plan,
Publish each clause, your union's laws, so break them if you can.
Rally to the union, boys, oh don't give up your stand
To vice-creating pig-tails in Australia's Happy Land.

Live on Kanaka Queensland, and boast your slavery tales,
Let us breathe the air of freedom at least in New South Wales.
Oh! Let us boast a union in every country town,
Capital then will have to cease to pull the workmen down.
Come, roll up to the union, let not one vacant stand,
You then can say 'I'll have fair play, in Australia's Happy Land.

Once more, boys, join the union, stand out you'll sure repent,
No squatter in Australia dare to face a union's strength.
Victoria boasts her union, South Aus' can do the same,
No need to come – but send the sum – five shillings – and your name.
Three colonies together, all walking hand in hand,
You then can cry in voices high – Australia's Happy Land!

We Travel a Lot of Country

TRAVELLING DOWN THE CASTLEREAGH

Words adapted from Banjo Paterson's 'A Bushman's Song' by Joe Cashmere.

I'm travelling down the Castlereagh, I am a station hand,
I'm handy with the roping pole, I'm handy with the brand,
And I can ride a rowdy colt, or swing an axe all day,
But there's no demand for a station-hand along the Castlereagh.

Shift, boys, shift, there's not the slightest doubt
It's time to make a shift to the stations farther out,
Your pack-horse running after, he follows you like a dog,
We travel a lot of country at the old jig-jog.

This old black horse I'm riding–if you wish to know his brand,
He's branded with the crooked R–none better in the land.
He takes a lot of beating; the other day we tried,
For a bit of a joke, with a racy bloke, for twenty pound a side.

It was shift, boys, shift, there wasn't the slightest doubt
We had to make him shift for our money was near run out,
But he cantered home a winner, while the other one had to flog–
He's a good old sort for the pick up, with his old jig-jog.

I asked a bloke for shearing once, down on the Marthaguy:
'We shear non-union here', he said. 'I call it scab', said I.
I looked along the shearing board before I chanced to go–
Saw eight to ten dashed Chinamen all shearing in a row.

It was shift, boys, shift, there's not the slightest doubt
For it's time I made a shift with the leprosy about.
I saddled up my horses, and I whistled to my dog;
I left that scabby station at the old jig-jog.

I called at Illawarra, where my brother keeps a farm;
He has to ask the landlord's leave before he'd raise an arm:
The landlord owns the countryside–man, woman, dog, and cat,
They haven't the cheek to dare to speak unless they raise their hat.

It was shift, boys, shift, there's not the slighest doubt
That squatter chap and I we would soon be falling out;
Was I to raise my hat to him?–was I a blooming dog?
I struck for up the country at the old jig-jog.

But it's time that I was movin', I've a mighty way to go.
Till I drink artesian water from a thousand feet below;
Till I meet the overlanders with the cattle comin' down–
And I'll work a while till I makes a pile, then have a spree in town.

So it's shift, boys, shift, for there isn't the slightest doubt
We've got to make a shift to the stations further out;
The pack horse runs behind us, for he follows like a dog,
And we cross a lot of country at the old jig-jog.

THE FLASH STOCKMAN

I'm a stockman to my trade, and they call me ugly Dave,
I'm old and grey and only got one eye;
In a yard I'm good, of course, but just put me on a horse,
And I'll go where lots of young uns daren't try.

I lead 'em through the gidgee over country rough and ridgy,
I lose 'em in the very worst of scrub;
I can ride both rough and easy, with a dewdrop I'm a daisy,
And a right-down bobby-dazzler in a pub.

Just watch me use a whip, I can give the dawdlers gyp,
I can make the bloody echoes roar and ring;
With a branding iron, well, I'm a perfect flaming swell,
In fact, I'm duke of every blasted thing.

To watch me skin a sheep, it's so lovely you could weep,
I can act the silvertail as if my blood was blue;
You can strike me pink or dead, if I stood upon my head,
I'd be just as good as any other two.

I've a notion in my pate, that it's luck, it isn't fate,
That I'm so far above the common run;
So in every thing I do, you could cut me fair in two,
For I'm much too bloody good to be in one.

LADIES OF BRISBANE
or Augathella Station

Farewell and adieu to you, sweet Brisbane ladies,
Farewell and adieu to you girls of Toowong,
For we've sold all our cattle, and have to be moving,
But we hope we shall see you again before long.

Chorus:
We'll rant and we'll roar like true Queensland drovers,
We'll rant and we'll roar as onwards we push,
Until we get back to the Augathella Station,
For it's flaming dry going through the old Queensland bush.

The first camp we make, we shall call it the Quart-pot,
Caboolture, then Kilcoy and Colinton's Hut;
We'll pull up at the Stone House, Bob Williamson's paddock,
And early next morning we cross the Blackbutt.

Then on to Taromeo and Yarraman Creek, lads,
It's there we shall make our next camp for the day,
Where the water and grass are both plenty and sweet, lads,
And maybe we'll butcher a fat little stray.

Then on to Nanango, that hardbitten township,
Where the out-of-work station hands sit in the dust,
And the shearers get shorn by old Tim the contractor –
Oh I wouldn't go near there but I flaming well must!

The girls of Toomancey, they look so entrancing,
Those young bawling heifers are out for their fun!
With the waltz and the polka and all kinds of dancing,
To the racketty old banjo of Bob Anderson.

Then fill up your glasses and drink to the lasses;
We'll drink this town dry, then farewell to them all;
And when we've got back to the Augathella Station
We'll hope you come by there and pay us a call.

THE MARANOA DROVER
or The Sandy Maranoa

The night is dark and stormy and the sky is clouded o'er,
Our horses we will mount and ride away,
To watch the squatter's cattle through the darkness of the night,
And we'll keep them on the camp till break of day.

Chorus:
Oh, we're going, going, going to Gunnedah so far,
And soon we'll be in sunny New South Wales,
And we'll shout hurray for Queensland with the swampy coolibah,
Happy drovers from the sandy Maranoa.

When the fires are burning bright through the darkness of the night,
And the cattle camping quiet, well I'm sure,
That I wish for two o'clock when I call the other watch–
This is droving from the sandy Maranoa.

With our beds made on the ground and we're sleeping all so sound,
We're wakened by the distant thunder's roar,
With the lightning's vivid flash followed by an awful crash,
Rough on drovers from the sandy Maranoa.

We're up at break of day and we're all soon on our way,
We've always got to do ten miles or so,
It don't do to loaf about, lest the squatter might come out,
He's rough on drovers from the sandy Maranoa.

We shall soon be on the Moonie, and we'll cross the Barwon, too,
Then we'll be out upon the rolling plains once more,
We'll shout hurrah for Queensland with its swampy coolibah,
And the cattle that come off the Maranoa.

Where The Brumbies Come To Water

Words based on verses by Will Ogilvie

There's a lonely grave half hidden
Where the blue-grass droops above,
And a slab that roughly marks it
For we planted it with love,
There's a mourning rank of riders
Closing in on every hand
O'er the vacant place he left us,
He was the best of all the band,
But he's lying cold and silent
With his hidden hopes unwon,
Where the brumbies come to water
At the setting of the sun.

There's a well worn saddle hanging
In the harness room at home,
And a good old stock-horse waiting
For the steps that never come,
His dog will lick some other hand,
And when the wild mob swings,
We'll get some slower rider
To replace him on the wings,
But who will kiss his little wife,
Who kneels beyond the long lagoon,
Where the brumbies come to water
At the rising of the moon.

We'll miss him in the cattle camp,
A trusted man and true,
For the daddy of all stockmen
Was 'Bold Jack' Donahue,
We'll miss the tunes he used to play
On his banjo, soft and low,
We'll miss the songs he used to sing
Of the days of long ago,
Where the shadow line is broken
'Neath the moon-beams silver bars,
Where the brumbies come to water
At the twinkling of the stars.

THE QUEENSLAND DROVER
or The Overlander

There's a trade you all know well,
It's bringing cattle over.
On every track, to the Gulf and back,
Men know the Queensland drover.

Chorus:
Pass the billy round, boys!
Don't let the pint-pot stand there!
For tonight we drink the health
Of every overlander.

I come from the northern plains
Where the girls and grass are scanty;
Where the creeks run dry or ten foot high
And it's either drought or plenty.

There are men from every land,
From Spain and France and Flanders;
They're a well-mixed pack, both white and black,
The Queensland overlanders.

When we've earned a spree in town
We live like pigs in clover;
And the whole year's cheque pours down the neck
Of many a Queensland drover.

As I pass along the roads,
The children raise my dander
Crying 'Mother dear, take in the clothes,
Here comes an overlander!'

Now I'm bound for home once more,
On a prad that's quite a goer;
I can find a job with a crawling mob
On the banks of the Maranoa.

THE DYING STOCKMAN

Parody on the music of Charles Coote on words of
C.J. Whyte Melville for 'The Tarpaulin Jacket'

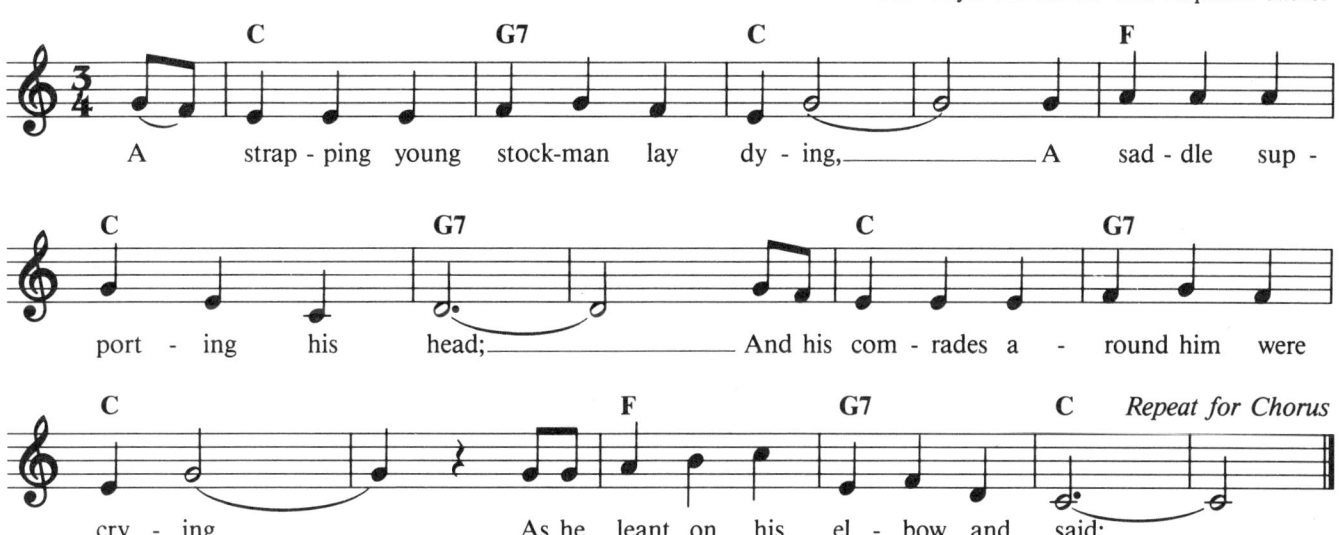

A strapping young stockman lay dying,
A saddle supporting his head;
And his comrades around him were crying
As he leant on his elbow and said:

Chorus:
Wrap me up in my stockwhip and blanket
And bury me deep down below,
Where the dingoes and crows will not find me,
In the shade where the coolibahs grow.

Cut down a couple of saplings,
Place one at my head and my toe;
Carve on them a stockwhip and saddle
To show there's a stockman below.

There's some tea in that battered old billy,
Place the pannikins all in a row,
And we'll drink to the next merry meeting,
In the place where all good stockmen go.

I hear the wail of a dingo,
In the gloom of the scrub down below,
And he rings the knell of a stockman,
Farewell, dear old pals, I must go.

If I had the wings of a pigeon,
Far over the plains I would fly;
I'd fly to the arms of my loved ones,
And there I would lay down and die.

I Was a Cane Cutter
Cane Killed Abel

Words by Merv Lilley. Music by Chris Kempster.

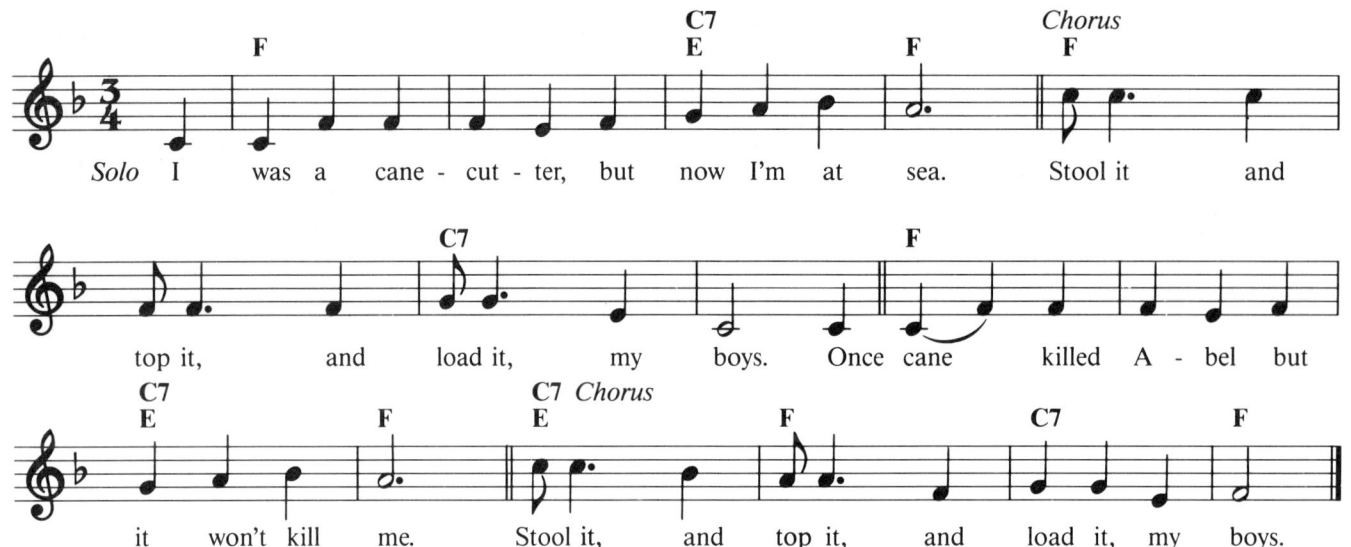

Solo: I was a cane cutter, but now I'm at sea,
Chorus: Stool it, and top it, and load it, my boys.
Solo: Once cane killed Abel, but it won't kill me,
Chorus: Stool it, and top it, and load it, my boys.

(Solo lines only)
There was an old seaman who sang this refrain,
He stood to the bar and he filled up again.

I rose every morning about half past three,
To cook me my breakfast, my dinner and tea.

I worked very hard until I went to sea,
Once cane killed Abel, and it almost killed me.

(Repeat verse 1 ad lib.)

The Cane Cutters' Lament

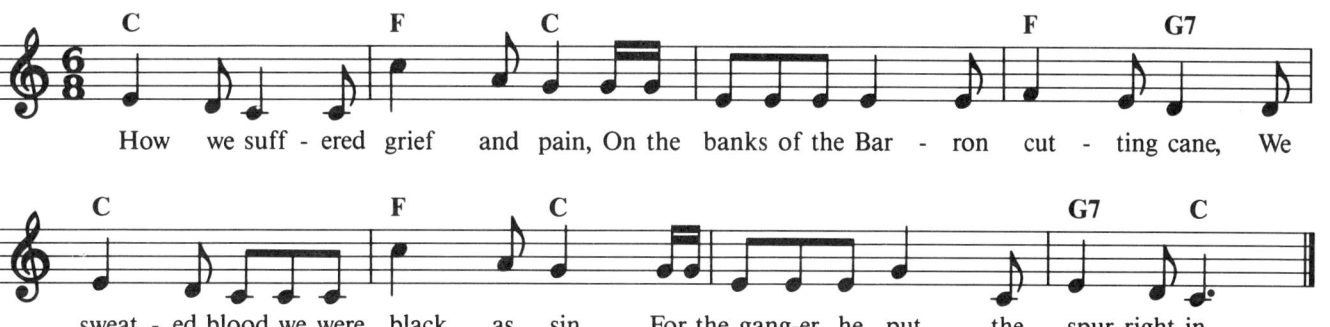

How we suffered grief and pain,
On the banks of the Barron cutting cane,
We sweated blood, we were black as sin,
For the ganger he put the spur right in.

The greasy cook with his sore-eyed look,
And the matter all stuck to his lashes,
He damned our souls with his half-baked rolls,
And he'd poison snakes with his hashes.

The first six weeks so help me Christ,
We lived on cheese and half-boiled rice,
Mouldy bread and cats-meat stew,
And corn beef that the flies had blew.

The cane was bad, the cutters were mad,
The cook had shit on the liver,
And I'll never cut cane for that bastard again,
On the banks of the Barron River.

So now I'm leaving that lousy place,
I'll cut no more cane for that bugger,
He can stand in the mud that's red as blood,
And cut his own bloody sugar.

THE CANE GANG

Words by Stan Dean

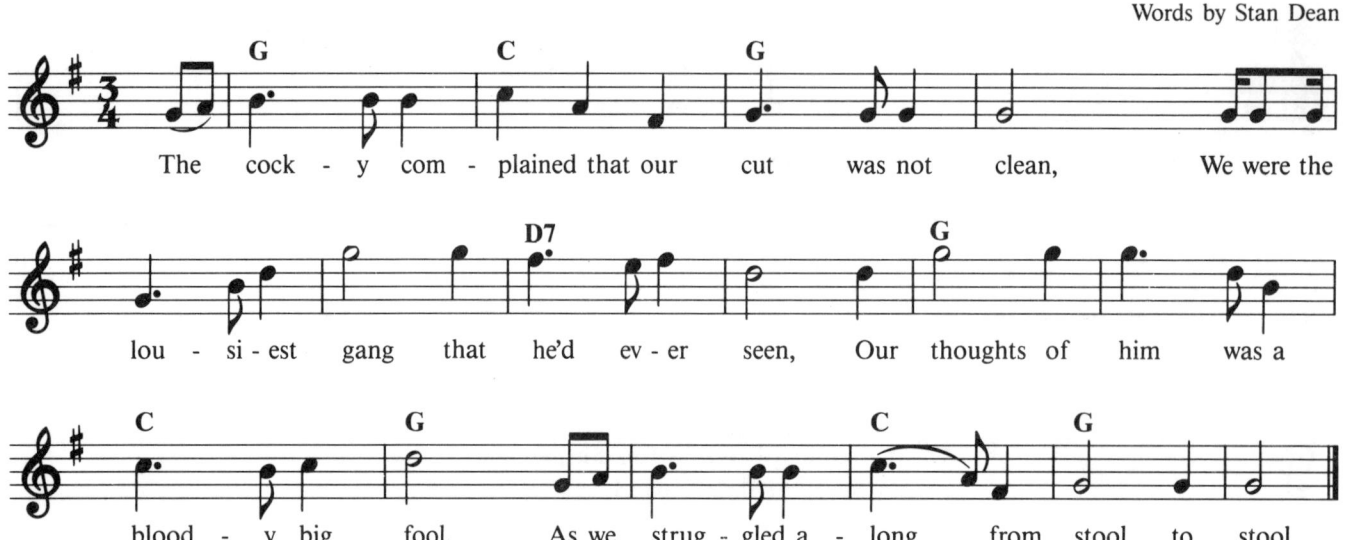

The cocky complained that our cut was not clean,
We were the lousiest gang he'd ever seen,
Our thoughts of him was a bloody big fool,
As we struggled along from stool to stool.

In some of the tangle no doubt we were slow,
But all we required was a fair ruddy go,
And that's just what the babbler gave us for tea,
Roasted go-anna, believe you me.

From then on all adders and snakes that we saw,
Were quickly dispatched to settle the score,
Until Yorky suggested, 'tis true by my soul,
A tucker change he'd prepare with Toad in t'hole.

Tramlines to shift, as we chop the last row,
When a dropped one can poison a man's main toe,
The overall work sends a man off the rails,
When he yearns for weekends, grog and the girls.

Cleaning a truck is no time to grin
When a key or a chain smacks one on the shin,
D-eleven it may be, but never OK,
As one limps with the chop for the rest of the day.

Ah, the blessed sight of the last truck of all,
Labelled all B–s, with 'you beaut' as our call,
With Blue's shirt, shorts and hat tied to the rear,
His rear quite black, 'Hear! Hear!' we cheer.

And I Whistle Through the Bush

MY TRAPS ARE ALL A - JANGLE
or The Rabbit Trapper's Song

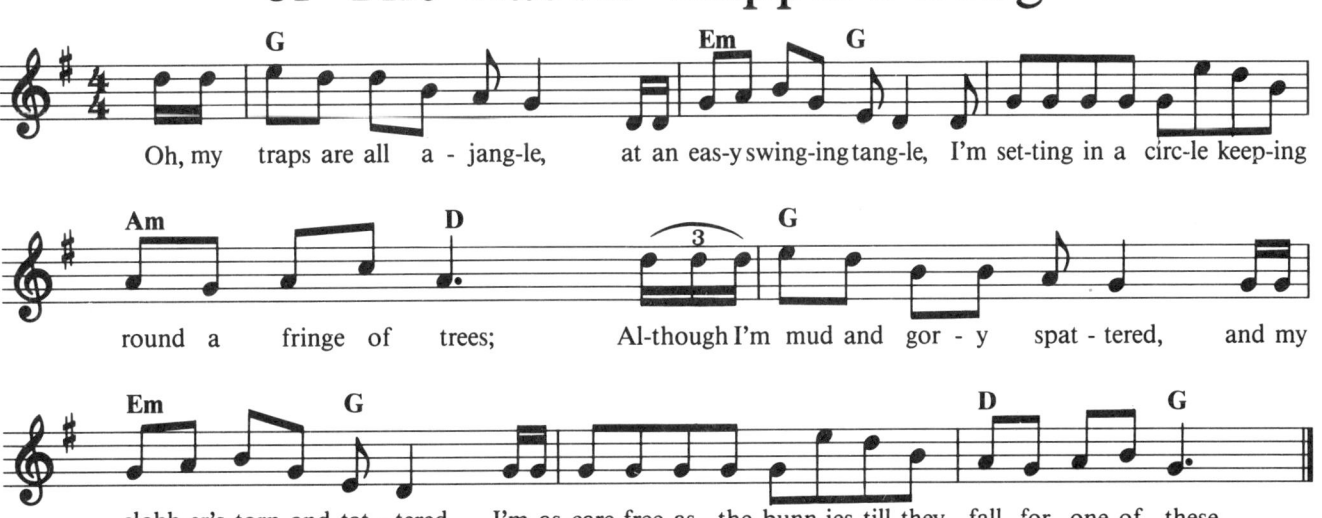

Oh, my traps are all a-jangle, at an easy swinging tangle,
I'm setting in a circle keeping round a fringe of trees;
Although I'm mud and gory spattered, and my clobber's torn and tattered
I'm as carefree as the bunnies till they fall for one of these.

Oh, I'm under no man's orders and I recognise no borders,
There's a welcome everywhere for me and my old dungarees;
I'm a _____ rabbit trapper, and a canny bunny snapper,
And I (whistle) through the bushland, though I'm wet up to the knees.

While you guys are courting tabbies, I'm out among the rabbies,
I can hear them bucking, squealing, oh, a dozen traps ahead,
And again while you are flirting at the last trap I am certain
To be bagging up my bunnies, keeping tally as I tread.

To 2nd half of tune:
So Ginger make the railway early, there's a shy and dinkum girlie
Let's me juggle with the cream cans as she write cheques out for me.

The Buyer On Our Run

Music supplied by Fai Hockley

Out across the Nullarbor, where roos and rabbits roam,
Just ninety miles from Eucla, there's a place that I call home,
I was very happy there, beneath the blazing sun,
Till I became acquainted with the buyer on our run.
Give you an example of the silly things he'd do,
Waited back to see him, on the day that he came through,
Pairing rabbits by the string, but I guess he didn't see,
Cause the silly so and so ran right over me.

Now, I am just a trapper, trapping for a crust,
Fighting for survival in the biting wind and dust,
And if these troubles aren't enough there is another one:
I can't divulge his name, but he's the buyer on our run.
I'll tell you that it's real good fun, to set two hundred traps,
To know that you'll get ninety or a hundred pair, perhaps;
To find when you come home at night, from the dust and heat,
That he's forgot your order and you're out of bread and meat.

Now if you plan on travelling, and across the plains you go,
Take a tip from me, I'm the guy that ought to know,
Plan your trip ahead my friend, be sure you plan it right,
So that you pass Madura in the middle of the night.
Chances are he'll be there, to have himself a whirl,
Has a taste for grape juice, has a taste for girls,
Avoid him like the plague, my friend; he is the devil's son,
You don't know trouble till you've met the buyer on our run.

Bullocky - O

I draw for Speckle's Mill, bullocky-O, bullocky-O,
And it's many a log I drew, bullocky-O.
I draw cedar, beech and pine, and I never get on the wine;
I'm the king of bullock-drivers, don't you know, bullocky-O!

Chorus:
I'm the king of bullock-drivers, don't you know, bullocky-O!

There's Guinea and Anderson too, bullocky-O, bullocky-O,
And it's many a log they drew, bullocky-O.
I can give 'em a thousand feet, axe 'em square and never cheat;
I'm the king of bullock-drivers, don't you know, bullocky-O!

There's Wapples too, he brags, bullocky-O, bullocky-O,
Of his forty rawboned stags, bullocky-O.
I can tell you it's no slander when I say I raise their dander,
When they hear the crack of me whip, bullocky-O, bullocky-O.

THE GREAT NORTHERN LINE

My love he is a teamster, a handsome man is he,
Red shirt, white moleskin trousers, and a hat of cabbage-tree;
He drives a team of bullocks, and whether it's wet or fine,
You will hear his whip a-cracking on the Great Northern Line.

Chorus:
Watch him, pipe him, twig him, how he goes,
With his little team of bullocks he cuts no dirty shows;
He's one of the flash young carriers that on the road do shine,
With his little team of bullocks on the Great Northern Line.

And when he swings the greenhide, he raises skin and hair,
His bullocks all have shrivelled horns, for Lordy, he can swear!
But I will always love him, the splendid man of mine,
With his little team of bullocks on the Great Northern Line.

When he bogged at Mundowie and the bullocks took the yoke,
They strained with bellies on the ground until the chain broke,
He fixed it up with fencing wire and brought wood from Bundamine,
With his little team of bullocks on the Great Northern Line.

When he comes into Tamworth you will hear the ladies sigh,
And parents guard their daughters for he has a roving eye;
But he signals with his bullock whip as he comes through the pine,
With his little team of bullocks on the Great Northern Line.

THE COCKIES OF BUNGAREE

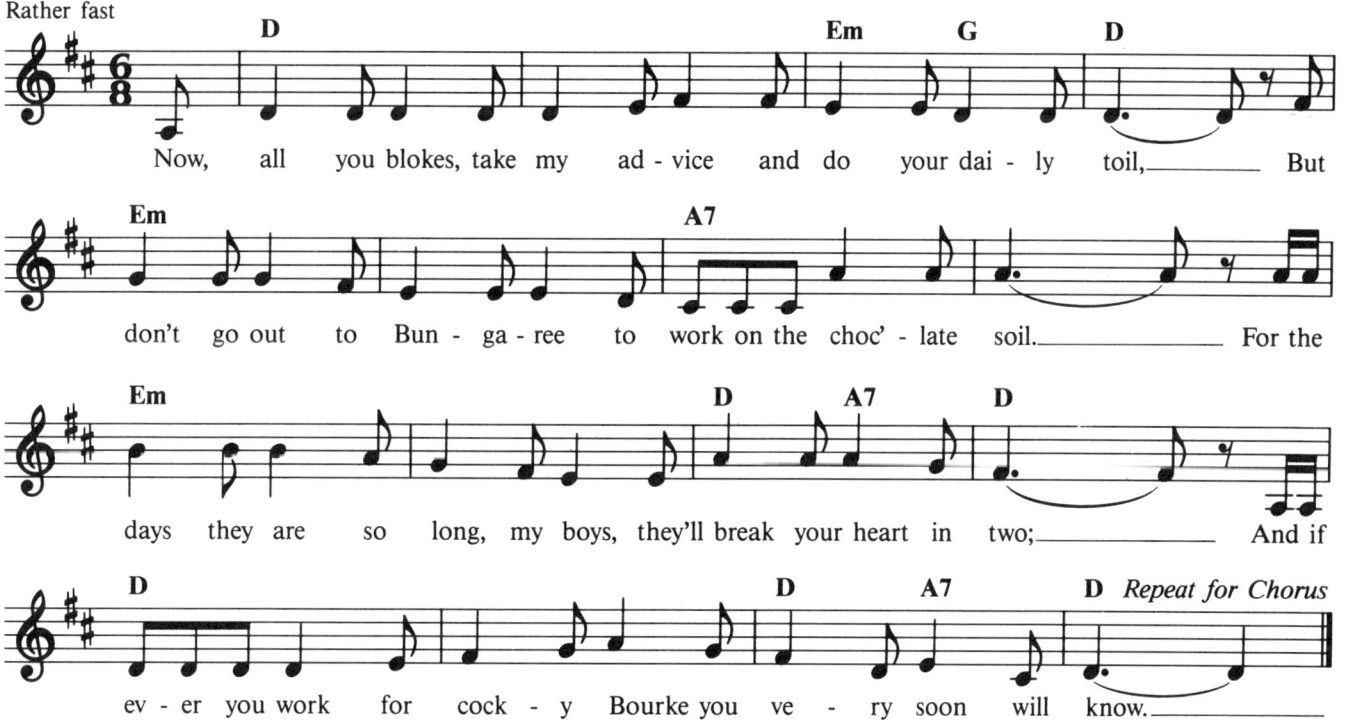

Now, all you blokes, take my advice and do your daily toil,
But don't go out to Bungaree to work on the chocolate soil.
For the days they are so long, my boys, they'll break your heart in two;
And if ever you work for cocky Bourke you very soon will know.

Chorus:
Oh we used to go to bed, you know, a little bit after dark.
The room we used to sleep in, it was just like Noah's Ark:
There were dogs and rats and mice and cats and pigs and poulteree.
I'll never forget the time we had while down in Bungaree!

On the thirsty Monday morning, sure, to work I had to go.
My noble cocky says to me, 'Get up! You're rather slow.'
The moon was shining gloriously, and the stars were out, you see,
And I thought before the sun would rise I'd die in Bungaree.

Oh, he called me to my supper at half past eight or nine,
He called me to my breakfast before the sun could shine,
And after tea was over, all with a merry laugh,
The _____ old cocky says to me, 'We'll cut a bit of chaff.'

'Now when you are chaff-cutting, boys, isn't it a spell?'
'Yes, be Jove,' says I, 'it is, and it's me that knows it well!'
For many of those fellows with me they disagree,
For I hate the jolly nightwork that they do in Bungaree.

THE CONSERVATIONIST

By Michael Flannagan

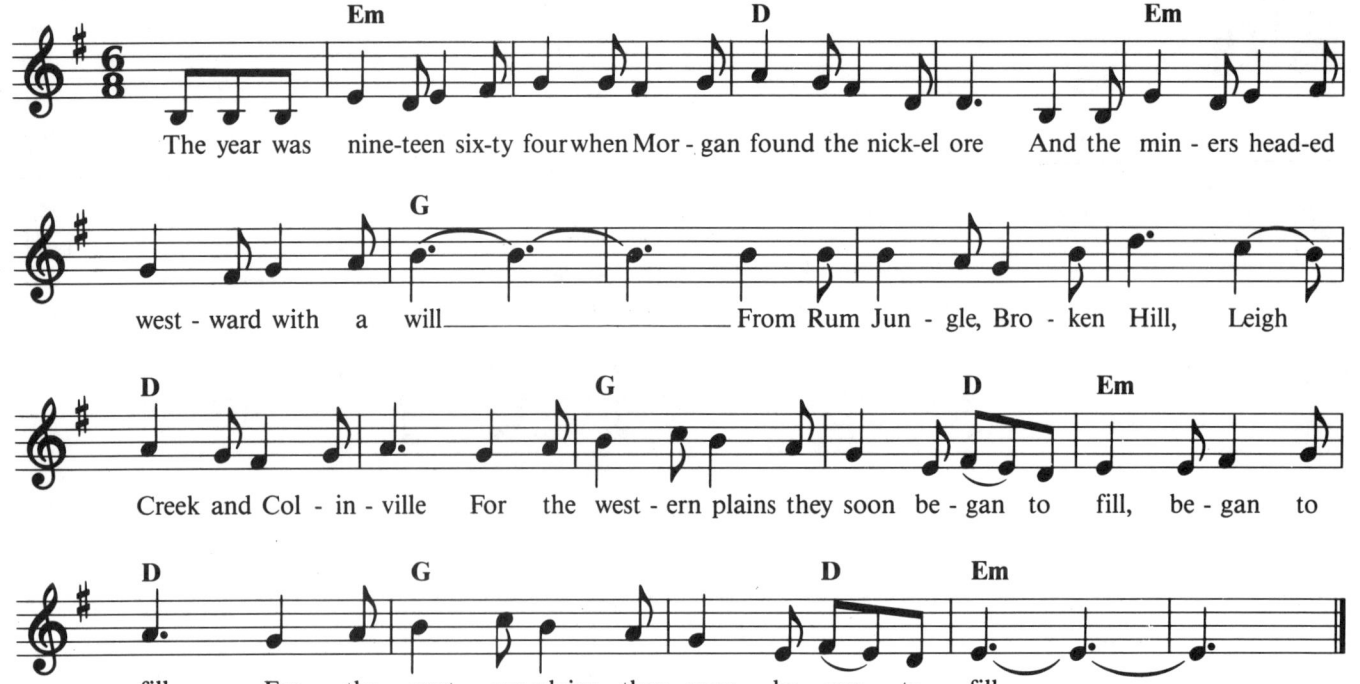

The year was nineteen sixty four when Morgan found the nickel ore
And the miners headed westward with a will
From Rum Jungle, Broken Hill, Leigh Creek and Colinville
For the western plains they soon began to fill, began to fill,
For the western plains they soon began to fill!

Oh the shafts are sinking fast, and their spreading through the west
And the beasts of nature don't know what to do
Soon the emu and the 'roo, there will be no room for you
Your extinction seems to be so close at hand, close at hand
Your extinction seems to be so close at hand.

Oh the Durkin shaft went down, and up sprang Cambalda town
With employment for a thousand mining men
Be you Aussies, Scotch or Turk, you are well paid for your work
Whether underground or working in the mill, in the mill
Whether underground or working in the mill.

Next Poseidon made a find, and the stockmarkets went wild
And the trading reached a fever on the floor
Ah, the brokers knees grew weak, as Poseidon reached its peak
For the likes of it they'd never seen before, seen before.
For the likes of it they'd never seen before.

Conservationists they say, if we carry on this way
It's no doubt that we are heading for our doom
For the companies don't mind with all the minerals they find
For the dollar god he rules them every day, every day
For the dollar god he rules them every day.

So stand up while you can, and think of your fellow man
And the children that will follow after you
I'm sure they'd like to see all the animals that we
Are killing every day throughout the land, throughout the land
Are killing every day throughout the land.

Oh the shafts are sinking fast, and they're spreading through the west
And the beasts of nature don't know what to do
Soon the emu and the 'roo, there will be no room for you
Your extinction seems to be so close at hand, close at hand
Your extinction seems to be so close at hand.

A – Digging I Will Go

Look Out Below!

By Charles Thatcher

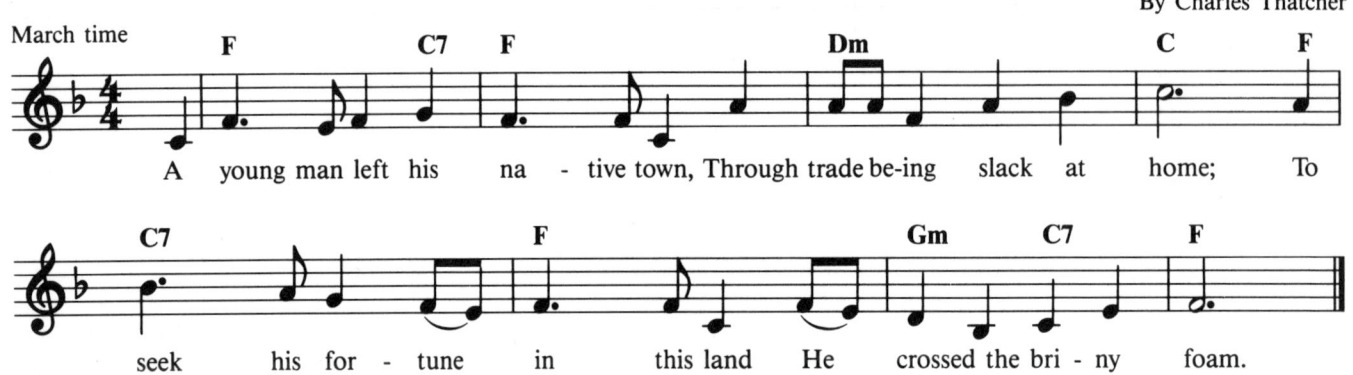

A young man left his native town,
Through trade being slack at home;
To seek his fortune in this land
He crossed the briny foam.

And when he came to the Lachlan,
His heart was in a glow,
To hear the sound of the windlasses,
And the cry 'Look out below'!

Where'er he turned his wondering eyes,
Strange sights he did behold
Of full and plenty in the land
And the magic power of gold.

He says: 'Now I am young and strong,
And a-digging I will go,
For I like the sound of the windlasses,
And the cry "Look out below!"

So now he's settled down again
With a charming little wife,
He says there's nothing can come up
To a jolly digger's life.

Ask him if he'll go home again
And he'll quickly answer 'No',
For he likes the sound of the windlasses
And the cry 'Look out below!'

THE MINER

The min-er he goes and he chang-es his clothes, And then makes his way to the shaft,

Each man well knows that he's go-ing be-low, To put in his eight hours of graft.

Repeat tune for Chorus

The miner he goes and he changes his clothes,
And then makes his way to the shaft,
Each man well knows that he's going below,
To put in his eight hours of graft.

Chorus: (same tune)
With his calico cap and his old flannel shirt,
And his pants with a strap round the knee,
His boots watertight, his candle alight,
His quid and his billy of tea.

The tapman, his driver, he looks free and wan,
The ropes to the windlass they strain,
As one shift comes up another goes down,
And working commences again.

He works hard each day for six bob a day,
He toils for his missus and kids,
And when work is over he thinks he's in clover,
To cut off his baccy and quids.

The Chinaman

by Charles Thatcher

There's a land that bears a well known name,
Though it's not a little spot;
'Tis the place from whence these Chinamen came,
And who shall aver it is not?
All I can say is, s'help me bob,
I think I'm not far wrong,
Those coves with pigtails round their knob,
To that spacious land belong.
It's a curious country, deny it who can—
'Tis the native home of a Chinaman.

The Chinese are trying themselves to free
From oppression's galling chain,
For they're under the Tartar dynasty,
But no longer they'll remain;
The emperor a duty puts
On tea, silk goods and rice,
But of the Chinese cocoa-nuts
He seems to set no price...
'Tis a jolly rum country, deny it who can,
Where they chop off the head of a Chinaman.

When John first came to the colony
He subsided alone in rice,
But being well off, he buys you see,
Fowls and pigs, no matter what price;
And sometimes, mounted on a horse,
Through the diggings he will ride,
And John at the blackguard boys looks cross
When they tell him to 'get inside'.
He's in a rage, deny it who can,
When insult's offered to a Chinaman.

The Chinaman traverses the wide world through,
On the diggings him you'll find,
Staggering under a big bamboo,
While his pigtail hangs behind:
Should a stranger be inquisitive,
And to ask him questions try,
A vacant stare them John will give,
And 'No sabby' he'll reply.
He's a peaceable fellow, deny it who can,
And there's many worse than a Chinaman.

MAN OF THE EARTH

Music by Phyl Lobl. Words by Jock Graham.

By profession and birth I'm a man of the earth,
I burrow in it like a mole;
I dig it and drill it, and blast it and fill it
For that great commodity coal.

To some I'm a brave man, to others a knave man
Who's putting the land in a hole;
A strike and attack man, a black man and slack man
Who plunders the country of coal.

It's narkin' at times to be blamed for their crimes,
And placed in the villainous role
Invented by story, press-jury and tory,
The profit-made agents of coal.

No story of men who are suffering pain;
Of heroes who starve on the dole;
Nought written or spoken of hearts that are broken:
The widows and orphans of coal.

The court is the gauge which determines my wage,
The parson looks after my soul;
My hands are my boss's, his gains are my losses;
My body is bartered in coal.

The gaps in our lines: 'Red roll of the mines',
Show death has been takin' his toll,
While snipers at maimed men and dead men and famed men
Grow fat on the blood on the coal.

Yet through muck and mire and lung-dust and fire,
More clearly I'm seein' my goal:
Of diggin' and drillin' and blastin' and fillin';
Supplyin' a socialised coal.

Give Us Our Two Pence Back

Music adapted by Graeme Smith from Harry Von Tilzer's
'When the harvest days are over Jessie Dear'

It is strike time in the dear old Lith-gow val-ley_____ The men on strike in-tend to do their best_____ A few scabs round the ty-rant seem to ral-ly_____ But there's not a spark of man-hood in their breast._____ When the ty-rant said he'd take them down for two-pence_____ Like a spi-rit each man seemed to dis-ap-pear_____ As they said fare-well they add-ed we'll re-turn a-gain_____

Chorus
_____ When you give that two-pence back Charl-ie dear_____ When you give that two-pence back Charl-ie dear_____ We can then re-turn to

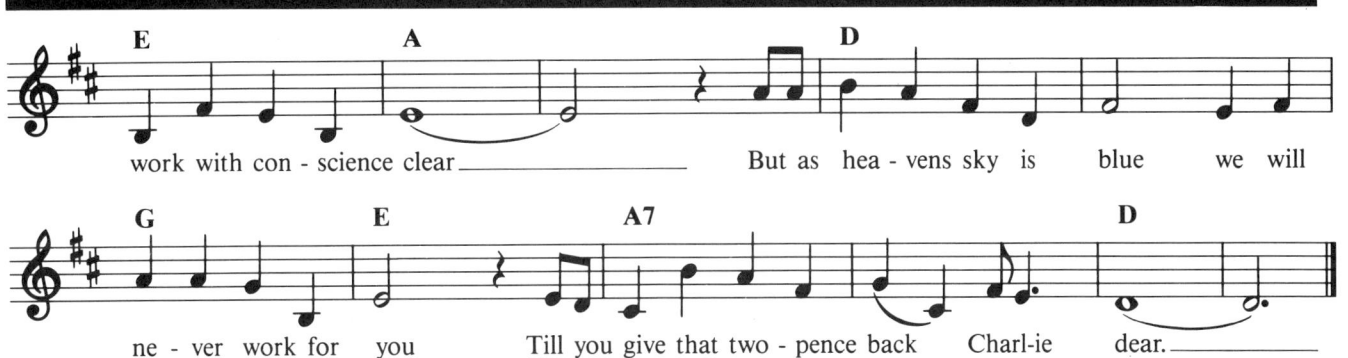

It is strike time in the dear old Lithgow valley
The men on strike intend to do their best
A few scabs round the tyrant seem to rally
But there's not a spark of manhood in their breast.
When the tyrant said he'd take them down for two pence
Like a spirit each man seemed to disappear
As they said farewell they added we'll return again
When you give that two pence back Charlie dear.

Chorus:
When you give that two pence back Charlie dear
We can then return to work with conscience clear
But as heaven's sky is blue we will never work for you
Till you give that two pence back Charlie dear.

As we wander up and down old Lithgow valley
The scenes of strife and want must give us pain
Standing for their rights like men of honour
Let us hope the struggle will not be in vain.
Then we wander down the roadway to the furnace
And it makes us sad to see scabs working there
They'd be better in the churchyard safely sleeping
Instead of being scabs for Charlie dear.

Here Comes a Union Boy

The Union Boy

When I first arrived in Quirindi, those girls they jumped with joy,
Saying one unto the other, 'Here comes a union boy!'

'We'll treat him to a bottle, and likewise to a dram,
Our hearts we'll freely give, too, to all staunch union men.'

I had not long been in Quirindi, not one week, two, or three,
When a handsome pretty fair maid she fell in love with me.

She introduced me to her mother as a loyal union man,
'Oh mother, dearest mother, now he's gently joined the gang!'

'Oh daughter, dearest daughter, oh this can never be,
For four years ago-oh he scabbed it at Forquadee.'

'Oh mother, dearest mother, now the truth to you I'll tell,
He's since then joined the union, and the country knows it well.'

'Now Fred, you've joined the union, so stick to it like glue,
For the scabs that were upon your back, they're now but only few.'

'And if you go blacklegging or scabbing it likewise,
It's with my long, long fingernails I'll scratch out both your eyes.'

'I'll put you to every cruelty. I'll stretch you in a vice,
I'll cut you up in a hay machine and sell you for Chinee rice.'

Come all you young and old men, oh, wherever you may be,
Oh it's hoist-oh the flag-oh, the flag of unity!

Then scabbing in this country will soon be at an end,
And I pray that one and all of you will be staunch union men.

THE BALLAD OF 1891

Words: Helen G. Palmer Music: Doreen Jacobs Bridges

The price of wool was falling in 1891;
The men who owned the acres saw something must be done;
'We'll break the shearers' union and show we're masters still,
And they'll take the terms we give them or we'll find the men who will!'

From Clermont to Barcaldine the shearers' camps were full,
Ten thousand blades were ready to strip the greasy wool,
When through the west like thunder rang out the union's call:
'The sheds'll be shore union or they won't be shorn at all!'

O Billy Lane was with them – his words were like a flame;
The flag of blue above them, they spoke Eureka's name.
'Tomorrow', said the squatters, 'you'll find it does not pay –
We're bringing up free labourers to get the clip away!'

'Tomorrow', said the shearers, 'they may not be so keen –
We can mount three thousand horsemen to show them what we mean.'
'Then we'll pack the west with troopers from Bourke to Charters Towers –
You can have your fill of speeches, but the final strength is ours!'

'Be damned to your six-shooters, your troopers and police –
The sheep are getting heavy, the burr is in the fleece!'
'Then if Nordenfeldt and Gatling won't bring you to your knees,
We'll find a law', the squatters said, 'that's made for times like these!'

To trial at Rockhampton the fourteen men were brought;
The Judge had got his orders: the squatters owned the court –
But for every one was sentenced, a thousand won't forget
When they gaol a man for striking, it's a rich man's country yet!

After The Strike

Music by Charles K. Harris

1. Once a lit-tle maid-en climbed an old man's knee; Asked for a sto-ry 'Please tell to me, why are you lone-ly, why are you sad, Why do your shed mates call you a scab?' 3. 'I thought it best pet, best to turn a scab, best to knock off strik-ing and go back to the job I had, That's why I'm lone-ly, That's why I'm sad, that's why my shed mates call me a scab.'

2. Brave men were fight-ing, fight-ing side by side; Fight-ing for jus-tice, fight-ing with pride, I then was with them, with them heart and soul. But when the test came I left them in a hole.

Chorus: Af-ter the strike is o-ver, af-ter the shear-ing's done, Af-ter the fight is end-ed, af-ter the bat-tle's won, Ma-ny a heart is wear-y, tired of all the strife, Ma-ny a scab is ban-ished, af-ter the strike.

Once a little maiden climbed an old man's knee;
Asked for a story, 'Please tell to me,
Why are you lonely, why are you sad,
Why do your shed mates call you a scab?'

'Brave men were fighting, fighting, side by side,
Fighting for justice, fighting with pride,
I then was with them, with them heart and soul,
But when the test came I left them in a hole.'

'I thought it best pet, best to turn and scab,
Best to knock off striking and go back to the job I had,
That's why I'm lonely, that's why I'm sad,
That's why my shed mates call me a scab.'

Chorus:
After the strike is over, after the shearing's done,
After the fight is ended, after the battle's won,
Many a heart is weary tired of all the strife,
Many a scab is banished, after the strike.

STRUGGLE IN THE WEST

There's a struggle going on in the West, boys,
A battle for Freedom and Right;
Tho' Tyranny's raising his crest, boys,
We'll conquer or die in the fight.
They may take from the hands that are free
The ballot that backs up his claim,
May land us in prison, but see, boys,
They never shall win at the game.

Chorus:
There's a struggle going on in the West boys,
A battle for Freedom and Right,
Tho' Tyranny's raising his crest boys,
We'll conquer or die in the fight.

They have sent to the plains of the West, boys,
The Gatling, the Nordenfeldt, too;
It seems that we must be suppressed, boys,
Says Price: 'Lay them out and fire low!'
The soldiers and troopers are here
To shoot down the men of their class;
Grim heroes with rifle and spear, boys,
To charge on a weaponless mass.

There are woolsheds and grass in the West, boys,
There's fences and sheep on the plain,
Would stranger to see us have guessed, boys,
They've sprung from our labour and pain?
Can they garrison plains with police?
Can they line the back tracks with their troops?
Can they watch the slow growth of the fleece, boys?
They are mad! They are fools! They are dupes!

They are sending the scabs to the West, boys,
At the sheds they are dumping them down;
For the man that the squatter likes best, boys,
Is the loafer and duffer from town.
Surrounded by troops and police,
Let them watch till the squatters go lame,
If they wait till we're suing for peace, boys,
They never shall win at the game.

So be true to yourself in the West, boys,
Be staunch to your colour and class;
The *'Brag'* of the squatters we'll test, boys,
By the power of the Union *'Hold Fast'*.
Let them hunt up the scum of the South,
Bring outcasts too wretched to name,
We'll give it to them straight from our mouths, boys,
They never shall win at the game.

HOGAN'S FLAT

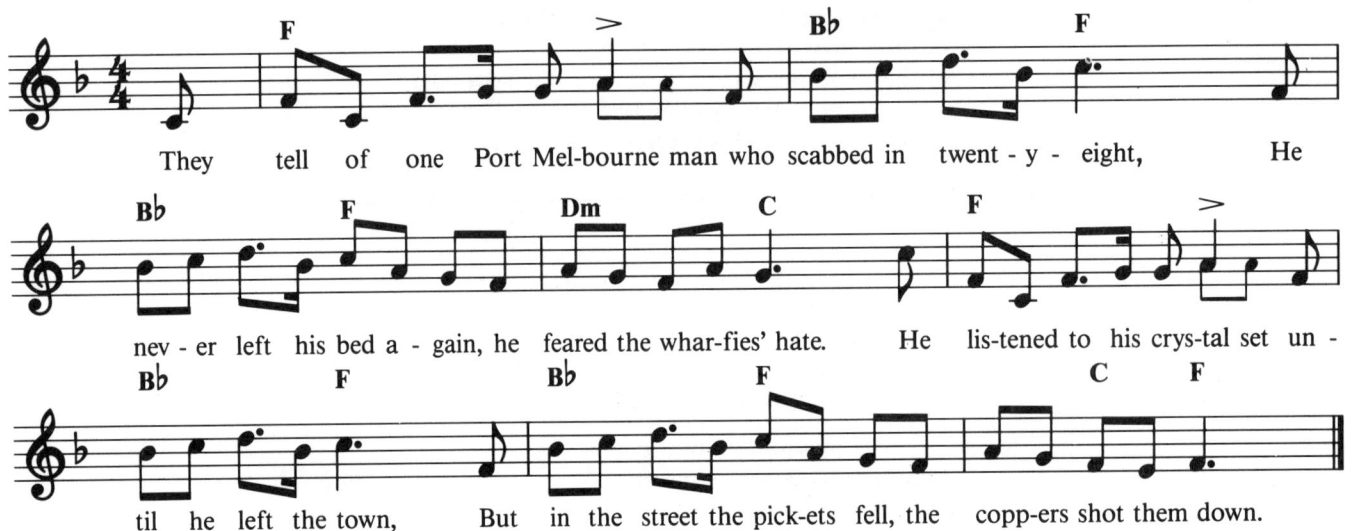

They tell of one Port Melbourne man who scabbed in twenty eight,
He never left his bed again, he feared the wharfie's hate.
He listened to his crystal set until he left the town,
But in the street the pickets fell, the coppers shot them down.

They signed the scabs in Bourke Street, they signed them off the boats,
As new-come men and foreigners who didn't know the ropes.
We ambushed them at Hogan's Flat, the coppers aimed and fired,
While Hogan's men in Parliament betrayed our trust and lied.

The ship owners were scornful, they'd let the wharfies starve,
Between the scabs and licences they squeezes the Union hard.
But worse there was to come my lads, if only we could know,
With starving kids and workless men and no-where else to go.

The waterfront was finished, there was no work at all,
The wharfies stood at Hogan's Flat to hear the foreman's call.
We stood there in the sleet and rain, so cold you can't believe,
But even those in work could barely get enough to eat.

Freedom in the Land

FREEDOM'S ON THE WALLABY

Words by Henry Lawson

Australia's a big country
An' Freedom's humping bluey,
An' Freedom's on the wallaby,
Oh, don't you hear 'er cooey?
She's just begun to boomerang,
She'll knock the tyrants silly,
She's going to light another fire
And boil another billy.

Our fathers toiled for bitter bread
While loafers thrived beside 'em,
But food to eat and clothes to wear,
Their native land denied 'em.
An' so they left that native land
In spite of their devotion,
An' so they came, or if they stole,
Were sent across the ocean.

Then Freedom couldn't stand the glare
Of royalty's regalia,
She left the loafers where they were
An' come out to Australia.

But now across the mighty main
The chains have come to bind her,
She little thought to see again
The wrong she left behind her.

Our fathers grubbed to make a home,
Hard grubbin' 'twas and clearin',
They wasn't troubled much with lords
When they was pioneerin'.
But now that we have made the land
A garden full of promise,
Old Greed must crook 'is dirty hand
An' come ter take it from us.

So we must fly a rebel flag
As others did before us,
And we must sing a rebel song
And join in rebel chorus.
We'll make the tyrants feel the sting
O' those that they would throttle;
They needn't say the fault is ours
If blood should stain the wattle.

The Ballad Of Eureka

Words by Helen G. Palmer. Music by Doreen Jacobs Bridges.

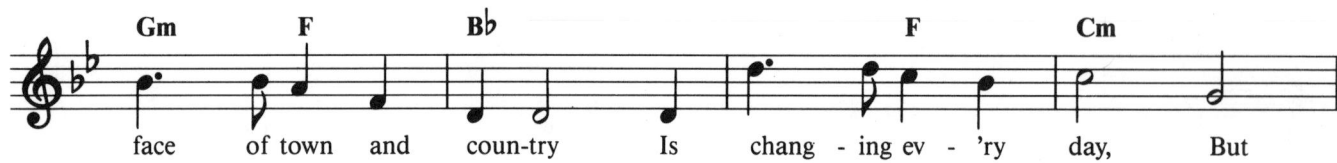

They're leaving ship and station,
They're leaving bench and fold,
And pouring out from Melbourne
To join the search for gold.
The face of town and country
Is changing ev'ry day,
But rulers keep on ruling
The old colonial way.

'How can we work the diggings
And learn how fortune feels
If all the traps forever
Are yelping at our heels?'
'If you've enough,' says Lalor,
'Of all their little games,
Then go and get your licence
And throw it on the flames!'

'The law is out to get us
And make us bow in fear.
They call us foreign rebels
Who'd plant the Charter here!'
'They may be right,' says Lalor,
'But if they show their braid,
We'll stand our ground and hold it
Behind a bush stockade!'

It's down with pick and shovel,
A rifle's needed now;
They come to raise a standard,
They come to make a vow.

There's not a flag in Europe
More lovely to behold,
Than floats above Eureka
Where diggers work the gold.

'There's not a flag in Europe
More lovely to the eye,
Than is the blue and silver
Against a southern sky.
Here in the name of freedom,
Whatever be our loss,
We swear to stand together
Beneath the Southern Cross.'

It is a Sunday morning.
The miner's camp is still;
Two hundred flashing redcoats
Come marching to the hill
Come marching up the gully
With muskets firing low;
And diggers wake from dreaming
To hear the bugle blow.

The wounded and the dying
Lie silent in the sun,
But change will not be halted
By any redcoat's gun.
There's not a flag in Europe
More rousing to the will
Than the flag of stars that flutters
Above Eureka's Hill.

I'm on me way down to the quay
Where the big ship now doth lay,
To command a gang of navvies
I was ordered to engage.
And I thought I would stop in for a while
Before I sailed away
To take a trip, on an immigrant ship,
To the shores of Botany Bay.

Chorus:
Farewell to your bricks and mortar
Farewell to your dirty lime
Farewell to your gangway and gang plank
And to hell with your overtime–
For the good ship Ragamuffin
She's lying at the quay
For to take old Pat, with a shovel on his back
To the shores of Botany Bay.

The best years of our lives we spend
At working on the docks
Building mighty wharves and quays
Of earth and ballast rocks
Our pensions keep our lives secure.
But I'll not rue the day
When I take a trip, on an immigrant ship,
To the shores of Botany Bay.

The boss came out this morning
And he said 'Why Pat, hello,
If you do not mix the mortar quick
Be sure you'll have to go.'
Well of course he did insult me
And I demanded all me pay,
And I told him straight I was going to emigrate
To the shores of Botany Bay.

And when I reach Australia
I'll go and search for gold
There's plenty there for digging up
Or so I have been told.
Or maybe I'll go back to me trade,
Eight hundred bricks I'll lay
For an eight-hour shift and an eight bob pay
On the shores of Botany Bay.

To Doctor Mannix

We welcome you back, and we greet you with love,
You're the man who defied all danger,
In your fight for the lives and the freedom of men,
As did He who was born in a manger.

As a man true and bold you despised their gold,
And you smiled at the loud orations
Of the traitors who tried to conscript our land,
While they gabbled about "small nations".

Though you fain would have pressed once again to your heart
Her who taught you your infant prayers,
You would not be an agent, a pimp or a part
Of your country's foul betrayers.

Long may you be spared to direct in their fight
All sects and creeds of toilers,
In resisting the forces of cash, combined
With the rats and the cloth despoilers.

The Ship's Under Way

Last Work We Go Home

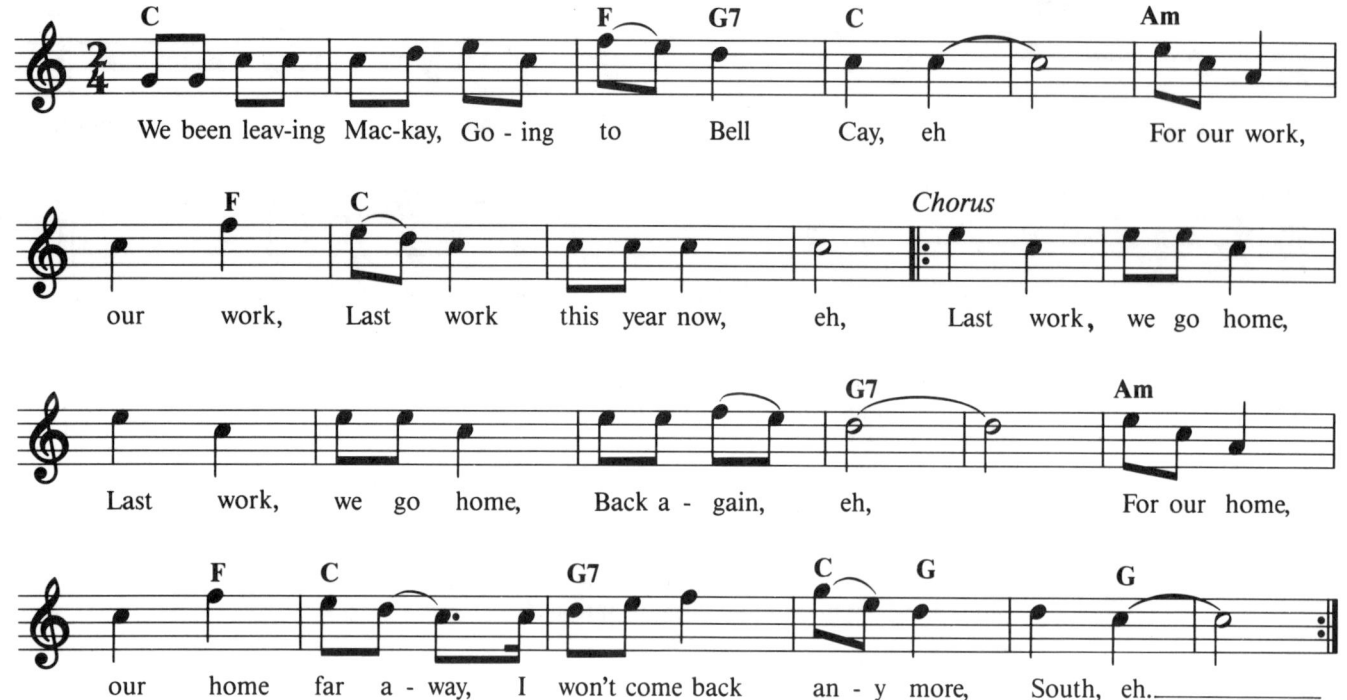

We been leaving Mackay,
Going to Bell Cay, eh
For our work, our work,
Last work this year now, eh,
Last work, we go home,
Last work, we go home,
Back again, eh,
For our home, our home far away,
I won't come back any more, South, eh,

Chorus:
Last work, we go home,
Last work, we go home,
Back again, eh,
For our home, our home far away,
I won't come back any more, South, eh.

QUEENSLAND WHALERS

Words and Music by Harry Robertson

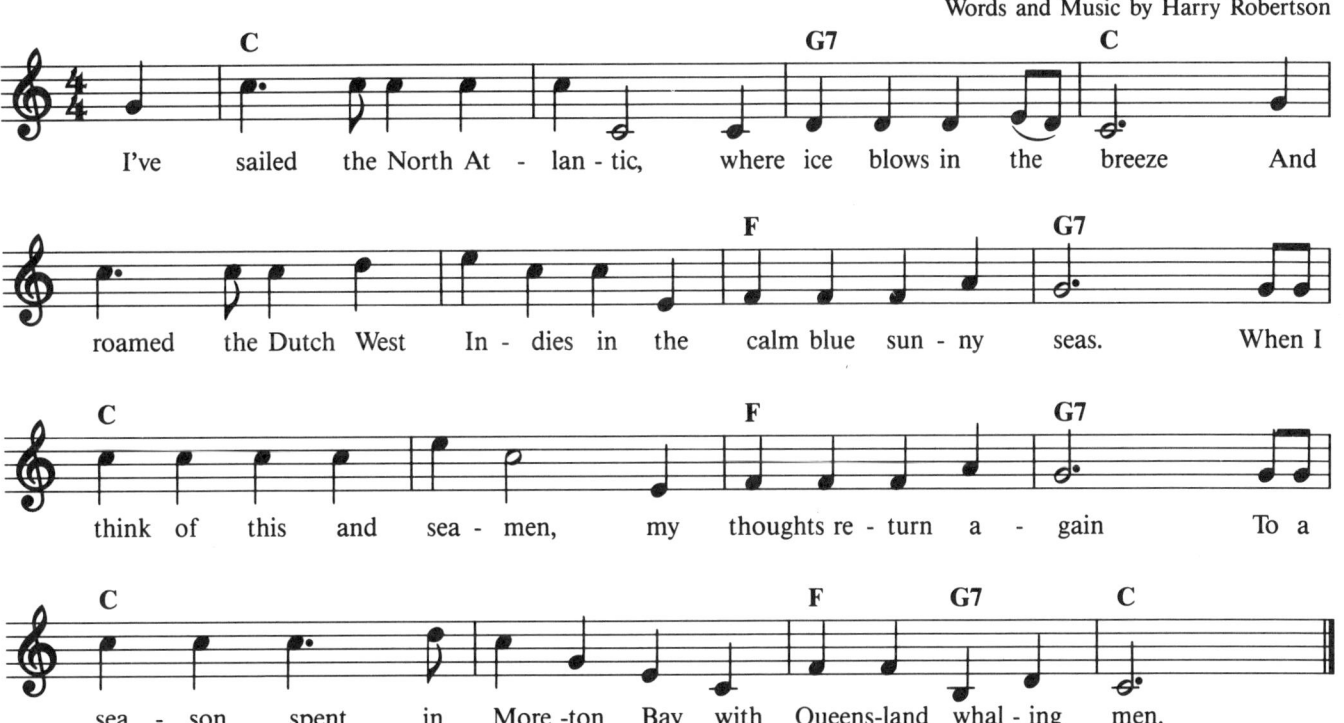

I've sailed the North Atlantic, where ice blows in the breeze
And roamed the Dutch West Indies in the calm blue sunny seas.
When I think of this and sea-men, my thoughts return again
To a season spent in Moreton Bay with Queensland whaling men.

Chorus:
Sing ho, you Queensland whalers, who have cut the sugar cane
And drove the herds of cattle o'er the dry and dusty plain.
You've dug the ore at Isa, laid countless miles of rail
And now you come to Moreton Bay, to catch the humpback whale.

For men who've chased the brumbies, caught bullocks by the tail,
It really is no problem to catch a humpback whale.
Just spur your iron sea-horse, put the gun through rigging struts,
And when he runs from the coral scrub, you belt him in the guts.

The man up in the crow's nest, as whaling legends go,
Looks out across the water and then cries 'Thar she blows',
But here in sunny Queensland you'll sometimes hear them shout,
'There goes a bloody beauty, mate, so get your finger out'.

From Moreton to Caloundra bronze whaler sharks abound.
They wait like dingoes in the scrub for a wounded beast that's down.
But their taste for blood and savagery, it never could compare
With the bite that Inland Revenue took from our bonus share.

When fuel tanks were running low, we'd sail to Brisbane town
And at the nearest boozer our sorrows we would drown,
With beer and fiery whisky and plonk of vintage rare
We'd steer a steady zigzag course without a blasted care.

Hooray, the season's over and we can all return
To treat our wives and sweethearts and have a little fun.
We'll rant like cattle drovers, we'll roar like whaling men.
But when the season starts next year you'll find us back again.

Cock Of The Morning
or Sailor Home From the Sea

Words by Dorothy Hewett. Music by Bill Berry.

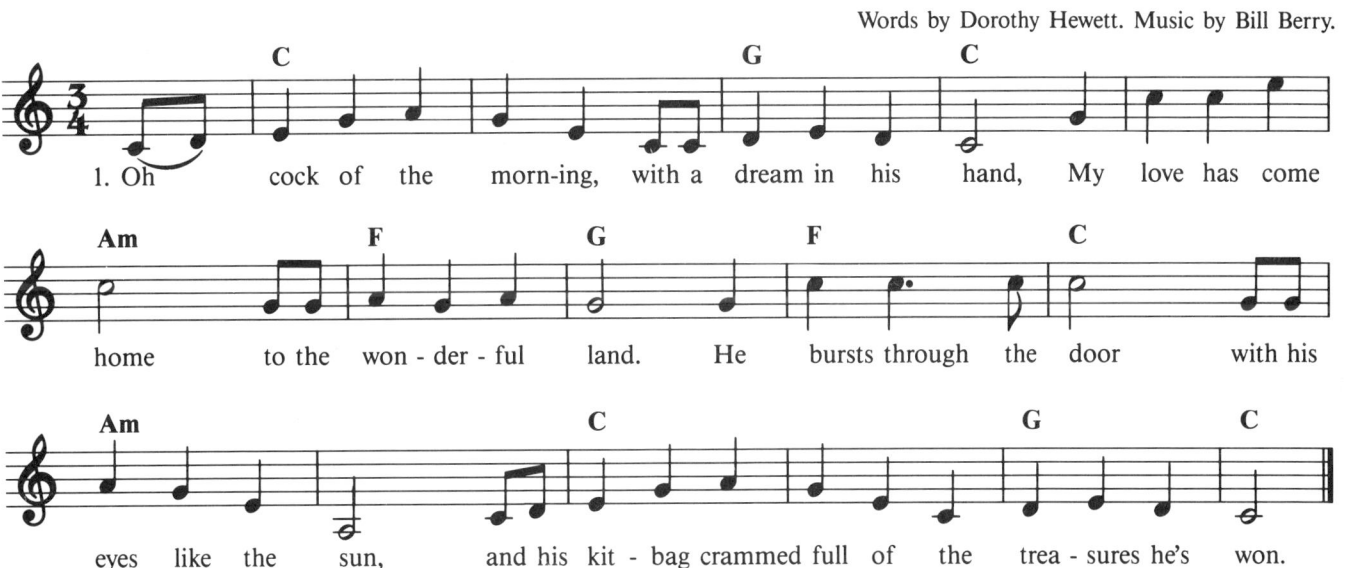

O cock of the morning,
With a dream in his hand,
My love has come home
To the wonderful land,
He bursts through the door
With his eyes like the sun,
And his kit-bag crammed full
Of the treasures he's won.

There's a pearl shell from Broome
And a tall Darwin tale
And coral and clam
And the jaws of a whale,
And my kitchen is full
Of the smell of the sea
And the leaping green fishes
My love brings to me.

O tumble your treasures
From Darwin to Broome
And fill with your glory
This straight little room
With the sun in the morning
Ablaze on his chest
My love has come home
From the North of No'West.

And deep-in our bed
We'll love and we'll be
We'll kiss and we'll listen
To the rain in the sky
Warm as the summer
We've lived winter long
My love has come home
Like King Solomon's song.

WE BUILT SOME GREAT SHIPS

Words by Ray Sowerby
From Peter Green's documentary film of the same name on the closure of the Whyalla ship yard, 1978.

They came from the Clyde
They came from the Tyne
To tell us of tales
Of life left behind.

Of the fights they had won
Of the fights they had lost
But never did they tell us
Of the pain and the cost

And when the BHP said
That the yard had to close
They didn't much care
How the town took the blows

For what can you do
When your job disappears
And you look at yourself
And you find you're arrears

We built some great ships
The best it is said
Not out of love
But for our daily bread

And all the thanks that we got
For building their fleet
Was to dismiss us all and
Chuck us out in the street

The moral of this story
Is very plain to see
Don't put your trust
In the BHP

For the dollar must come first
To hell with the town
And its hard to get up
When you've been knocked down.

Ship Repairing Men

Words and Music by Harry Robertson

From the workshops off we go, tool-kits heavy in our hands,
To the big one that's come in from a trip to foreign lands,
Salty streaks of rust have marked her, but the moorings hold her right,
And we'll work to fix her engines all today and half the night.

Chorus:
Don't wait up for me this evening, I'll be out all night again,
Working on the Brisbane River, with the ship repairing men.

Oil fired boilers throb with power drinking up the furnace heat,
Water turns to driving steam to make the engines beat,
But the feed pumps sighing wail to us, cuts through all other sound.
And sings a song of triumph for the valves that we have ground.

Engine bearings that knocked and hammered through the wild and stormy seas
Will be machined and fitted till they run with silent ease,
And the winch that rattles every time the piston turns her shaft,
Will hum along and sing its song to men skilled in their craft.

When you see an ocean liner glide between the river banks,
And the captain in his gold braid, orders men of lesser ranks,
Have you ever thought that stately craft might never sail again,
If it weren't for the toil and sweat of ship repairing men.

THE ANTI - FOULING ROLL

Words by Merv Lilley. Music by Bill Berry.
This song took first prize in a competition for a song about the Sydney branch of the Waterside Workers' Federation, c.1967.

Some men are pink or yellow
And some are black as coal
The rich man has the money
And the poor man has the soul

Chorus:
Keep rolling anti-fouling
Anti-fouling roll
Keep rolling anti fouling
In the dockyards of my soul
In the dockyards of my soul

I am a painting docker
I paint the poor man's goal
To stop the rich man's fouling
From entering my soul

Some men are anti others
And anti this and that
But I am anti rich man
From my feet up to my hat

Some names are writ in charcoal
Some names are drawn instead
Some names are writ in pencil
When the pencil has some lead

Oh Hear the Railway Whistle

THE LAUNCESTON AND DELORAINE RAILWAY

Music by Henry Clay Work

Oh, hear the railway whistle boys; it's notes are shrill and clear;
Just jump into the carriage, sir, there's nothing you may fear,
And let your voice re-echo as you shout it through the air,
The Launceston and Deloraine Railway.

Hurrah! Hurrah! for the men that worked so hard,
Hurrah! Hurrah! for I'm the railway guard,
You'd like to know the stoker, so I have brought his card,
On the Launceston and Deloraine Railway.

The farmers they will bless them when they hear the joyful sound,
Of the Launceston and Western rolling o'er the ground;
And the native youths, God bless them, some work at last have found,
On the Launceston and Deloraine Railway.

Hurrah! Hurrah! for the men that set us free–
Hurrah! Hurrah! for Mr Adye D.
A reserved seat we'll always keep for Mr Johnny C.,
On the Launceston and Deloraine Railway.

Oh yes, we'll keep a seat for them and Mr Norwood too,
And others who were friends to us shall bear the flag of blue;
And England when we sent to her she found us all the screw;
For the Launceston and Deloraine Railway.

Hurrah! Hurrah! for the horse that goes by steam;
Hurrah! Hurrah! for the railway whistle's scream.
The people down in Hobart can use the four-horse team
While we go to Deloraine by Railway.

They gave us lots of trouble, boys, before we passed the Bill;
The main line was a bubble boys, our fondest hopes to kill;
But now they've got the double boys, although against their will,
By the Launceston and Deloraine Railway.

Hurrah! Hurrah! for the debentures they are sold,
Hurrah! Hurrah! for the use of England's gold.
For soon we will repay them and those that shares do hold
By the Launceston and Deloraine Railway.

But soon they sent to us to sing their railway policy
And sent them back already filled to Mr Charles To-be;
Why don't they get a man to work like our Sir Richard D.,
For their Main Trunk Railway.

Hurrah! Hurrah! the Trunk is all my eye;
Hurrah! Hurrah! do you know the reason why?
They haven't the men to work like Dowling, Crookes and Dry,
For the great Shoe Trunk Railway.

Tenders have been accepted, and the work will soon begin,
And soon we'll feel the benefit of the Melbourne company's tin;
Yes, every shop in Launceston good stock must now lay in,
For the Launceston and Deloraine Railway.

Hurrah! Hurrah! for Overend and Robb,
Hurrah! Hurrah! for soon they'll do the job,
And Launceston will soon be filled with people–such a mob;
For the Launceston and Deloraine Railway.

So let's return our thanks to them who love the native youths,
And who, to gain some work for them have stood such vile abuse,
But crowned their efforts with success, which soon we will adduce
By the Launceston and Deloraine Railway.

Hurrah! Hurrah! for the men who helped us through;
Hurrah! Hurrah! for the gallant railway crew!
And every one whose motto is the never fading blue
And the Launceston and Deloraine Railway.

BILLY SHEEHAN

Arr. Paviour

On the forty-pound rails steamed a C-16,
Commanded by its driver, Mister Billy Sheehan.
The G.M. gave him orders on the strict Q.T.
To run a faster schedule than the Spirit of P.
'Keep that regulator open, watch the black smoke roll,
Pile on all the floorboards if we run out of coal.
If we don't beat that record; Billy said to his mate,
'Send my memos care of Peter at the golden gate!'

Chorus:
Billy Sheehan, ran a faster schedule,
Billy Sheehan, a mighty man was he.
Billy Sheehan, ran a faster schedule,
Out to break the record of the Spirit of P.

His fireman was a punting boy from Narrabeen,
He said, 'I'll lay the odds against the C-16'.
Billy flashed a roll of notes that was a bear;
The boiler then exploded, blew them both in the air.
Said Billy to his fireman as they left the wreck,
'I dunno where we're going but we're neck and neck!'
The fireman then said, 'Billy, I'll tell you what I'll do,
I'll bet another fifty I go higher than you!'

The wife of Driver Sheehan was at home in bed
When the railway wired that old Bill was dead.
She called her children to her, said, 'Listen, honey lambs,
The next old man you get'll be a Guard in the van!'
The railway's all in mourning now for Billy Sheehan,
No more we'll hear the puffing of his C-16.
There's crepe on all the locos, both the goods and mails,
From Ingham and Mount Isa down to New South Wales.

The Granville Rail Disaster

Moderately quickly
Words and Music Tom Bridges (1977)

1. The early morning train from Mt. Victoria — Headed for the city and the grime — But no-one was to know that the train that ran so slow was riding on the tracks for the last time. answers come too late.

The early morning train from Mt Victoria
Headed for the city and the grime
But no-one was to know
that the train that ran so slow
Was riding on the tracks for the last time.

At eight am the train neared Granville Station
The loco hit a bump and left the rails
And it never made the town
For the Bold St bridge crashed down
Who's guilty when a worn out system fails?

The papers greedily took up the story
For any news is entertainment now
'It's carnage' screamed the press.
'How many dead; oh can you guess?'
To the mourners does it matter anyhow.

As they cleared away the bodies and the wreckage,
People started asking how and why;
But nobody dared name
The ones who shared the blame
They knew full well that they'd get no reply.

When the public transport network's in a shambles
When the system's fifty years out of date
It was the government's neglect
That had that poor train wrecked
For so many now these answers come too late.

THE POISON TRAIN

Words and Music by Michael O'Rourke

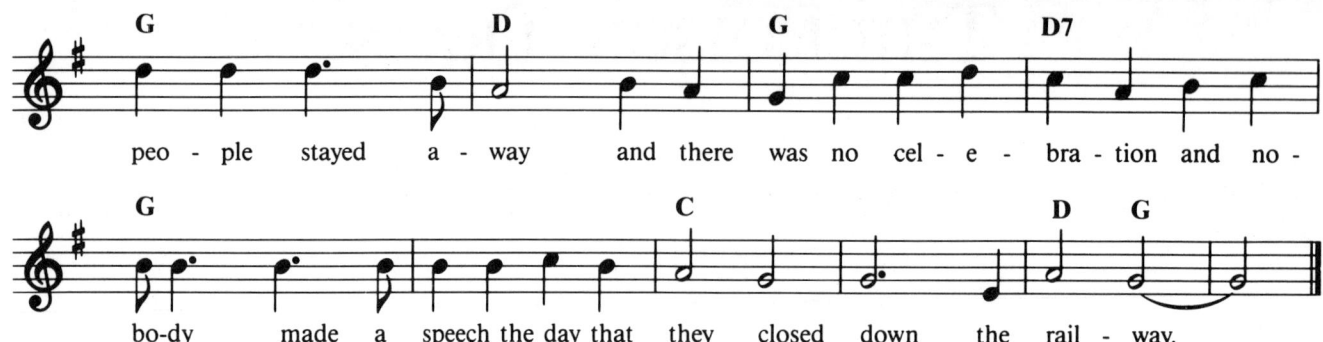

peo - ple stayed a - way and there was no cel - e - bra - tion and no - bo-dy made a speech the day that they closed down the rail - way.

This old town has had its day, all the people moved away,
And the houses standing empty in the dry and dusty day.
No-one cares for this old town, now the money's not around
And the railway lines are rusty
And the station's falling down.

Chorus:
There's a light down the line.
Let it shine, shine, let it shine.
There's a camp down the way.
All the fettlers will be coming home today.

When the railway opened here, all the gutters flowed with beer
And the people stood beside the line to watch and wave and cheer.
All the speeches that were made, when the bosses smiled and said
The good times are just beginning,
follow us and you'll go ahead.

Well they built the street so wide, it would be a thing of pride
To walk across it drunk or throw a stone to the other side.
And the building grew so tall, you would tremble at their fall,
But they just dried out and you'd never know
there was any one there at all.

I can hear the tall man say to the children at their play
You'd better go home early and you'd better stay away.
Stay away from the line, can't you hear the railway humming,
The grass has grown too tall
and the poison train is coming.

You feel sorry for the grass, all it did was grow too fast
All the weapons raised against it, it was never made to last
And the man and his offsider are all dressed in black
As the poison train goes through the town
and blisters all the track.

Well it never lasted long, half the town was packed and gone,
And everybody was afraid to be left there alone.
All the people stayed away, and there was no celebration,
And nobody made a speech
the day they closed down the railway.

The Pinch of Want
THE HUNGRY MILE

Freely - Parlando Rubato
Words by Ernest Anthony and Music set by Peter Parkhill

They tramp there in their legions on the mornings dark and cold
To beg the right to slave for bread from Sydney's lords of gold
They toil and sweat in misery, it would make the devil smile
To see the Sydney wharfies tramping down the hungry mile.

On ships from all the seas they came, that others of their kind
May never know the pinch of want or feel the misery blind
That makes the lives of men a hell in those conditions vile:
The hopeless lot of those who have to tramp the hungry mile.

The slaves of men who know no thought of anything but gain,
Who wring their brutal profits from the blood and sweat and pain
Of all the disinherited who slave and starve the while
Upon the ships beside the wharves along the hungry mile.

But every stroke of that grim lash that sears the souls of men
With interest due from years gone by will be paid back again
To those who drive those wretched slaves to build the golden pile
And blood shall blot the memory out of Sydney's hungry mile.

The time will come, and come it must when those same slaves shall rise
And through the revolution's smoke ascending to the skies
The master then will show the fear he hides behind his smile
At those his slaves who on that day shall scorn the hungry mile.

(To the tune of the last two lines)
The master then will show the fear he hides behind his smile
And blood shall blot the memory out of Sydney's hungry mile.

WALTZING MATILDA

Reproduced by permission of the publisher Allans Music Australia Pty Ltd
The Marie Cowan version

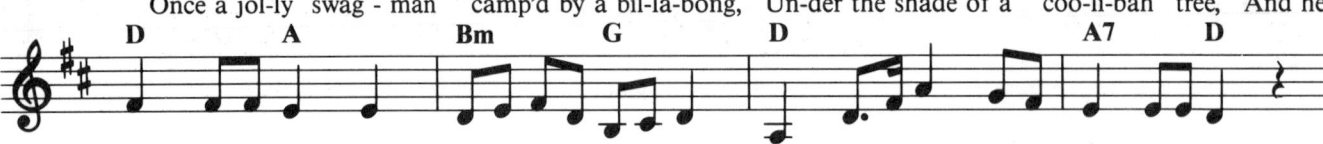
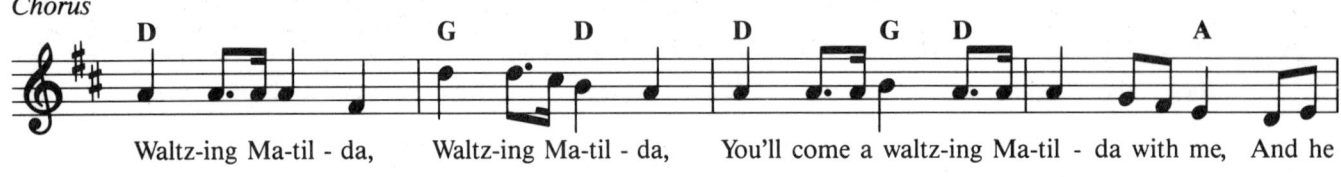

Once a jolly swagman camp'd by a billabong,
Under the shade of a coolibah tree,
And he sang as he watch'd and waited till his billy boiled,
You'll come a waltzing Matilda with me.

Chorus:
Waltzing Matilda, Waltzing Matilda,
You'll come a-waltzing Matilda with me,
And he sang as he watched and waited till his billy boiled,
You'll come a waltzing Matilda with me.

Down came a jumbuck to drink at that billabong,
Up jumped the swagman and grabbed him with glee,
And he sang as he shoved that jumbuck in his tucker bag,
You'll come a waltzing Matilda with me.

Chorus:
Waltzing Matilda, Waltzing Matilda,
You'll come a-waltzing Matilda with me,
And he sang as he shoved that jumbuck in his tucker bag,
You'll come a waltzing Matilda with me.

Up rode the squatter mounted on his thoroughbred,
Down came the troopers, one, two, three,
Whose that jolly jumbuck you've got in your tucker bag?
You'll come a waltzing Matilda with me.

Chorus:
Waltzing Matilda, Waltzing Matilda,
You'll come a-waltzing Matilda with me,
Who's that jolly jumbuck you've got in your tucker bag?
You'll come a-waltzing Matilda with me.

Up jumped the swagman, sprang into the billabong,
You'll never catch me alive said he,
And his ghost may be heard as you pass by that billabong,
You'll come a waltzing Matilda with me.

Chorus:
Waltzing Matilda, Waltzing Matilda,
You'll come a-waltzing Matilda with me,
And his ghost may be heard as you pass by that billabong,
You'll come a-waltzing Matilda with me.

WALTZING MATILDA
Alternative version

Reproduced by permission of the publisher Allans Music Australia Pty Ltd

The Queensland version

Oh, there once was a swag-man camped by a bil-la-bong, Un-der the shade of a coo-li-bah tree; And he

sang as he looked at his old bil-ly boi-ling, 'Who'll come a-walt-zing Ma-til-da with me?'

Chorus

Who'll come a-walt-zing Ma-til-da, my dar-ling? Who'll come a-walt-zing Ma-til-da with me?

Walt-zing Ma-til-da and lea-ding a wa-ter bag, Who'll come a-walt-zing Ma-til-da with me?

Oh, there once was a swagman camped by a billabong,
Under the shade of a coolibah tree;
And he sang has he looked at his old billy boiling,
'Who'll come a-waltzing Matilda with me?'

Chorus:
Who'll come a-waltzing Matilda, my darling?
Who'll come a-waltzing Matilda with me?
Waltzing matilda and leading a water-bag,
Who'll come a-waltzing Matilda with me?

Down came a jumbuck to drink at the water-hole,
Up jumped the swagman and grabbed him with glee;
And he sang as he stowed him away in his tucker-bag,
'You'll come a-waltzing Matilda with me.'

Down came the Squatter a-riding his thoroughbred;
Down came Policemen – one, two and three.
'Whose is the jumbuck you've got in the tucker-bag?
You'll come a-waltzing Matilda with me.'

But the swagman he up and he jumped in the water-hole,
Drowning himself by the coolibah tree;
And his ghost may be heard as it sings in the billabong
'Who'll come a-waltzing Matilda with me?'

The Sandy Hollow Line

Words by Duke (H.P.) Tritton

The sun was blazing in the sky and waves of shimmering heat
Glared down on the railway cutting, we were half dead on our feet,
And the ganger stood on the bank of the cut and snarled at the men below,
'You'd better keep them shovels full or all of you cows will go.'

'I never saw such a useless mob, you'd make a feller sick.
As shovel men you're hopeless and you're no good with the pick.'
There were men in the gang who could belt him with a hand tied at their back
But he had the power behind him and we daren't risk the sack.

So we took his insults in silence, for this was the period when
We lived in the great depression and nothing was cheaper than men,
And we drove the shovels and swung the picks and cursed the choking dust;
We'd wives and hungry kids to feed, so toil in the heat we must.

And as the sun rose higher the heat grew more intense,
The flies were in their millions, the air was thick and dense.
We found it very hard to breathe, our lungs were hot and tight
With the stink of sweating horses and the fumes of gelignite.

But still the ganger drove us on, we couldn't take much more,
We prayed for the day, we'd get a chance to even up the score.
A man collapsed in the heat and dust, he was carried away to the side;
It didn't seem to matter a damn if the poor chap lived or died.

'He's only a loafer', the ganger said, 'A lazy useless cow.
I was going to sack him anyway, he's saved me the trouble now.'
He had no thoughts of the hungry kids, no thought of a woman's tears
As she struggled and fought to feed her brood all down the weary years.

But one of the Government horses fell down and died in the dray;
They hitched two horses to him and dragged his corpse away.
The ganger was a worried man and he said with a heavy sigh,
'It's a bloody terrible thing to see a good horse die.'

'You chaps get back to your work, don't stand loafing there.
Get in and trim the batter down, I'll get the engineer.'
The engineer came and looked around and said as he scratched his head,
'No horse could work in this dreadful heat or all of them will be dead.'

'They're much too valuable to lose, they cost us quite a lot,
And I think it's a wicked shame to work them while it's hot.
So we will take them to the creek and spell them in the shade.
You men must all knock off at once. Of course you'll not be paid.'

And so we plodded to our camps and it seemed to our weary brains
We were not better than convicts, though we didn't wear the chains.
And in those drear depression days we were unwanted men,
But we knew that when a war broke out we'd all be heroes then.

(Sung to tune of verse lines 3 and 4.)
And we'd be handed a rifle and forced to fight for the swine
Who tortured us and starved us on the Sandy Hollow Line.

Soup
or My Bonnie Lies Over The Sea

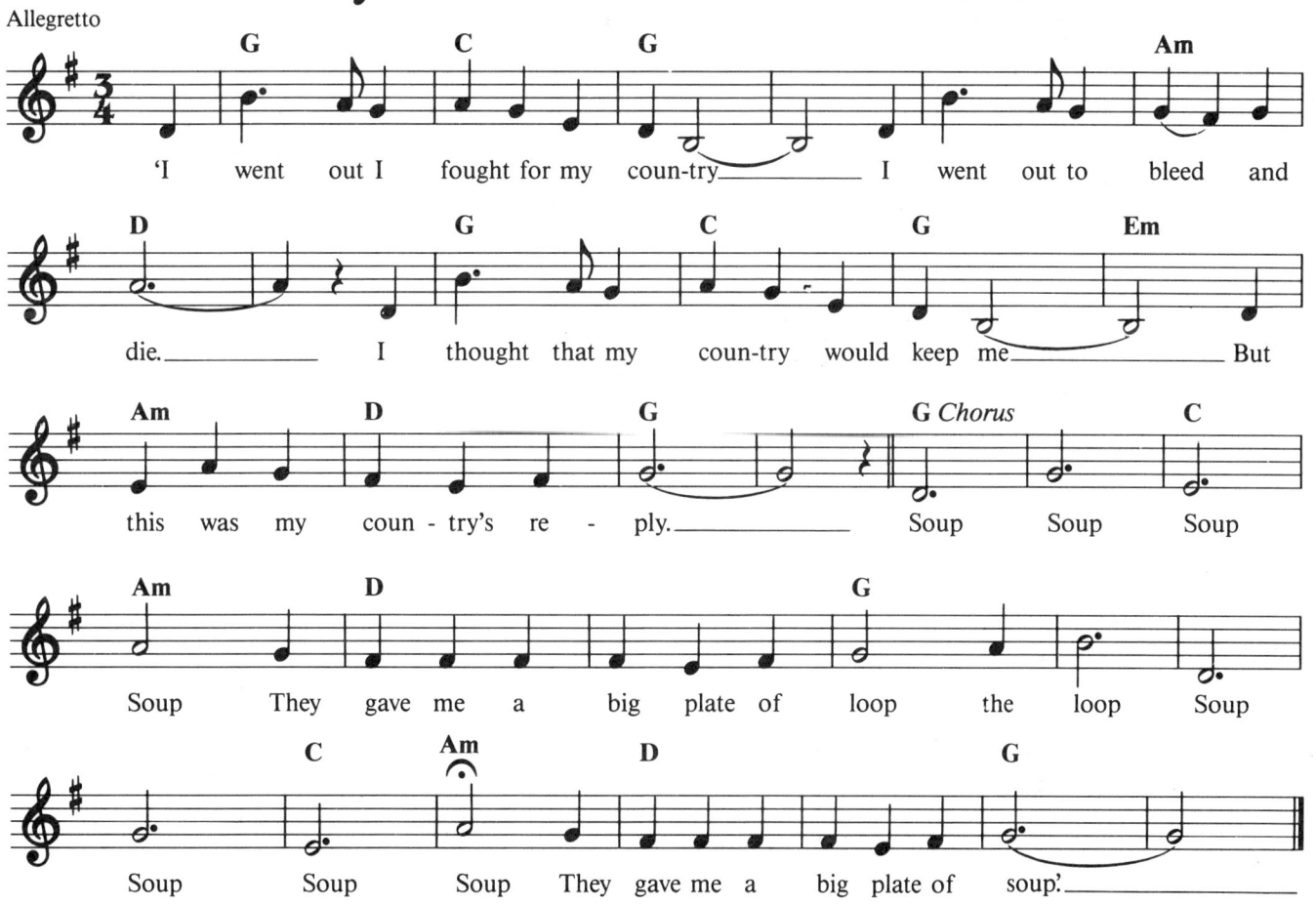

'I went out, I fought for my country,
I went out to bleed and die,
I thought that my country would help me,
But this was my country's reply: . . .
Soup, Soup, Soup, Soup,
They gave me a big plate of loop-the-loop.'

Chorus:
Soup, Soup, They gave me a big plate of loop-the-loop
Soup, Soup, They gave me a big plate of soup.

'I'm spending my nights in the doss house
I'm spending my days in the street
I'm looking for work but I find none
How I wish I had something to eat.

'I saved twenty pound with my banker
To buy me a car and a yacht
When I went to draw out my money
Then this was the answer I got: . . .

'I went off to fight for my country
I went off to bleed and to die
When I asked for my country to help me
Then this was my country's reply . . .

You are just a lonely battler
And you're waiting for a rattler –
You wish to heaven that you were never born,
For you ran to dodge a copper,
And you came an awful cropper
And the skin on both your hands is cut and torn;

Chorus:
Hobo, round you go
You are just a rolling stone,
Even though you're stony broke
If you still can laugh and joke,
You're good as any king upon his throne.

You are tired and you are weary
Lack of sleep makes your eyes bleary
And the soles of both your shoes are worn right through.
Your heart is sore and achin'
And your back is nearly breakin'
And your coat and shirt and pants have had it too.

With fury you are boiling
And your muscles need no oiling –
As you duck to dodge the headlight's brilliant glare,
For you've seen the copper's woodheap
And you know that it's a good heap
And you know the tucker's not the best in there.

Then you step upon a thistle,
You get tangled up with signal wires and points –
Then you blunder in the gutter
And angrily you mutter
'Stike me pink! Of all the flamin' joints.'

Then you see the green lights flashin'
And you hear the bumpers crashin'
And you see the great big engine that's rushin' by.
With your swag held at the ready,
Your nerves are none too steady
For you know you've got to take her on the fly.

Then your swag you try to throw in,
But the flamin' thing won't go in,
Bounces off the truck, it hits you, and you fall
Pick the remnants of your swag up,
Pick your billy can and bag up,
And you say, 'I missed the bastard after all!'

Chorus
Hobo, round you go
You are just a rolling stone,
Though your pants are wearin' thin
If you still can raise a grin,
You're better than a king upon his throne.

Last Chorus
Hobo, round you go
You are just a rolling stone,
Even though the skies are mighty grey
There surely will come a day,
You'll own a bloody railway of your own
You'd be good as any king upon his throne
We'll be better than a king upon his throne.

Weevils In The Flour

Words by Dorothy Hewett. Music by Michael Leyden.

On an island in a river
How that bitter river ran,
I grew on scraps of charity
In the best way that you can –
On an island in a river
Where I grew to be a man.

And just across the river
Stood the mighty BHP.
It poured pollution on the water,
All the lead of misery,
And its smoke was black as hades
Rolling hungry to the sea.

Chorus:
For dole bread is bitter bread,
Bitter bread and sour.
There's grief in the taste of it
There's weevils in the flour
There's weevils in the flour.

In those humpies by the river
We lived on dole and stew
While just across the water
Those greedy smokestacks grew,
And the hunger of the many
Filled the bellies of the few.

On an island in a river
How that bitter river ran
It broke the banks of charity
And baked the bread of man –
On that island in a river
Where I grew to be a man.

Champions All

MANDRAKE

A Tex Morton Song

Chorus:
Screw down the saddle, make 'er good and tight,
Back from the ropes boys, ask him is he right,
Pick up your mate lads, he's had a nasty fall.
They're all the same to Mandrake, champions and all.

You've heard about Aristocrat and dear old Rocky Ned
Their names we will remember long after they are dead
But when it comes to horses, there's one that bucks so fine
So now then I will tell you of this new outlaw of mine.

The Yankees have their strawberry roans and horses fancy-hued
But when they come to Mandrake they'll want their trousers glued
He tries a new trick every time and he never bucks the same
He really is a wizard and that's how he got his name.

'Now all you local riders, come here and gather round,
Stay on his back ten seconds and I'll pay a hundred pound.'
The champion of Queensland got on to ride him round.
He lasted just two seconds – one up, one coming down.

A fellow came in the other night to show what he could do,
He thought that he'd be clever, so he painted his pants with glue.
Mandrake threw him easily, he says: 'huh, I don't mind!
I says, 'Old chap, take a look at yourself, you've left your pants behind.'

I have a little saying it's one you ought to know
It's always been the motto of my travelling rodeo.
There never was a rider who never could be throwed
And there never was a bronco that never could be rode.

Les Darcy

Words by P.F. Collins (Percy the Poet) Music by Walter Donaldson

Way down in Tennessee
There lies poor Les Darcy,
His mother's pride and joy
Yes Maitland's fighting boy.

All I can think of tonight
Is to see Les Darcy fight,
How he beats them,
Simply eats them,
Every Saturday night.

And people in galore
Said they had never saw,
The likes of Les before
Upon the stadium floor.

They called him a skiter
But he proved to them a fighter,
But we lost all hope
When he got that dope
Way down in Tennessee.

KEEP YOUR TAIL UP KANGAROO

Verse 1

We've got a little song to sing, it's just the very thing, now cricket is on the wing.
We've got a little song to sing, and when the Tests commence, we'll sing together. Oh!

Chorus:
Keep your tail up, Kangaroo! Keep it up in the air, and you'll come smiling through.
Keep your tail up Kangaroo, keep it up in the air, that's all you've got to do.
Lancashire, Gloucestershire, Yorkshire, Surrey and Kent;
Show them all with the bat and ball that you're one hundred per cent! Oh!
Keep your tail up Kangarooo, keep it up in the air, and you'll come smiling through.

(In the first repeat of the Chorus lines 3 and 4 are:
  Husbands go, then say, 'Oh! been so busy today'.
  Wifie sighs, then replies,
  'I saw you watching the play'. Oh!)

(In the second repeat of the Chorus lines 3 and 4 are:
  People shout, 'Run him out!' 'Why?' says Missis O'Flynn,
  'If my Paddy threw a brick like that, they'd talk of running him in'. Oh!)

Verse 2

We'll sing this happy little song, 'twill cheer the boys along, and entertain the throng.
We'll sing this happy little song, it's just the song to sing in any weather. Oh!

Chorus: (with first repeat lines)

VERSE 3. As for VERSE 1.

Chorus: (with second repeat lines)

TEST NEWS

Who's the only one who can bowl Bradman out? His wife.
Tate is coming. No, he isn't. Yes, he is. Why hesi-Tate?
What's the last thing in cricket? Tea.
Is it right for Bradman to write?
Who are the most bored at a Test? The Board.
Why do they call it The Stand? Because it's the only place you're not supposed to.

Extra Chorus

Keep your tail up, Kangaroo,
Keep it up in the air, and you'll come smiling through;
Keep your tail up, Kangaroo,
Keep it up in the way you always do.
" It's a cert, I'll bet my shirt," yelled a fellow from Hay;
"Right," said Bill, "if you only will PERSIL it right away."
Oh, keep your tail up, Kangaroo.
Keep it up in the air, and you'll come smiling through.

PERSIL HAS WON THE **TEST** IN ENGLAND WASHING & AUSTRALIA

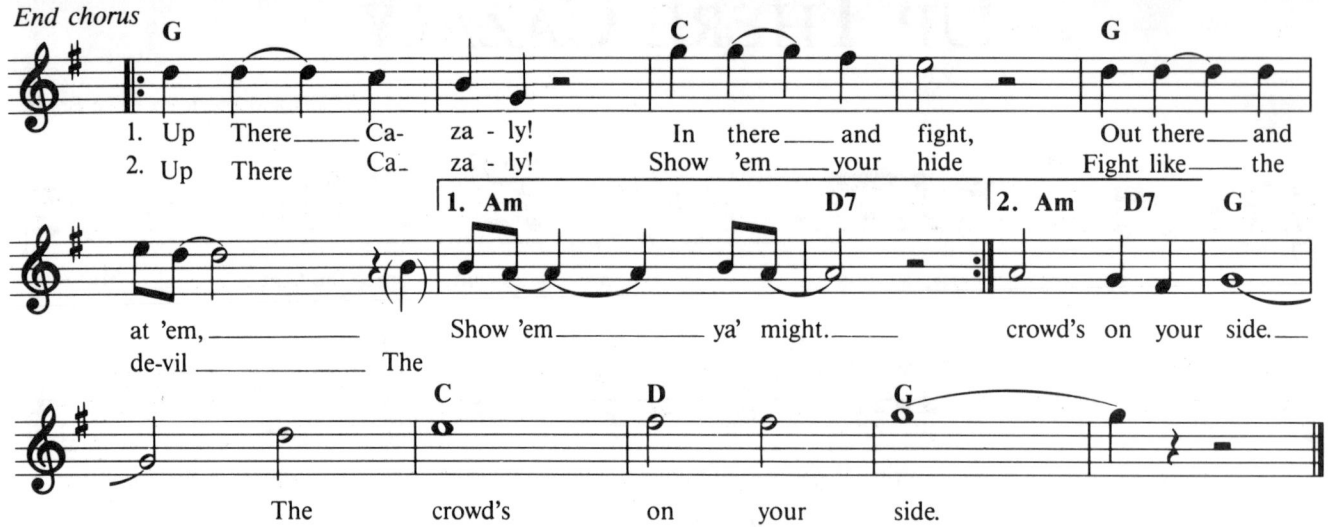

Well you work to earn a living, but on weekends comes the time
You can do whatever turns you on, get out and clear your mind.
Me, I like football, well there's a lot a'things around,
When you line them up together the footy wins hands down.

Chorus:
Up There Cazaly!
In there and fight,
Out there and at 'em,
Show 'em your might.
Up There Cazaly!
Don't let 'em in,
Fly like an angel,
You're out there to win.

Now there's a lot more things to football than really meets the eye,
There are days when you could give it up, there are days when you could fly.
You either love or hate it, depending on the score,
But when your team's run out, or they kick a goal, how's the mighty roar.

Chorus:
Up There Cazaly!
In there and fight,
Out there and at 'em,
Show 'em your might.
Up There Cazaly!
Don't let 'em in,
Fly like an angel,
You're out there to win.

(Repeat Verses)

End Chorus:
Up There Cazaly!
In there and fight,
Out there and at 'em,
Show 'em your might.
Up There Cazaly!
Show 'em your hide,
Fight like the devil,
The crowd's on your side.
The crowd's on your side.

THE TAB PUNTERS' SONG

Words by John Dengate. Music by W.S. Hays

Each Saturday morning I crawl out of bed
Hung-over from Friday's excess,
Feeling crook in the "comics" and crook in the head
With a mountain of sins to confess,
But then I remember it's race day again
And I collect up my clothes from the floor;
I tune into Mahoney's selections at ten –
The adrenalin's pumping once more.

Chorus:
At Warwick Farm, Randwick or Rosehill they race,
It's a sign of our moral decay,
But wipe that superior look off your face,
I expect a trifecta today.

I have a quick piss, I give breakfast a miss,
Wallet and form guide I grab,
Then I suddenly bolt like a two-year old colt
Away down the road to the Tab.
It's number of units and number of race,
The numbers spin round in my brain,
And I stand there blaspheming and cursing the place,
The biro is broken again.

Chorus:

Oh, the long shots are rough and the favourites are short
And I never know what's running dead
So I ring up my mate, but he got home so late
His mother won't rouse him from bed.
Ron Quinton could win on a horse made of tin
So I back everything that he rides
And the big Melbourne grey is a good thing each way,
And a couple of others besides.

Chorus:
And fellas, quinellas are always a chance
And doubles are sometimes a go
So when I walk out I feel light in the pants
For the Tab has got most of my dough.

A short break for grub, then I'm into the pub
And I stand there and weep in my booze
For the horses I back veer all over the track
And they lose and they lose and they lose.
Oh! seek not escape in the gambling my friend
Though life may be hum-drum and drab;
Seek solace in psalms or in fair ladies' arms
But never go into a Tab.

Chorus:

I'm Tall Dark and Lean
The Land Where The Crow Flies Backwards

A spoken delivery is used by Dougie Young

Words and Music by Dougie Young

Well I was born in the scrub of the out-back, On a riv-er they call the Bar-coo; My par-ents left me when I was quite young To pad-dle my own can-oe. They took me lon-ga Yon-da-ma sta-tion, And with a stock-whip they tanned my hide, They threw me in the sad-dle of a buck-ing horse, And that's how I learned to ride.

Chorus
Yes, I'm tall dark and lean, And ev-'ry place I've been the white man calls me Jack; It's no crime, I'm not a-shamed I was born with my skin so black. When it comes to rid-ing rough hors-es Or work-ing cat-tle I'll mix it with the best, In the land where the crow flies back-wards, And the pel-i-can builds his nest.

Well I was born in the scrub of the outback;
On a river they call the Barcoo;
My parents left me when I was quite young
To paddle my own canoe.
They took me longa Yondama station,
And with a stockwhip they tanned my hide,
They threw me in the saddle of a bucking horse,
And that's how I learned to ride.

Chorus:
Yes, I'm tall dark and lean,
And every place I've been the white man calls me Jack;
It's no crime,
I'm not ashamed I was born with my skin so black.
When it comes to riding rough horses
Or working cattle I'll mix it with the best,
In the land where the crow flies backwards
And the pelican builds his nest.

Well, I've knocked about a lot of places
In this land called the great outback,
Many times I've drove a herd of cattle
Along the Birdsville track.
With the mosquitoes and flies coming at you
And the sun beating down so hot,
You might think it's a hell of a place,
But to me it means a lot.

Well, they laugh in my face, they say I'm a disgrace,
They say I've got no sense;
The white men took this country from me –
He's been fighting for it ever since.
Well, these governments and presidents they're arguing
And every day they're starting a brawl;
If there's going to be a nuclear war
What's going to happen to us all?

Chorus:
Yes, I'm tall dark and lean,
And every place I've been the white man calls me Jack;
It's no crime,
I'm not ashamed I was born with my skin so black.
So I'll just linger on, when from this world I've gone,
This'll be my last request,
Bury me where the crow flies backwards
And the pelican builds his nest.

PRISON'S NOTHING SPECIAL

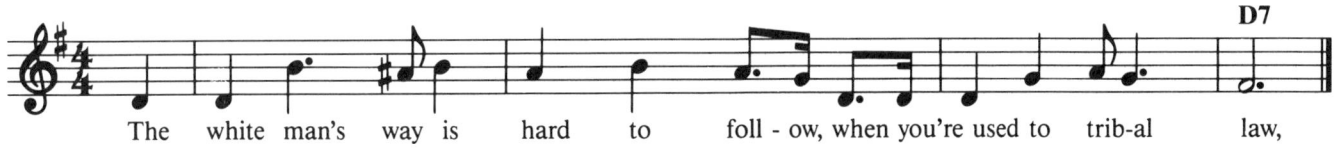

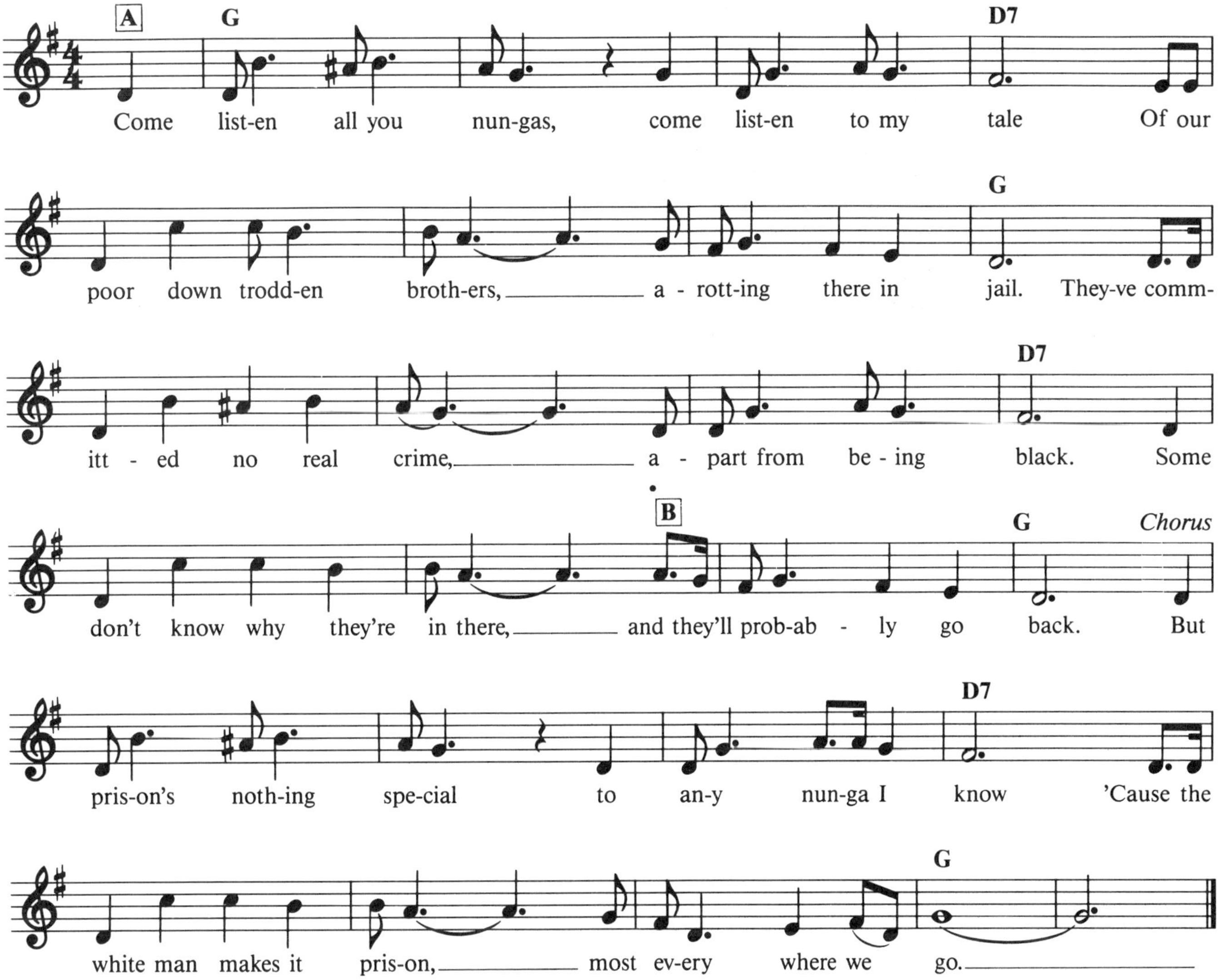
A
G
Come list-en all you nun-gas, come list-en to my
D7
tale Of our poor down trodd-en broth-ers, a - rott-ing there in
G
jail. They-ve comm-itt - ed no real crime, a - part from be - ing
D7
black. Some don't know why they're in there,
B
and they'll prob-ab - ly go
G
Chorus
back. But pris-on's noth-ing spe-cial to an-y nun-ga I
D7
know 'Cause the white man makes it pris-on, most ev-ery where we
G
go.

A In Verse 2 The first line is altered to:

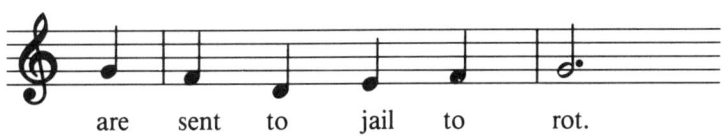

The white man's way is hard to foll - ow, when you're used to trib-al
D7
law,

B In Verses 2 and 3 substitute these notes at this point:–

are sent to jail to rot.

Come listen all you Nungas, come listen to my tale
Of our poor down-trodden brothers, a-rotting there in jail.
They've committed no real crime, apart from being black.
Some don't know why they're in there, and they'll probably go back.

Chorus:
But prison's nothing special to any Nunga I know
'Cause the white man makes it prison, most everywhere we go.

The white man's way is hard to follow, when you're used to tribal law,
And so before you know it, the cops have got you for sure,
And then from just the one arrest, seven convictions can be got,
So the poor down-trodden nungas, are sent to jail to rot.

We'd really like to find out, just how to apply for bail
But then we cannot raise it, so it's back again to jail
That's where my story started, and probably will end
So don't be too downhearted, at least we don't pretend.

VICTOR PODHAM'S RUSTY HUT

A spoken delivery is used by Dougie Young

Words and Music by Dougie Young

The Wil-cannia boys are all down this year Pick-in' grapes by the hun-dreds, so have no fear Gon-na be some trou-ble brew-in' at the week-end. Yes we gam-ble all night, we drink and fight Next day we're all good friends. Well, we have great times with the gall-ons of wine We have no trou-ble with the law The boys all shout when the grog runs out Hey, ring a tax-i and we'll get some more (spoken) that's for sure

Chorus
Come down to Vic-tor Pod-ham and his rust-y hut When he gets drunk, he los-es his nut Talk a-bout the fun that fell-a real-ly has He's a real cool cat, and he digs that kind of jazz.

Come down to Vic-tor Pod-ham and his rust-y hut Its full of emp-ty gall-ons and cig-ar-ette butts You'll meet the boys there on the razz-a-ma-taz Yes they're all cool cats and they dig that kind of jazz.

The Wilcannia boys are all down this year
Pickin' grapes by the hundreds, so have no fear
Gonna be some trouble brewin' at the week end...

Yes we gamble all night, we drink and fight
Next day we're all good friends.
Well, we have great times with the gallons of wine
We have no trouble with the law
The boys all shout when the grog runs out
Hey, ring a taxi and we'll get some more (that's for sure!).

Chorus:
Come down to Victor Podham and his rusty hut
When he gets drunk, he loses his nut
Talk about the fun that fella really has
He's a real cool cat, and he digs this kind of jazz.

Every Friday night, when they get their pay
They get the bus to Mildura on Saturday
In the Waterson pub they drink their share of beer
As they sink one down, they look around with a grin ear to ear.
Yes we have great times with the gallons of wine
We have no trouble with the law
The boys all shout when the grog runs out
Hey, ring a taxi and we'll get some more (that's for sure!)

Chorus:
Come down to Victor Podham and his rusty hut
It's full of empty gallons and cigarette butts
You'll meet the boys there on the razzamatazz
Yes they're all cool cats and they dig this crazy jazz.

In Mildura at the weekend, Walter Clark
Was drunk as a monkey, sleepin' in the park
Until Detective Barrett came along
He said 'You're doggone pissed, I place you under arrest
So don't try to bung it on.'
Yes we have great times with the gallons of wine
We have no trouble with the law
The boys all shout when the grog runs out
Hey, ring a taxi and we'll get some more (that's for sure!).

Chorus:
Come down to Victor Podham and his rusty hut
It's full of empty gallons and cigarette butts
You'll meet the boys there on the razzamatazz
Yes they're all cool cats and they dig this kind of jazz.

So come along to Scobie if you want to learn
Got a brand new drink called 'the three sharp turns'
Talk about the fun that fella really has
He's a real cool cat and he digs this crazy jazz.
Yes we have great times with the gallons of wine
We have no trouble with the law
The boys all shout when the grog runs out
Hey, ring a taxi and we'll get some more (that's for sure!)

Chorus:
Come down to Victor Podham and his rusty hut
It's full of empty gallons and cigarette butts
You'll meet the boys there on the razzamatazz
Yes they're all cool cats and they dig this crazy jazz.

GURINDJI BLUES

A Ted Egan Song

Poor bugger me, Gurindji,
Me bin sit down this country
Long time before the Lord Vestey
Allabout land belong to we
Oh, poor bugger me, Gurindji
Poor bugger blackfeller Gurindji
Long time work no wages we
Work for the good old Lord Vestey
Little bit plour, chugar and tea
For the Gurindji
From Lord Vestey
Oh poor bugger me.

Poor bugger me, Gurindji,
Man called Vincent Lingiari
Talk long allabout Gurindji
Daguragu place for we
Home for we, Gurindji
But poor bugger blackfeller Gurindji
Government boss him talk long we
Build you house with electricity
But at Wave Hill, for can't you see
Wattie Creek belong to Lord Vestey
Oh poor bugger me.

Poor bugger me, Gurindji
Up come Mr Prank Hardy
ABSCHOL too, and we talk long we
Givit hand long Gurindji
Buildim house and plantim tree
Longa Wattie Creek for Gurindji
But poor bugger blackfeller Gurindji
Government law him talk long we
Can't givit land long blackfeller, see,
Only spoilim Gurindji
Oh poor bugger me.

Poor bugger me, Gurindji,
Peter Nixon talk long we
Buy you own land, Gurindji,
Buyim back from the Lord Vestey
Oh poor bugger me, Gurindji
But poor bugger blackfeller Gurindji
Suppose we buyim back country
What you reckon proper fee?
Might be plour, chugar and tea
From the Gurindji
To lord Vestey
Oh poor bugger me.

Nothing Is As I Would Wish It To Be

THE HOUSEWIFE'S LAMENT

One day I was walking, I heard a complaining,
I saw a poor woman the picture of gloom.
She gazed at the mud on her doorstep ('twas raining),
And this was her song as she wielded her broom:

Chorus:
'O life is a toil, and love is a trouble,
Beauty will fade and riches will flee,
Wages will dwindle and prices will double
And nothing is as I would wish it to be'.

'There's too much of worriment goes to a bonnet,
There's too much of ironing goes to a shirt.
There's nothing that pays for the time you waste on it,
There's nothing that lasts us but trouble and dirt.

'In March it is mud, it's slush in December,
The midsummer breezes are loaded with dust.
In fall the leaves litter, in muddy September
The wallpaper rots and the candlesticks rust.

'There are worms on the cherries and slugs on the roses,
And ants in the sugar and mice in the pies.
The rubbish of spiders no mortal supposes,
And ravaging roaches and damaging flies.

'It's sweeping at six and it's dusting at seven,
It's victuals at eight and it's dishes at nine.
It's potting and panning from ten to eleven.
We scarce break our fast till we plan how to dine.

'With grease and with grime from corner to centre,
Forever at war and forever alert.
No rest for a day lest the enemy enter,
I spend my whole life in the struggle with dirt.

'Last night in my dreams I was stationed forever,
On a far distant rock in the midst of the sea.
My one task of life was a ceaseless endeavor,
To brush off the waves as they swept over me.

'Alas! 'Twas no dream – ahead I behold it,
I see I am helpless my fate to avert!'
She lay down her broom, her apron she folded.
She lay down and died and was buried in dirt.

THE OLD MAN AND HIS WIFE

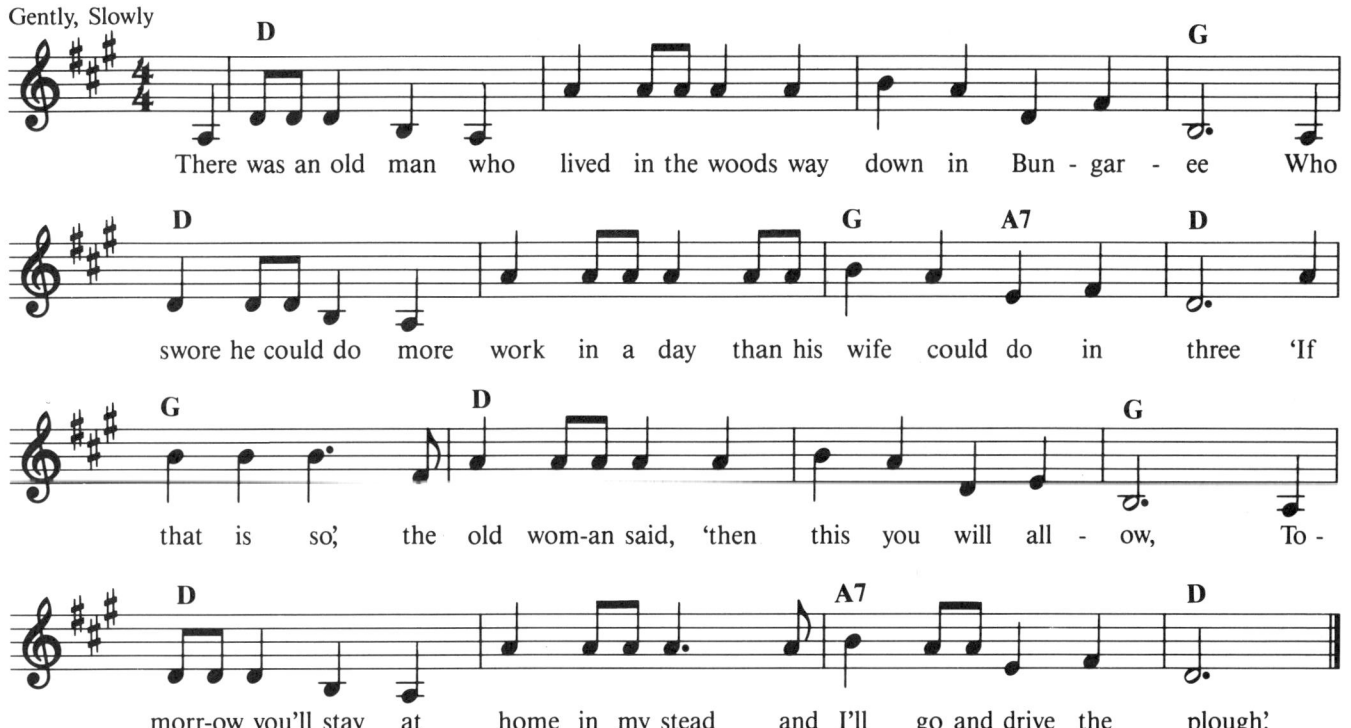

There was an old man who lived in the woods
Way down in Bungaree
Who swore he could do more work in a day
Than his wife could do in three
'If that is so', the old woman said,
'Then this you will allow,
Tomorrow you'll stay at home in my stead
And I'll go and drive the plough.

But you must milk Tidy the cow
For fear that she go dry.
And you must feed the little pigs
That are within the sty.
And you must mind the speckled hen
For fear she lays astray.
And you must wind the spool of yarn
That I spun yesterday.

The old woman took a staff in her hand
And went to mind the plough:
The old man took a pail in his hand
And went to milk the cow

But Tidy hinched and Tidy flinched
And Tidy broke his nose.
And Tidy gave him such a blow
That the blood ran down to his toes.

'Hi Tidy Hi! Tidy Ho!
Tidy stand you still!
If ever I milk you Tidy again
It'll be against my will.'
He went to feed the little pigs
That were within the sty
He hit his head against a beam
That made the blood to fly.

He went to mind the speckled hen
For fear she'd lay astray
But he forgot the spool of yarn
His wife spun yesterday.
So he swore by the sun, the moon and the stars
He'd never more rule his wife
Nor grumble if she never did
Another day's work in her life.

Wallaby Stew

Arr. by P. Evans

Poor Dad, he got five years or more as everybody knows,
And now he lives in Maitland gaol, broad arrows on his clothes.
He branded old Brown's cleanskins, and he never left a tail.
So I'll relate the family's fate since Dad got put in gaol.

Chorus:
So stir the wallaby stew, make soup with the kangaroo's tail.
I tell you things are pretty crook since Dad got put in gaol.

Our sheep all died a month ago, they all got flamin' fluke,
Our cow was boozed last Christmas by my big brother, Luke;
I sold the buggy on me own–the place is up for sale,
That won't be all that's up the spout when Dad gets out of gaol.

Our Bess got shook upon some bloke, he's gone, we don't know where,
He used to act around the shed, but he ain't acted square;
And mother's got some shearer cove forever at her tail–
The family will have grown a bit when Dad gets out of gaol.

They let him out before his time to give us a surprise;
He looked around at all of us, and gently blessed our eyes;
He shook hands with the shearer cove, and said that things seemed stale,
Then left him there to shepherd us, and headed back to gaol.

GENTLE ANNIE

Peter Hamilton
Used by permission. All right reserved

When the harvest time comes, Gentle Annie,
And the wild oats are scattered round your door,
You'll be anxious to know, Gentle Annie,
How your little stack of oats is going to yield.

Oh, your mutton's very sweet, Gentle Annie,
And I'm sure it can't be packed in New South Wales.
But you'd better put a fence round those cabbages
Or they'll all be eat up by the snails.

And you'll take me advice, Gentle Annie,
And you'll watch the old chaffie going away.
With his pack-bag hung on his saddle
And he stole some knives and forks the other day.

Ah, the bullocks they are yoked, Gentle Annie,
And with you I can no longer stay.
I'll bid you one and all farewell, Gentle Annie,
And I hope we'll meet you on another threshing day.

THE REBEL GIRL

A March, spirited
Words by Joe Hill

There are women of many descriptions
In this queer world, as every one knows,
Some are living in beautiful mansions,
And are wearing the finest clothes.
There are blue-blooded queens and princesses,
Who have charms made of diamonds and pearl;
But the only and Thoroughbred Lady
Is the Rebel Girl.

Chorus:
That's the Rebel Girl. That's the Rebel Girl.
To the working class she's a precious pearl.
She brings courage, pride and joy
To the Fighting Rebel Boy.
We've had girls before
But we need some more
In the Industrial Workers of the World,
For it's great to fight for freedom
With a Rebel Girl.

Yes, her hands may be harden'd from labor
And her dress may not be very fine;
But a heart in her bosom is beating
That is true to her class and her kind.
And the grafters in terror are trembling
When her spite and defiance she'll hurl.
For the only and Thoroughbred Lady
Is the Rebel Girl.

Bread And Roses

Music by Caroline Kohlsart Words by James Oppenheim

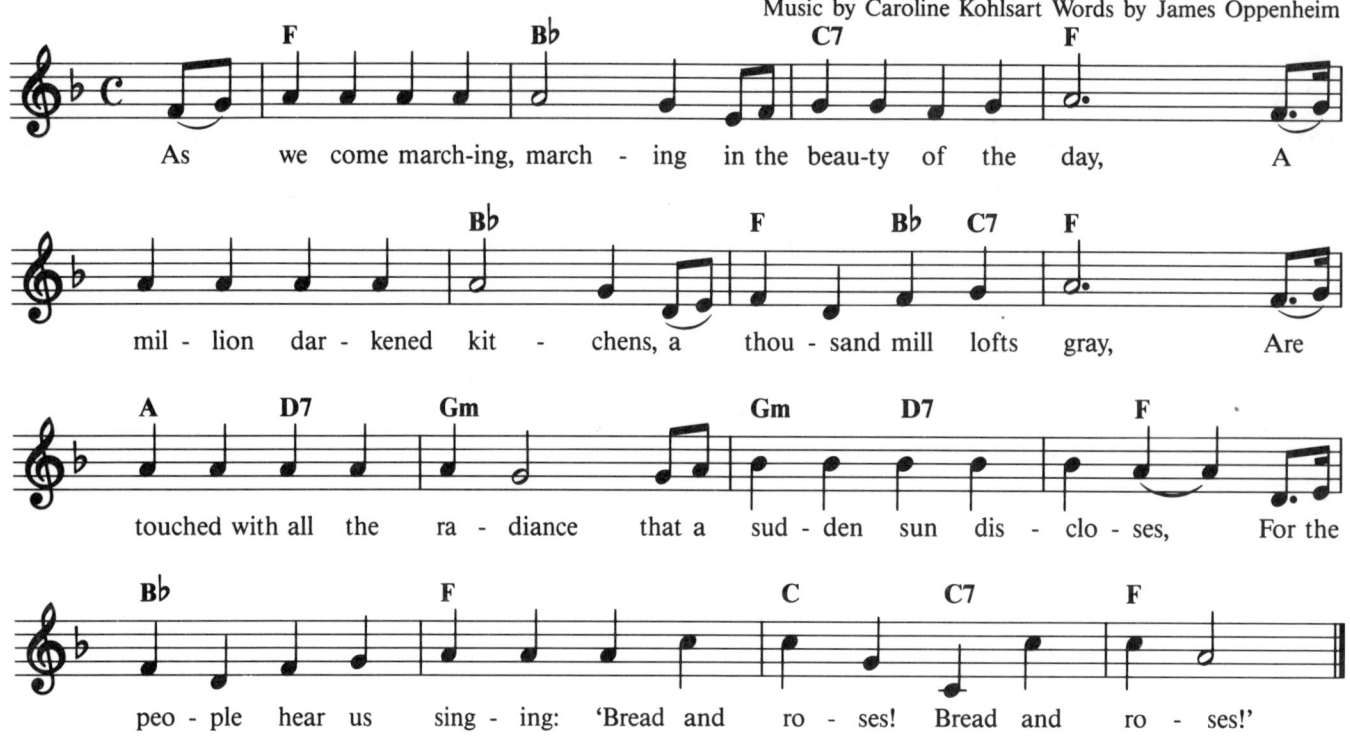

As we come marching, marching in the beauty of the day,
A million darkened kitchens, a thousand mill lofts gray,
Are touched with all the radiance that a sudden sun discloses,
For the people hear us singing: 'Bread and roses! Bread and roses!'

As we come marching, marching, we battle too for men,
For they are women's children, and we mother them again.
Our lives shall not be sweated from birth until life closes;
Hearts starve as well as bodies; give us bread, but give us roses!

As we come marching, marching, unnumbered women dead
Go crying through our singing their ancient cry for bread.
Small art and love and beauty their drudging spirits knew.
Yes, it is bread we fight for – but we fight for roses, too!

As we come marching, marching, we bring the greater days.
The rising of the women means the rising of the race.
No more the drudge and idler–ten that toil where one reposes,
But a sharing of life's glories: Bread and roses! Bread and roses!

Wife To A Cocky Farmer

A Richard Keam song
Registered APRA
Recorded by Judy Small on Old Friends
New Faces (Sidetrack TMS 010)

I am the one that has carried the can
Since time before time began
Or that's the way that its often seemed
Since I married a dairying man
We've had our times and we've had our strife
–It's a good but an awful hard, hard life
And the one thing sure is you'll pay the price
When you're wed to a cocky farmer.

I was the one got the bookwork done
When the kids were in bed at night
Rose every morn before the sun
When the winter frosts would bite
And I swapped m'good clothes long ago
For gumboots and an overcoat
And a lifetime bailing a sinking boat
For the sake of a cocky farmer.

And the sound of the scenes in m'very dreams
Is the sound of milk can lids
I never knew how we'd get through
But we managed to raise four kids
And the time that we've had away from here
Is less than a month in twenty years
–Now the kids've gone, and they shed no tears
For the life of a cocky farmer.

And the price we get never keeps in step
With the prices that we pay
But you can't tell cows that they're out on strike
You're a slave to them night and day
We've seen the neighbours all around
Toss it in and shift to the local towns
But you talk of this and he only frowns
He'll die as a cocky farmer.

Oh they used to say that I wore the pants
In the days when they said such things
But I was a one when I was young
For a bit of a wild old fling
Ah, the times we had at the Shire Hall Dance
Stars in me eyes and a head for romance
Some times I think that I'm still young Nance
Not the wife of a cocky farmer.

Hush Little Baby

Words by Pam Collier

Hush little baby, don't say a word,
Father's asleep, you must not be heard.
He's been on night-shift up at the mine,
Now he must sleep 'til a quarter to nine.

This house that they gave us, with no thought at all
Of shift-workers with young children to call.
He needs his sleep to earn his pay,
Children demand, there's nowhere to play.

The sun's too hot, it's forty degrees,
Inside the cool house to watch T.V.
Dad shouts it's too loud, he's awake again,
Who planned this house? It's a crying shame.

Mum's nerves are frayed, what can she do
To keep the peace, or start anew?
Why did we come to this awful place?
The last outpost of the human race.

We came for two years, and now it's three,
Whatever is happening to you and me?
Our savings all went in the stike last year,
Can I go on?... Not without you dear.

I miss your Nan, no-one to help,
In times of strife when he gives me the belt.
The pub, it calls your Dad away,
The beer, it takes all his shift-working pay.

(Unaccompanied)... Hush little baby, don't say a word,
Father's asleep, you mustn't be heard.

DON'T BE TOO POLITE GIRLS!

Words by Glen Tomasetti

We're really on the way, girls, really on the way!
Hooray for equal pay, girls, hooray for equal pay!
They'll give it to ten percent of us in spite of all their fears,
But do they really need to make us wait three years?

Chorus:
Don't be too polite, girls, don't be too polite!
Show a little fight, girls, show a little fight!
Don't be fearful of offending in case you get the sack,
Just recognise your value and we won't look back.

Though equal pay in principle is now a woman's right,
To turn it into practice, we must show a little fight,
We fear male disapproval, if to argue we decide,
The boss fears for his bank account, the husband for his pride.
I'm a lady journalist, I work upon The Age,
I've become a feature writer after years on the social page,
The editor tells me 'Sweet, you're almost better than the men,
But if you think you'll get A grading, you'd better think again'.

I work as a waitress. My working mates are men,
Do I have to go to court to prove I work as hard as them?
The diner knows the food, the bill, the tips are just the same?
Well, tell me why my pay is less and how am I to blame?
I sew up shirts and trousers in the clothing trade,
Since men don't do the job I can't ask to be better paid.
The people at the top have rarely offered something more
Unless the people underneath are walking out the door.

They say a man needs more to keep his children and his wife,
What are the needs of a woman who leads a double working life?
When the whistle blows for knock-off, it's not her time for fun,
She goes home to start the job that's not yet paid and never done.
The employer needs his profit, but the argument is weak,
Compared with how a woman needs eight dollars more a week,
Eight dollars more of butter and eggs and fruit and bread and meat,
And a bit aside to buy some shoes for all the growing feet.

'We can't afford to pay you', say the masters in their wrath,
But woman says, 'Just cut the coat according to the cloth!
If the economy won't stand it, here's the answer boys,
Cut out the wild extravagance on the new war toys!'
All among the bull, girls, all among the bull,
Keep your hearts full, girls, keep your hearts full!
What good is a man as a doormat, or following at heel?
It's not their pants we're after, it's a fair square deal.

The Job is Hard

THE PINEAPPLE TRIMMERS

A Don Henderson song

The job is hard, but hard or not,
A job is more than some have got
I'll swing my knife and sing my song
Till something better comes along.

Chorus:
I trim the tops, cut out the eyes,
All day the supervisor cries
As she looks down along the lines,
'Ladies, please pick up your pines.'

Twelve girls work, sometimes sixteen,
In two lines, and in-between
An endless belt, fed by a chute,
Brings and takes away the fruit.

Rattling tins go overhead;
You cannot talk or hear what's said.
The noise goes through and through my brain,
My song is all that keeps me sane.

The day drags on. Time passes slow,
I count the minutes as they go.
When day is done and I get paid,
I wonder how the hell I stayed.

THE BONING ROOM LADIES

Words by Des Byers

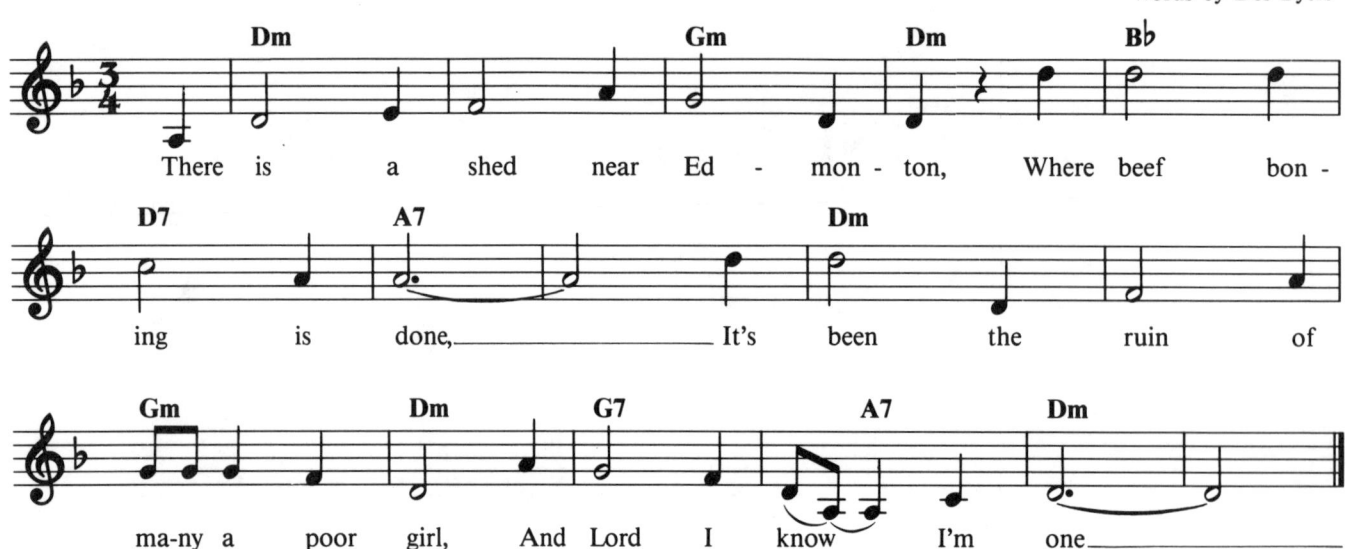

There is a shed near Edmonton,
Where beef-boning is done,
It's been the ruin of many a poor girl,
And Lord I know I'm one.

My father was a slicing man,
My mother worked the scales,
And they weighed and sliced in every shed,
From here to New South Wales.

My matadors are wearing thin,
My boots will wear out soon,
For I must wear them every day
In this cold boning room.

The boners they are cheeky,
They think that we are bold,
They think we wear pants just for them,
And not because we're cold.

And if I cut my fingers,
No hospital for me,
Just cart me down to Woree pub,
And there just let me be.

There is a shed near Edmonton,
Where beef-boning is done,
And I know that I'll go there again.
For Lord I need the mon.

THE BASIC WAGE DREAM

A Don Henderson song

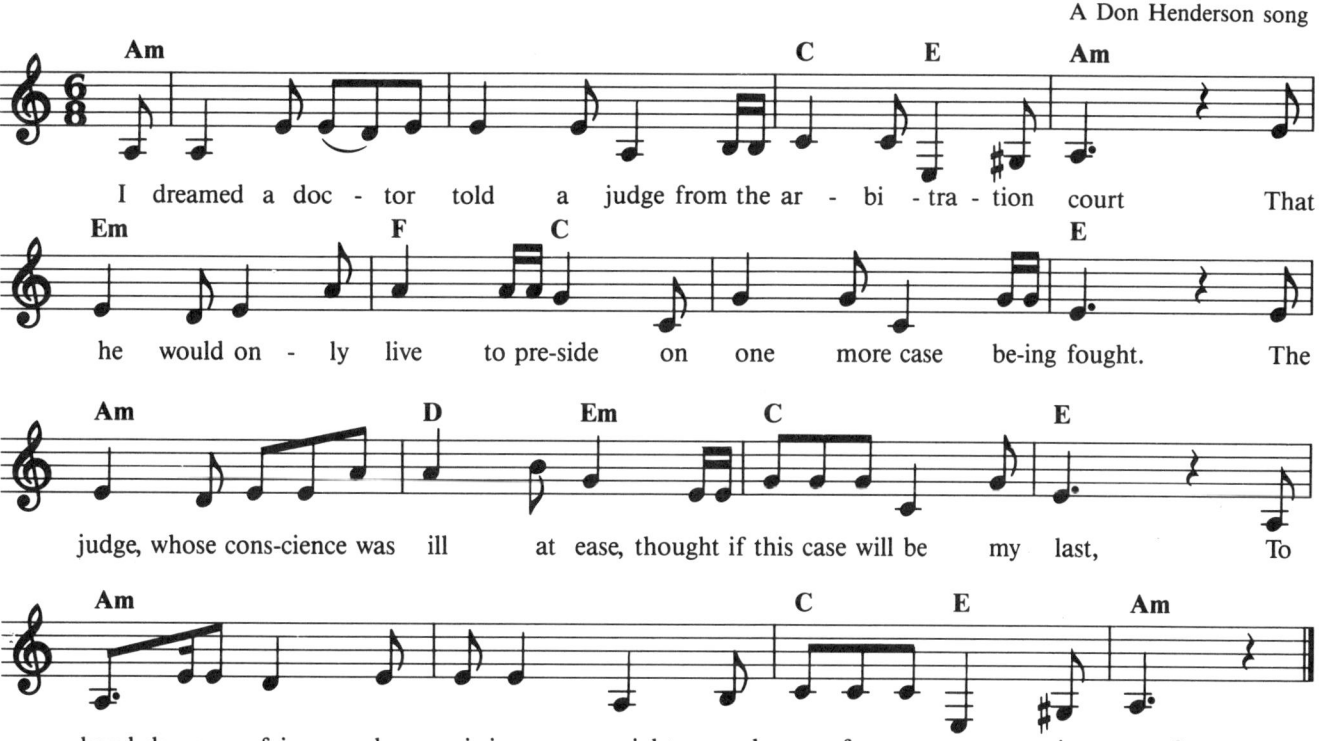

I dreamed a doctor told a judge
  from the arbitration court
That he would only live to preside
  on one more case being fought.
The judge, whose conscience was ill at ease,
  thought 'If this case will be my last,
To hand down a fair decision
  might make up for my unjust past.'

The very next case that was to come before
  this very worried sage,
was a request to raise by fifty two bob
  the weekly basic wage.
The old chap granted the raise in full
  and to assure his place in heaven,
Made the payment retrospective
  to nineteen hundred and seven.

On the first pay day after the trial,
  I couldn't believe my luck.
The paymaster brought my wages out
  on a fork lift truck.
I dreamed we got paid on a Friday
  and on that lovely night,
Mayne Nickless sent out an armoured car
  to get me home all right.

On the way we stopped at the R.S.L.
  and as I walked inside,
A poker machine took a look at my pay
  and committed suicide.
I turned around as I heard a man
  behind me softly speak.
It was Dr Coombs trying to borrow a quid
  to seem him through the week.

Then the alarm went off and I recall
  as I was waking up,
How people dream they saw the horse
  that won the Melbourne Cup,
But they can't remember what number it was.
  Well my dream was just the same,
For I can't for the very life of me
  Remember that judge's name.

A First Class Boiler Maker

A Don Henderson song

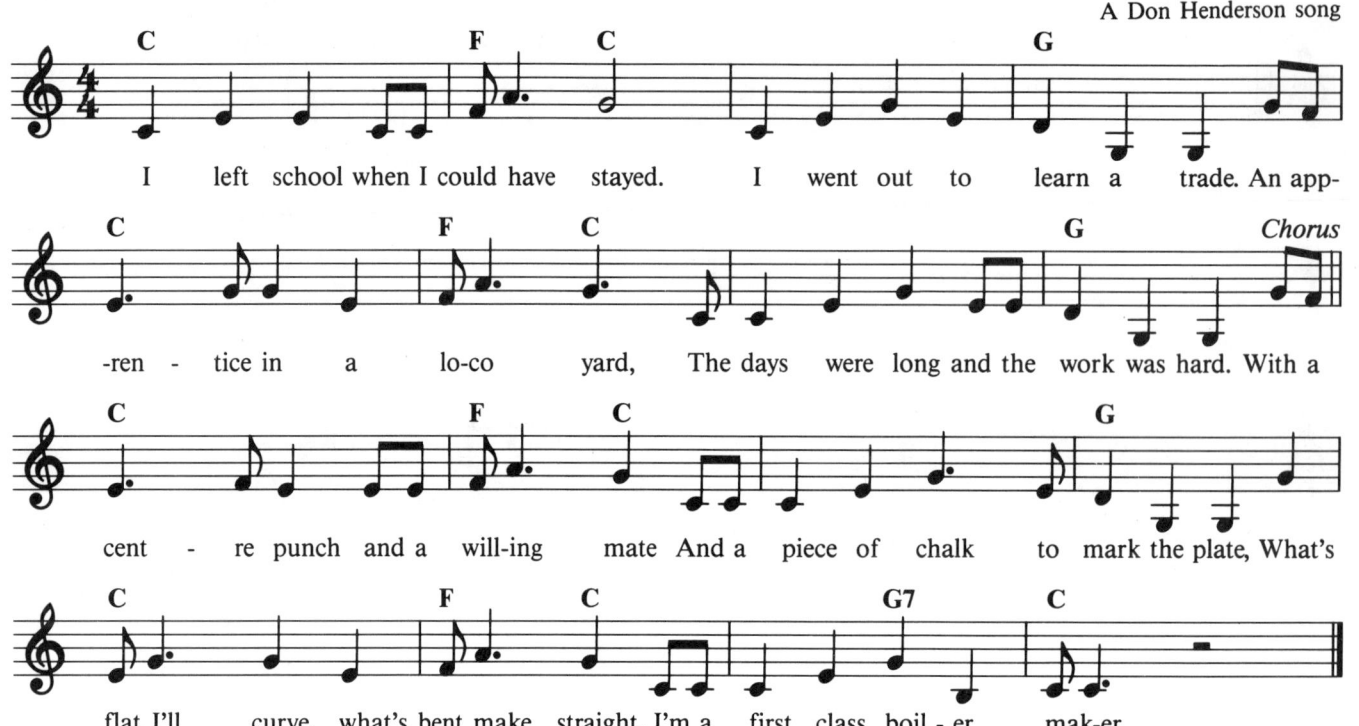

I left school when I could have stayed,
I went out to learn a trade.
An apprentice in a loco yard,
The days were long and the work was hard.

Chorus:
With a centre punch and a willing mate
And a piece of chalk to mark the plate,
What's flat I'll curve
What's bent make straight.
I'm a first class boiler maker.

Well, I read my books and I served my time,
Had my indentures sealed and signed.
What I did then I'd do again
And I've always been a Union Man.

I make machines for crushing rock,
I build railway rolling stock.
I build boilers, hoppers, frames,
Trailer chassis, tanks and cranes.

I worked in iron and then in steel.
The file gave way to the emery wheel.
Riveting went when welding came,
I am a boiler maker just the same.

ISA

Words and Music by Don Henderson

Where a giant copper mine feeds a hungry railway line
with all that the earth can give
There were buildings there and all,
but still you couldn't call it
a decent place to live.
And they took a lot before
the men who dug the ore
looked again at their bitter bread
And they knew from what they saw
that life could offer more
and some among them said
'We will make a town of Isa.'

The union met and talked,
Some southern leaders baulked
but the miners would not yield.
The meeting rose and turned
and southern leaders learned
there were strong men of the field.
Two shifts were sacked
for refusing to contract.
The day we will remember
When the company locked the gate
on the evening shift, the date
was the 14th of December
When they made a town of Isa.

When the craftsmen came next day
a locked gate barred their way
– it's own story told
Soon the smokestack that looked
in the sky no longer fumed
and the smelter had gone cold
And the eyes that met on the street were set
While men sized up each other.
The women came then
and stood beside their men
and each man's name was 'brother'
Whey they made a town of Isa.

The company and a judge
met the union, but a grudge
had split their tongue in two.
Half-strength didn't hold,
One union had sold out
– it was the A.W.U.
And the miners were betrayed
When the judgement were made
and judgement made the law
and the law was tried
and the law was defied
for the people still were sure
they could make a town of Isa.

A plane-load of police
can keep pickets off the lease,
They can hold the leaders down
They can run men off until
their dirty prisons fill,
but they can't arrest a town
and there's too much at stake
for batons to make
fighters turn and run
When the men who fight know
that even though
there'll be more fights lost than won
They'll still make a town of Isa.

Song Of The Sheet - Metal Worker

Words by John Dengate. Tune: The Valley of Knockanure.

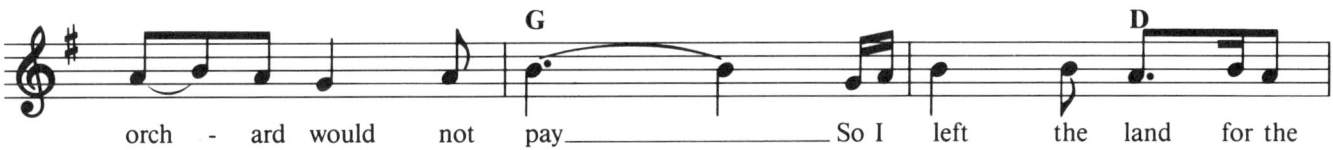

Oh, when I was a boy in Carlingford all sixty years ago,
The eucalypts grew straight and tall and the creeks did sweetly flow.
But times were hard when the old man died and the orchard would not pay
So I left the land for the factory bench and I'm working there still today.

I have earned my bread in the metal shops for forty years and more –
My hands are hard and acid-scarred as the boards on the workshop floor.
My soul is sheathed in Kembla steel and my eyelids have turned to brass
And the orchard's gone, and the apple trees where the wind whispered through the grass.

The workshop is my altar where I come to take the host.
Copper, brass and fine sheet steel – father, son and holy ghost.
The sacramental wine of work grows sour upon my tongue;
Oh, the fruit was sweet on the apple trees when my brothers and I were young.

PETER THE CABBY

A John Schumann song in the Redgum version set for the group's resources

Oh, Peter's a cabby on Adelaide's roads
And in five o'clock traffic that's a hard road to hoe
And he hunts for his family in a Holden with
   a two-way and meter.

There's no airconditioning where he plies his trade
On the green-plate stand by the Rundle Arcade
Where he sits and waits for the privilege of
   driving you home.

There's no Mr Muzak in the front of his cab
Just a crackling voice and a dog-eared road map
And a torch and biro sliding around on the dash.

Your life's in his hands when they're gripped on the wheel
The water-pump rattles and the Michelins squeal
He's been driving for years and sometimes it
   feels like forever.

He knows very well your city of gardens
He'll take you from town and drop you at Marden
Peak hour, five minutes, and if you think that's
   easy, well try it.

He can change a spare tyre in three minutes flat
And he lubes his own car lying flat on his back
And he tunes up his motor with a timing light
   in his ear.

You could be at Woodville you could be at Stirling
The sun may be burning the fog may be swirling
But Peter's still driving all down that endless
   white line.

It may be at midday, the morning or midnight
He'll sell you a ride with his yellow roof-light
'Til the drag-operator gives him a job to go home.

JOURNEYIN'

Words and Music: Chris Landon

Chorus:
The bore wheel's a turnin'
In the north-west wind,
And I'll be a journeyin'
With my best friend.

I've been around this country
Workin' here and there,
Stayin' for a season,
No ties, no cares.
Savin' up my wages,
Waitin' for the day
When tomorrow is endless
And I'll be on my way.

Well, my best friend don't say much,
That's why we get along,
He just wags his tail when he's happy,
Hangs his head when he's done wrong.
We travel round together,
Stopping where we please,
We sit around the campfire
Underneath the trees.

Well, I guess he's pretty happy,
And I guess that I am too;
As long as he's beside me
I never could be blue.
He's trusty and courageous,
He'll be with me to the end,
And what more could I ask for
Than a brave and loyal friend.

Pickin' Up Spuds

Words: Col Webb. Tune: 'Rosin the Bow'

I heard a week before Christmas
Me uncle was diggin' the spuds;
Bein' short of a quid then for Christmas
I put on me old workin' duds.
By six I was down in the paddock –
The tractor was goin' around,
Diggin' up rows of potatoes
And leaving 'em there on the ground.

Well, he gave me some bags and a bucket,
And he told me bout green ones and chats;
I looked round the paddock all over
There was spud-bags and backsides and hats –
There were backsides of every description,
And hats bobbin' up and down.
Then I heard him yell 'Come on young fella,
You won't make much just standin' around!'

So I wired right in to them 'taters –
I was goin' at 'em like fire!
Till me head started hurtin' and I slowed down –
In five minutes I started to tire.
The sun was a-blazin' down on me,
I started to feel quite a thirst,
Me back and me legs were both achin':
I wondered what would cave in first.

But when I saw that I'd filled five or six bags,
Why, then I felt like a young bull!
Till he came round and shook 'em down properly
And he said 'These here bags are half-full!' '
Well, I felt me heart sink within me
When I thought what I would have to do,
But I filled 'em right up to the top, and
I threw in a green spud or two.

Oh, the paddock was as rough as blazes –
There were thistles and snakes in me socks;
And I noticed the fella beside me
Was fillin' his bag up with rocks.
He was lobbin' 'em in there like crazy,
And it brought a smile to me lips
When I thought about the poor bloke
Who'd be buyin' them spuds to make chips!

When me uncle went home for his dinner
I sat down in the shade of the fence;
When I felt me sore muscles and sunburn
I tell you, it fair made me wince.
I prayed for a storm as I lay there,
And we had one – it came down a flood!
I thought 'Beauty, we'll pack up and go home'.
But no, we picked spuds in the mud.

Yes, we worked spuds till eight that evenin',
Then I loaded his truck up and all;
But when I asked my uncle to pay me
He gave me five dollars, that's all.
Well, I'm told green potatoes are poison;
That night, I had a dream –
Me uncle was eatin' spuds, and
Every potato was green!

THE SOUTHERN CROSS IS CALLING ME

Words and Music by Joe Paolacci

He hasn't had a break you know for 27 years
Non-stop, in a barber shop, he owns near Station Pier
He came from sunny Naples, just after World War II
And with aching heart he played his part and bid his folks adieu

Chorus:
So goodbye sunny Naples, my loving family too
The Southern Cross is calling me to build a life that's new
I'm off to see Australia, the work is plenty there
My bag is packed, I won't look back, I'll make a pile, I swear.

He took a boat to Melbourne, employment was in plenty
And he got a job, with a yankee mob, in motor car assembly
He rented up in Carlton, and money carefully spent
And with families four and sometimes more he shared his every cent.

'G'day mate!' they say to him, he answers 'Same to you'
He feels so queer they all drink beer and yell 'It's your shout Blue!'
And this goes on till six o'clock when the barman yells 'It's time!'
And it's down the hatch, there's a bus to catch on the Gardenvale line.

He met a girl from Williamstown and courted her at Mass
She stole his heart right from the start, a freckled Aussie Lass
They looked up Father Murphy, got married with great haste
And they honeymooned, in a tiny room they found in Elgin Place.

(Repeat Verse 1.)

THE WEST GATE BRIDGE DISASTER

Words by Ken Mansell. Music adapted from
'The Young Trooper Cut Down in His Prime' by Graeme Smith.

Oh time is a power that is precious and golden
That's needed so much by a working class bloke.
It's ours in the cradle then sold, seized and stolen.
If you're caught off your guard it is snuffed at a stroke.
Oh time is our own when we wake in the morning,
When stomachs are empty we clock on each day.
And high on the scaffold you are given no warning;
If a pylon comes crashing it will take you away.

There are men with more time than they know what to do with;
Who decided one day that a bridge we would build.
We rushed the job through to save costs on its finance;

The structure it split and cost thirty five killed.
It's safe in the boardroom when wind a bridge seizes.
When you hear the bolts snapping you can't strike for more pay.
They can hire more and fire more, start again when it pleases,
But the man who builds bridges, he is crushed in the clay.

The concreted decks bore down hard on the girders;
The foremen were blind when we looked down with fear.
While experts debate, who will punish these murderers?
'It's tragic', some say, 'for our two engineers',
For each one that forgets us there'll be two who remember
That profit, the culprit, in its greed was revealed.
Though many will stand by me, now I'm only an ember,
The lips of the judges have a price, and are sealed.

You can speed through the Westgate, Altona and Newport,
Past widows and children whose memories can't fade,
And use it for business or use it for pleasure,
Spare a thought for the men from whose flesh it was made.
Don't wait for the inquest or coroner's verdict;
Don't send for the priest to place me below;
But tell all my mates, if there's any still breathin'
To fight for the day when our time is our own.

Working until Friday night on city council rounds,
Writing parking tickets out as down the pavement he pounds,
Wears Adidas when he runs, his hair is short and sleek,
Writes his parking tickets out and murders in his sleep.

Chorus:
He is the weekend warrior, sharp-eyed and mean,
He is the kind of cowboy who irons his jeans,
Squinting down the barrel of a smoking twenty two,
He is out in the bush to kill those weekend blues.

Friday night the greens are out – his camo, gun and hat,
Leaves behind the city street and heads for the open flats,
Swinging on a spotlight in the night's darkest hour,
Pilot in a fighting plane – the hero feels the power.

Cripple another bounding 'roo – leave it there for dead,
Vietnam's fighting jungle kings – living in his head,
See the sun is rising now and his cartridges are spent,
He climbs between his silken sheets and seals the flap of his tent.

The victim's blood drips warm and wet to the river's bed,
Wounded – cringing in shadows of pain, cradles of burning lead,
Victor of wild creature's fear – Death won this sporting toss,
The mournful dingoes howling to the sinking Southern Cross.

Chorus:
(Repeat first two lines only).

Now Digger was a Soldier

FREIHEIT

Words by Karl Ernst Music by Peter Daniel

Spanish heavens spread their brilliant star-light
High above our trenches in the plain;
From the distance morning comes to greet us,
Calling us to battle once again.

We'll not yield a foot to Franco's fascists,
Even though the bullets fall like sleet;
With us stand those peerless men, our comrades,
And for us there can be no retreat.

Chorus:
Far off is our land,
Yet ready we stand.
We're fighting and winning for you.
Freiheit

I'm Going Back Again To Yarrawonga

Moderate

Words and Music by Neil McBeath and Claude McGlynn
J. Albert & Son, 9 Rangers Road Neutral Bay 2089
Used by permission,
all rights reserved

Now Digger was a soldier, and he sailed across the sea
With the first Anzac Brigade,
And Digger was a soldier as brave as one could be,
And a grand old name he's made.
From the landing at Gallipoli till the war clouds left the skies
He wandered round the Continent, a tourist in disguise,
Then after years of battling, when three parts full of lead,
The MO said 'We'll send you home': 'twas then old Digger said,

Chorus:
'I'm going back again to Yarrawonga,
In Yarrawonga, I'll linger longer,
I'm going back again to Yarrawonga,
Where the skies are always blue
And when I'm back again in Yarrawonga
I'll soon be stronger than old Mahonga.
You can have all your Tennessee and Caraline,
France and Belgium thrown in, take the whole lot for mine.
I'm going back again to Yarrawonga
And the land of the Kangaroo'.

Now Digger was a soldier, so he went back home again
In the good ship *Majarine,*
And Digger was a soldier, he couldn't settle down,
For a dinkum Anzac he'd been.
He daily read the papers of doings at the front,
Of all the latest victories and every blooming stunt.
One day he re-enlisted, he did without a doubt,
And out in France when peace had come again they heard him shout.

Go To The War Toiler

Words by William Robert Winspear

War is in Europe, toiler, blasting the land;
Workers stand facing workers, rifles in hand;
Masters have quarrelled, toiler: their cannons roar,
Slaying slaves in millions, toiler; go to the war!!

Chorus:
Go to the way, toiler, go to the war;
Heed not the Socialists, but wallow in gore.
Save not your helpless children, care for them
* no more;*
Leave your wife and family, and go to the war!!

Trust in the land-sharks, toiler, they own the land,
Slay for your kind employer, you are his 'hand'.
Stab for your 'pious' landlord till life is spent;
Whilst you raise your deadly rifle, he'll raise your rent!!

Heed not the sixth commandment, 'Thou shalt not kill',
Flout Christ, like jingo parsons, say 'Yes I will'!
Kill starving children's fathers; fill them with lead.
Cheer up, lad; don't be downhearted, you'll soon be dead!!

Follow your martial monarch; see how he goes,
Mounted on gallant charger, fronting his foes;
Safe from the distant foemen, bravely he fell:
If you follow his example, all will be well!!

THE PEATBOG SOLDIERS

Far and wide as the eye can wander,
Heath and bog are ev'rywhere.
Not a bird sings out to cheer us,
Oaks are standing, gaunt and bare.

Chorus:
We are the peat-bog soldiers,
We're marching with our spades
To the bog. (Repeat)

Up and down the guards are pacing,
No one, no one can go through;
Flight would mean a sure death facing,
Guns and barbed wire greet our view.

But for us there is no complaining,
Winter will in time be past;
One day we shall cry rejoicing:
'Homeland dear, you're mine at last!'

Last Chorus:
Then will the peat-bog soldiers
March no more with their spades
To the bog.

Wohin auch das Auge blicket,
Moor und Heide nur ringsheram.
Vogelsang uns nicht erquicket,
Eichen stehen kahl und krumm.

Chorus:
Wir sin die Moorsoldaten
Und ziehen mit dem Spaten
Ins Moor. (Repeat)

Auf und nieder geh'n die Posten,
Keiner, keiner kann hindurch.
Flucht wird nur das Leben kosten!
Vierfach ist umzäunt die Burg.

Doch für uns gibt es kein Klagen,
Ewig kann's nicht Winter sein.
Einmal werden frob wir sagen:
"Heimat, du bist wieder mein."

Last Chorus:
Dann zieh'n die Moorsoldaten,
Nicht mehr mit dem Spaten
Ins Moor.

If the guitar player wishes to transpose use Capo on 1st fret =

Fm	Db	Bbm	C7	Ab	Eb7	Eb	Bbm6
Em	C	Am	B7	G	D7	D	Am6

Kevin Conway

Words and tune by Clem Parkinson

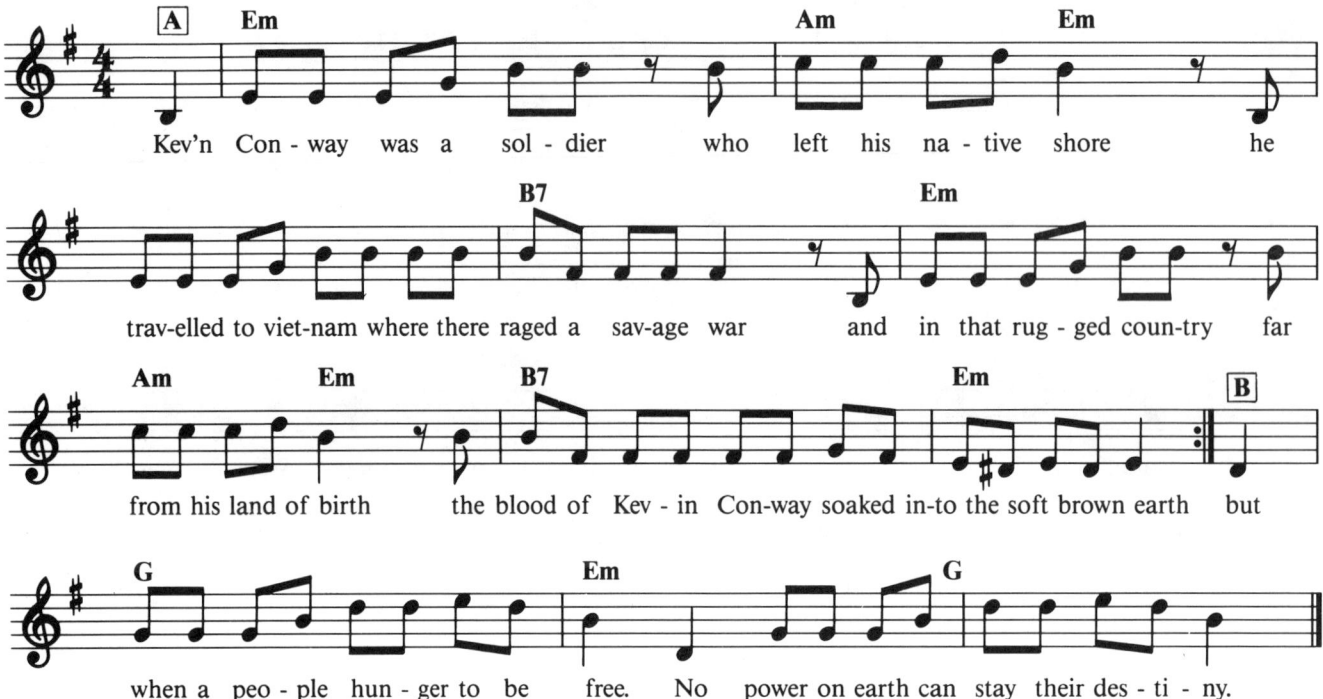

- [A] Kevin Conway was a soldier who left his native shore
  He travelled to Vietnam where there raged a savage war
  And in that rugged country far from his land of birth
  The blood of Kevin Conway soaked into the soft brown earth
- [A] The peasants fought for freedom throughout the countryside
  And a billion U.S. dollars couldn't buy a people's pride
  So men from foreign countries use napalm to kill and maim
  They call themselves 'advisers' but they're killers just the same.
- [B] But when a people hunger to be free
  No power on earth can stay their destiny
- [A] And what of Kevin Conway as he drew his final breath
  Did he curse the men who sent him to meet his tragic death?
  Were his masters filled with sorrow when they learned about his fate?
  Is there such a thing as sorrow in men who thrive on hate?
- [B] A man should be a brother to all men
  For we will never pass this way again
- [A] Now in a mine disaster, or a bushfire or a flood
  Men risk their lives for others – it's in the human blood
  They give their lives for others, it happens every day
  But he who dies for tyranny has thrown his life away.

Fixin' To Die Rag

Well come on all of you big strong men
Uncle Sam needs your help again,
He's got himself in a terrible jam,
Way down yonder in Viet Nam,
So put down your books and pick up a gun,
We're gonna have a whole lot of fun.

Chorus:
And it's one, two, three, what are we fighting for,
Don't ask me I don't give a damn,
Next stop is Viet Nam.
And it's five, six, seven, open up the pearly gates.
Well, there ain't no time to wonder why, Whoopee
We're all gonna die.

Come on Wall Street don't be slow.
Why, Man, this is war a-Go-Go.
There's plenty good money to be made
By supplyin' the Army with the tools of their trade
But just hope and pray that if they drop the bomb,
They drop it on the Viet Cong.

Come on Mothers through the land,
Pack your boys off to Vietnam.
Come on Fathers, don't hesitate,
Send your sons off before it's too late.
And you can be the first ones on your block
To have your boy come home in a box.

Come on Generals, let's move fast;
Your big chance has come at last.
Now you can go out and get those Reds - -
Cause the only good Commie is one that's dead.
And you know that peace can only be won,
When we've blown 'em all to kingdom come.

ÇANAKKALE IÇINDE — AT GALLIPOLI

A Song From Thrace

The accompanying instrument for this song is usually the saz. Guitarists could attempt a similar sound with an open D tuning DADADD and playing the melody on the upper strings with a continuous open string sound. The E's are performed slightly flatter than is usual.

At Gallipoli

There is a mirrored market at Gallipoli.
Mother, I am going to fight the enemy,
Alas, my youth alas!

At Gallipoli, there is a tall cypress tree,
Some of us are engaged, some are married,
Alas, my youth alas!

I was shot at Gallipoli,
Burried alive.
Alas, my youth alas!

Çanakkale Içinde

Çanakkale içinde aynali çarşi (repeat)
Ana ben gidiyam düşmana karşi
Of gençliğim eyvah (repeat)

Çanakkale içinde bir uzun selvi
Kimimiz nisanli kimimiz evli
Of gençliğim eyvah

Çanakkale içinde vurdular beni
Ölmeden mezara koydular beni
Of gençliğim eyvah

The Banners of Union
El Pueblo Unido

EL PUEBLO UNIDO JAMAS SERVA VENCIDO

1. De pie, cantar
   que vamos a triunfar
   avanzan ya
   banderas de unidad
   y tu vedrás
   machando junto a mi
   y así verás
   tu canto y tu bandera
   florecer, la luz
   de un rojo amanecer
   anuncian ya
   la vida que vendrá.

2. De pie, luchar
   al pueblo va a triunfar
   será mejor
   la vida que vendrá
   a conquistar
   muestra felicidad
   y en un clamor
   mil voces de combate
   se alzaran, dirán
   canción de libertad
   con decisión
   la patria vencerá.

3. La patria está
   forjando la unidad
   de norte a sur
   se movilizará
   desde el salar
   ardiente y mineral
   al bosque austral
   unidos en la lucha
   y el trabajo iran.
   La patria cubriran
   su paso ya
   anuncia el porvenir.

4. De pie cantar
   el pueblo va a triunfar
   millones ya
   imponen la verdad
   de acero son
   ardiente batallon
   sus manos van
   llevando la justicia
   y la razón, mujer
   con fuego y con valor
   ya estás aquí
   junto al trabajadro.

CHORUS:
Y ahora, el pueblo
que se alza en la lucha
con voz de gigante
gritando : ! Adelante!

El pueblo unido jamás
sera vencido.

1. Stand up and sing for victory will come,
   The banners of unions assemble in the sun.
   And you'll be there beside me on the march,
   Then you'll see the banners and the singing bursting forth,
   The dawn whose coming we proclaim,
   Red as blood, its rays set us aflame.

2. Stand up and fight, our hearts are all aflame,
   A new life is coming to put the past to shame,
   Your happiness is part of this our fight,
   A thousand cries will rise into a clamour that will
   Proudly sing, and we cannot be wrong,
   Freedom is the content of our song.

CHORUS:
*It's time for the people
To rise up in struggle
Against their oppressors
And shout all together.*
*EL PUEBLO UNIDO JAMAS SERA VENCIDO!
THE PEOPLE UNITED WILL NEVER BE DEFEATED!*

3. Our country is rising, its unity is strong.
   From north and south they come to join the throng.
   From nitrate fields the men are streaming in,
   Streaming from the forests in the south,
   They are together now, their struggle has begun,
   Their union foretells the shape of things to come.

4. Stand up and sing in a million blending parts,
   The people will win for the truth is in their hearts,
   Of steel our will, battalions we must build,
   Justice and reason will be our battle cry,
   Now look, the women too, their hearts so bold and brave,
   Unite to form the worker's mighty wave.

Bella Ciao

Bella Ciao

One morning I awoke
O bella ciao bella ciao
bella ciao ciao ciao
One morning I awoke
And I found the invader.

Oh partisan, take me away
O bella ciao, bella ciao,
bella ciao, ciao, ciao.
O partisan, take me away
I feel that I am about to die.

And if I die
O bella ciao, bella ciao,
bella ciao, ciao, ciao.
And if I die
You must bury me.

Bury me deep in the mountains
O bella ciao, bella ciao,
bella ciao, ciao, ciao.
Bury me deep in the mnountains
Under the shade of a beautiful flower.

This is the flower of the partisan
O bella ciao, bella ciao,
bella ciao, ciao, ciao.
This is the flower of the partisan
Who died for freedom.

Bella Ciao

Una mattina mi sono alzata
O bella ciao bella ciao
bella ciao ciao ciao
Una mattina mi sono alzata
e ho trovato l'invasor.

O partigiano portami via
O bella ciao bella ciao
bella ciao ciao ciao
O partigiano portami via
che me sento di morir.

E se muolo da partigiano
O bella ciao bella ciao
bella ciao ciao ciao
E se muolo da partigiano
tu mi devi seppellir.

Seppellire lassu' in montagna
O bella ciao bella ciao
bella ciao ciao ciao
Sepellire lassu' in montagna
sotto l'ombra di un bel fior.

E questo e'il fiore del partigiano
O bella ciao bella ciao
bella ciao ciao ciao
E questo e'il fiore del partigiano
morto per la liberta'.

SEBBEN CHE SIAMO DONNE
Given that we are Women

Sebben che siamo Donne

Sebben che siamo donne
paura non abbiamo
per amor dei nostri figli
per amor dei nostri figli
Sebben che siamo donne
paura non abbiamo
per amor dei nostri figli
in lega ci mettiamo

Chorus:
O lio lio la
a le lega la crescera
e noialtri lavaratori
e noialtri lavoratrici
O lio lio la
e la lega la crescera
e noir altri lavoratori
vogliamo la liberta.

E la liberta non viene
perche non c'e l'unione
crumiri col padrone
crumiri col padrone
a la liberta non viene
perche non c'e l'unione
crumiri col padrone
son tutti d'ammazzar.

E voi altri signoroni
che ci avete tanto orgoglio
abbassate la superbia
abbassate la superbia
e voi altri signoroni
che ci avete tanto orgoglio
abbassate la superbia
e aprite il portafoglio.

Given that we are Women.

Given that we are women
We have no fear
For the love of our children
For the love of our children
Given that we are women
We have no fear
For the love of our children
We will organise.

Chorus:
O lio lio la
The union will grow
We who are workers
We who are workers
O lio lio la
The union will grow
We who are workers
We demand our freedom.

And liberty does not come
Because there is no union
The scabs of the bosses
The scabs of the bosses
And liberty does not come
Because there is no union
The scabs of the bosses
Should all die.

And you 'gentlemen'
With so much pride
Drop your arrogance
Drop your arrogance
And you 'gentlemen'
With so much pride
Drop your arrogance
And open your wallets.

GÜNEŞI IÇENLERIN TÜRKÜSÜ
Ballad Of The Sunworshippers

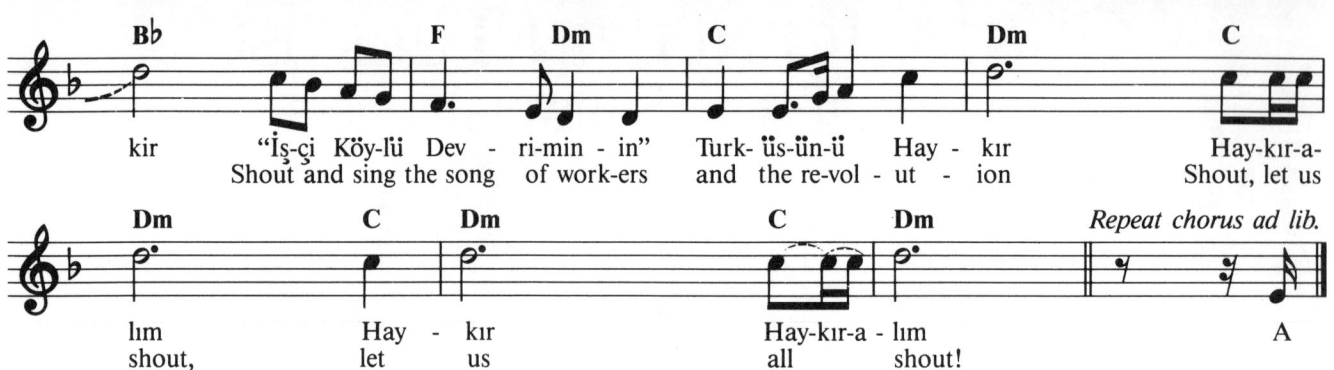

GÜNEŞI IÇENLERIN TÜRKÜSÜ

Chorus:
Akin var
    güneşe akin
Güneşi zaptedeceğiz
    güneşin zapti yakin...
.....

1. Biz topraktan, ateşten, sudan, demirden doğduk
   "Devrimleri emzirir, emekçi analarimiz"..

.....
Chorus

2. A Düşmesin bizimle yola
     evinde ağlayanlarin
         göz yaşlarini boynunda -bir-
             zincir
                 gibi taşiyanlar

...
Chorus

3. A Ölenler döğüşerek öldüler
       güneşe gömüldüler
   Vaktimiz yok onlarin matemini tutmaya

Chorus

4. A Toprak bakir
       gök bakir
   Hayir "Işci - Köylü Devriminin" Türküsünü
   Hay-kir
   Haykiralim...
   Hay-kir
   Haykiralim...

Chorus
Attack, Attack the sun
We will capture the sun

1. Soon we will capture the sun,
   We were born from earth, water, fire and iron
   Our working mothers breast fed revolutions

Chorus

2. Do not come with us if
   You have crying ones at home
   If you carry the chain of tear drops
   Round your neck then do not come

Chorus

3. Those who died fighting
   Were buried in the sun
   We have no time to grieve for them

Chorus

4. Copper the earth,
   Copper the sky
   Shout and sing the song of workers
   And the revolution
   Shout, let us shout, let us all shout!

BIR MAYIS
May Day

Gün-ler- in bu-gün get-tir-di-ği Bas-ki zu-lüm ve kan-dir Gün-ler-
It is on - ly o-ppress-ion that the days bring, These days it is

in bu-gün get-tir-di-ği Bas-ki zu-lüm ve kan-dir Anon - ly terr-or and blood that the days bring these days. But

cak bu böy-le git-mez Sö-mü-rü de-vam et-mez An-
this will not con-tin-ue. Ex-ploi-ta-tion will stop but

cak bu böy-le git-mez Sö-mü-rü de-vam et-mez Yep-ye-
this will not con-tin-ue. Ex-ploi-ta-tion will stop. A

ni bir günes po-ğar Be-de ve ül-ke-ler-de Yep-ye-
brand new sun will rise for us and for oth-ers A

ni bir-günes do-ğar Be-de ve ül-ke-ler-de Bir may
brand new sun will rise for us and for oth-ers may

Chorus

is bir may is is-cin-in em-ek-cin-in bay-ra-mi Dev-ri-
day May day the hol-i-day of work-ers and the

min san-li yol-un da I-ler-le-yen hal-kin bay-ra-mi. Dev-ri-
peo-ple who are march-ing on the glor-ious road to rev-olut-ion the

min san-li yol-un da I-ler-le-yen hal-kin bay-ra-mi.
peo-ple who are march-ing on the glor-ious road to rev-olut-ion.

Günlerin bugün getirdiği
Baski zulüm ve kandir
Günlerin bugün getirdiği
Baski zulüm ve kandir.

Ancak bu böyle gitmez
Sömürü devam etmez
Ancak bu böyle gitmez
Sömürü devam etmez.

Yepyeni bir günes doğar
Bizde ve ülkelerde
Yepyeni bir günes doğar
Bizde ve ülkelerde

Chorus:
Bir mayis bir mayis
Iscinin emerkinin bayrami
Devrimin sanli yolunda
Ilerleyen halkin bayrami
Devrimin sanli yolunda
Ilerleyen halkin bayrami.

Vermeyin insana izin
Susmasi ve kanmasi icin
Vermeyin insana izin
Susmasi ve kanmasi icin.

Hakkini almasi icin
Kitleyi bilinclendrin
Hakkini almasi icin
Kitleyi bilinclendrin.

Yurdumon mutlu günleri
Ancak gelen gündedir
Yurdumon mutlu günleri
Ancak gelen gündedir.

Translation:

It is only oppression, that the days bring,
These days it is only terror and blood
that the days bring, these days.
(Repeat)

But this will not continue,
Exploitation will stop.
(Repeat)

A brand new sun will rise
For us and for others.
(Repeat)

May day, may day,
The holiday of workers and
The people who are marching
On the glorious road to revolution.
The people who are marching
On the glorious road to revolution.

Don't let the people
Be silenced and be fooled.
(Repeat)

Raise the consciousness of the masses
So they can claim their rights.
(Repeats)

The happy days of my country
Lie in the future.
(Repeat)

Ο Μπελογιάννης ζει
Bellogiannis Lives

On the recording cited the song is attributed to D. Hatzi and D. Penti

Τον ξέρουνε τα ελάτια, τα πλατάνια
ίδιος μ' αυτά περήφανος, στητός
αχούνε απ' τη φωνή του τα Ρουμάνια
μπρός για τη νίκη, για το κόμμα μπρός.

Ο Μπελογιάννης ζει μεσ' την καρδιά μας
ο Μπελογιάννης ζει πάνω στις κορφές
ο Μπελογιάννης ζει κι είναι κοντά μας
στων τραγουδιών τις λεύτερες στροφές.

Ζει σ' όλους τους καιρούς, σ' όλους τους τόπους
το κάθε σπίτι, σπίτι του δικό.
Ζει ο Μπελογιάννης, ζει με τους ανθρώπους
που χτίζουνε ένα κόσμο Σοσιαλιστικό.

Ο Μπελογιάννης ζει μεσ' την καρδιά μας
ο Μπελογιάννης ζει πάνω στις κορφές
ο Μπελογιάννης ζει κι είναι κοντά μας
στων τραγουδιών τις λεύτερες στροφές.

by (Δ. Χατζή — Δ. Ρεντή)

The fir trees and plane trees they know him
Like them he is outstanding and tall
They heard him shout heard him from Roumania
For victory, for the party.

Belogiannis lives in our hearts
Belogiannis lives in our breast
Belogiannis lives and is with us
In the verse and song of freedom

He lives in all seasons, in all places
And every house is his house.
Belogiannis lives with men
Who are building the socialist world.

STILVORK AUSTRALISKI
Australian Steelworks

To be ornamented in performance

A Macedonian song by Vaska Ilieva

A bre stilvork, stilvork Australiski
Ti narodot što go izmači
Po furnite čerkezi Galerii
Kako lamja narod pocrna,
Staro mlado seto se prelaga
Se za taja prokleta para.

Oh you steelworks, steelworks of Australia,
Look at these faces, you have worn these people out.
With your dragon's breath you blacken every man and woman,
Exhausted men and women blackened by your furnaces.
We have been deceived, young and old alike have been deceived,
And all that for damned money, all because of money.

A bre stilvork, stilvork Australiski
Denje noké ognovite gorat
Po furnite žeški i krvavi
I vo dvata teški obertai
Mnogu narod zdravje izgubija
A i dosta kuki zatvorija

Oh you steelworks, steelworks of Australia,
Day and night those fires burn, those fires burn.
Hot and bloody burn those furnaces, those furnaces.
But we must work and work again for overtime
Falling ill from work, too much work, for overtime.
And now the houses stand empty, stand empty.

Proleta da e životta pečalbarska	Oh damned is life for a fortune seeker.
Taja pečalba mladost ni zema	Exiled all, the exile's work has claimed our youth.
Ostavivme deca siračinja	We have left our children, left them orphans,
Mladi ženi crni vdovici	Our young women, black widows,
Cela život kukavički živeeme	Living all our lives in exile, in exile,
Cela život oddeleni od roda.	Yet all our lives to live without our dear ones.

When the Earth is Owned by Labour

The Commonwealth Of Toil

In the gloom of mighty cities, midst the roar of whirling wheels, We are toiling on like chattel slaves of old, And our masters hope to keep us Ever thus beneath their heels, And to coin our very life blood into gold.

Chorus
But we have a glowing dream Of how fair the world will seem When each man can live his life secure and free; When the earth is owned by labor And there's joy and peace for all In the Commonwealth of toil that is to be.

In the gloom of mighty cities,
Mid the roar of whirling wheels,
We are toiling on like chattel slaves of old,
And our masters hope to keep us
Ever thus beneath their heels,
And to coin our very life blood into gold.

Chorus:
But we have a glowing dream
Of how fair the world will seem
When each man can live his life secure and free;
When the earth is owned by labor,
And there's joy and peace for all
In the Commonwealth of Toil that is to be.

They would keep us cowed and beaten,
Cringing meekly at their feet.
They would stand between each worker and his bread.
Shall we yield our lives up to them
For the bitter crust we eat?
Shall we only hope for heaven when we're dead?

They have laid our lives out for us
To the utter end of time.
Shall we stagger on beneath their heavy load?
Shall we let them live forever
In their gilded halls of crime,
With our children doomed to toil beneath their goad?

When our cause is all triumphant
And we claim our Mother Earth,
And the nightmare of the present fades away,
We shall live with love and laughter,
We who now are little worth,
And we'll not regret the price we have to pay.

Suggested accompaniment: Simplified version of the melody with an A minor chord used as a drone.

Today, black is the sky, today black is the day
Today a great event happened in Canberra.

It is Tuesday the eleventh of November
And the poet of the old Psillorittis writes again.

Those things that he sees and listens to are taking place
Right in this continent, in Australia, now.

Two wolves burst forth; two wolves enraged.
They ate the democracy elected by the people,

They ate the leader of democracy.
For years and times past they had been looking for an excuse.

The honoured leader, the genuine democrat,
The wolves devoured with lies and fraud.

Like the Jews who crucified Christ
And our contemporary Hebrews who betray justice,

They betrayed justice and trampled on it;
Fright and indignation they cast on the people.

Kennedy the second entered their eye,
That's why they defeated him with lies and fraud.

Gangsters and defrauders
A story written to stay through centuries

A story, unfortunately a black story
In Australia, written by evil spirits.

All the people knew from East to West
That the general has dismissed Whitlam,

Because the gangsters and the plutocracy orders
The death of justice and democracy.

But it will not be long before the sun shines and gives light
And plays its role in our democracy.

I will give unanimous victory to the just struggle
Which will give light to the people in all centuries.

Man, give the stick to hatred and fraud
And devote yourself wholeheartedly to a democrat.

Help the man that will help you
And will give a solution to your problem.

We must help, all, young and old
To accomplish the great victory,

A victory which will be crowned with success,
Which will give us joy as well as happiness.

Consider it well then, consider it well.
Vote for Whitlam and trust him

For the one whom God sent to help us
To grant happiness and joy to all.

Σήμερο μαύρος ουρανός σήμερο μαύρη μέρα,
σήμερο μέγα γεγονός συνέβη στην Καμπέρα

Νοέμβρης έχει ένδεκα ημέρα είναι Τρίτη,
και γράφει πάλι ο ποιητής του γέρο Ψηλορίτη.

Αυτά που βλέπει και γρικά και που λαβαίνουν χώρα,
σ' αυτή εδώ την ήπειρο την Αυστραλία τώρα.

Δυό λύκοι εξεσπάσανε δυό λύκοι λυσσασμένοι
δημοκρατία φάγανε απ' τον λαό βγαλμένη.

Εφάγανε τον αρχηγό απ' την δημοκρατία,
γιατί από χρόνια και καιρούς γυρεύανε αιτία.

Τον τιμημένο αργηγό γνήσιο δημοκράτη,
οι λύκοι καταφάγανε με ψεύδος και απάτη.

Ως οι Εβραίοι κάμανε και τον Χριστό σταυρώσαν,
κι οι σύγχρονοι Εβραίοι μας το δίκαιο προδώσαν.

Προδώσανε το δίκαιο και το καταπάτησαν,
φρίκη και αγανάκτηση εις τον λαό σπορπίσαν.

Ο Κένεντης ο δεύτερος τους έμπαινε στο μάτι,
γι' αυτό τον καταρρίψανε με ψεύδος και απάτη.

Μια σπείρα από μάφιες κι από απατεώνες,
μια ιστορία γράψανε να μένει στους αιώνες.

Μια ιστορία δυστυχώς μια μαύρη ιστορία
στην Αυστραλία γράψανε κακοποιά στοιχεία.

Όλος ο κόσμος τόμαθε σ' ανατολή και δύση,
πώς τον Γουίτλαμ ο τζένεραλ τον έχει απολύσει.

Γιατί προστάζει η μάφια και η πλουτοκρατία,
τον θάνατο στο δίκαιο και στην δημοκρατία.

Μα δεν θ' αργήσει ο ήλιος να λάμψει και να φέξει,
και στην δημοκρατία μας τον ρόλο του να παίξει.

Θα δώσει νίκη παμψηφεί στον δίκαιο αγώνα,
που θα φωτίζει τους λαούς στον άπαντα αιώνα.

Άνθρωπε δώσε ράπισμα στο μίσος, στην απάτη,
κι αφιερώσου ολόψυχα σε ένα δημοκράτη.

Βοήθησε τον άνθρωπο που θα σε βοηθήσει,
και στο δικό σου πρόβλημα θα δώσει μια λύση.

Πρέπει να βοηθήσουμε όλοι μικροί μεγάλοι,
σε πέρας για να φέρομε τη νίκη την μεγάλη.

Μια νίκη όπου θα στεφθεί από επιτυχία,
που θα μας δώσει τη χαρά συνάμα κι ευτυχία.

Σκεφθείτε το λοιπόν καλά, καλά να το σκεφθείτε,
Γουίτλαμ να ψηφίστε και να εμπιστευθείτε.

Σ' αυτόν που έστειλεν ο Θεός να μας εβοηθήσει,
την ευτυχία την χαρά σε όλους να χαρίσει.

THE MARSEILLAISE

Arise, ye sons of France to glory!
Your day of freedom bids you rise!
Your children, wives, and grandsires hoary,
Behold their tears and hear their cries,
Behold their tears and hear their cries,
Shall hateful tyrants, mischief breeding,
With hireling hosts, a ruffian band,
Affright and desolate the land,
While Peace and Liberty lie bleeding?

Chorus:
To arms! you sons of France!
To arms! your ranks advance!
March on! march on!
All hearts resolved
On liberty or death!

LA MARSEILLAISE (1792)

Allons, enfants de la Patrie,
Le jour de gloire est arrivé;
Contre nous de la tyrannie
L'étendard sanglant est levé. (bis).
Entendez-vouz dans les campagnes
Mugir ces féroces soldats?
Ils viennent jusque dans nos bras,
Egorger nos fils, nos compagnes!

Chorus:
Aux armes, Citoyens!
Formez vos bataillons,
Marchons, marchons,
Qu'un sang impur
Abreuve nos sillons!

THE INTERNATIONALE

Arise ye workers from your slumbers,
Arise ye prisoners of want,
For reason in revolt now thunders
And at last ends the age of can't
So away with all your superstitions
Servile masses arise – arise,
We'll change forth with the old conditions,
And spurn the dust to win the prize.

Chorus:
So comrades come rally,
And the last fight let us face
The International unites the human race.
So comrades come rally,
And the last fight let us face,
The International unites the human race.

Ye peasants-artisans and others,
Enroll among the sons of toil,
We'll claim the earth forth with as brothers,
Drive the indolent from our soil.
On our flesh too long was fed the Raven
We've too long been the Vulture's prey.
So now farewell to spirits craven
The dawn brings forth a brighter day.

No saviour from on high deliver.
No trust we have in Prince or Peer.
Our own strong hands the chains must sever
Chains of hatred-greed and fear.
N'ere the thieves will ere forgo their booty,
And to each give a happier lot.
Each at his forge must do his duty,
And strike while the iron is hot.

THE RED FLAG

To the Tune of Tannenbaum
Words by Jim Connell

To the Tune of The White Cockade

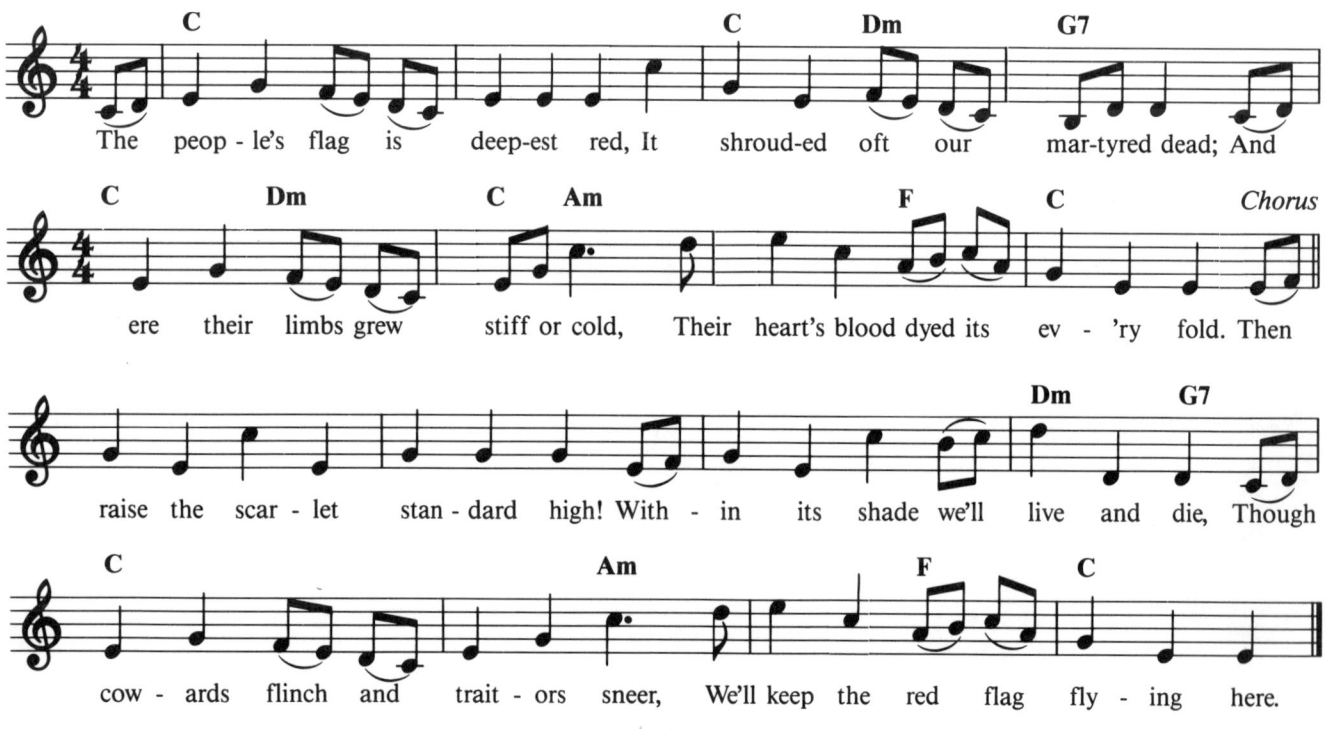

The people's flag is deepest red,
It shrouded oft our martyred dead;
And ere their limbs grew stiff or cold,
Their hearts' blood dyed its ev'ry fold.

Chorus:
Then raise the scarlet standard high!
Within its shade we'll live and die.
Though cowards flinch and traitors sneer,
We'll keep the Red Flag flying here.

Look round, the Frenchman loves its blaze,
The sturdy German chants its praise;
In Moscow's vaults its hymns are sung;
Chicago swells the surging throng.

It waved above our infant might,
When all ahead seemed dark as night;
It witnessed many a deed and vow–
We must not change its colour now.

It well recalls the triumphs past;
It gives the hope of peace at last.
The banner bright, the symbol plain
Of human right and human gain.

It suits to-day the weak and base.
Whose minds are fixed on pelf and place,
To cringe before the rich man's frown,
And haul the sacred emblem down.

With heads uncovered swear we all
To bear it onward till we fall;
Come dungeon dark, or gallows grim,
This song shall be our parting hymn!

SOLIDARITY FOREVER

Words by Ralph H. Chaplin

When the Union's inspiration through
the worker's blood shall run,
There can be no power greater
anywhere beneath the sun.
Yet what force on earth is weaker than
the feeble strength of one?
But the Union makes us strong.

Chorus:
Solidarity for ever!
Solidarity for ever!
Solidarity for ever!
For the Union makes us strong.

Is there aught we hold in common with
the greedy parasite.
Who would lash us into serfdom and
would crush us with his might?
Is there anything left for us but to
organise the fight?
For the Union makes us strong.

Is it we who ploughed the prairies, built
the cities where they trade.
Dug the mines and built the workshops;
endless miles of railway laid.
Now we stand, outcast and starving,
'mid the wonders we have made;
But the Union makes us strong.

All the world that's owned by idle drones
   is ours, and ours alone.
We have laid the wide foundations; built
   it skywards stone by stone.
It is ours, and not to slave in, but to
   master and to own
When the Union makes us strong.

They have taken untold millions that
   they never toiled to earn,
But without our brain and muscle not a
   single wheel can turn.
We can break their haughty power;
   gain our freedom when we learn
That the Union makes us strong.

In our hands is placed a power greater
   than their hoarded gold,
Greater than the might of armies
   magnified a thousandfold;
We can bring to birth the new world
   from the ashes of old,
When the Union makes us strong.

GUITAR CHORDS

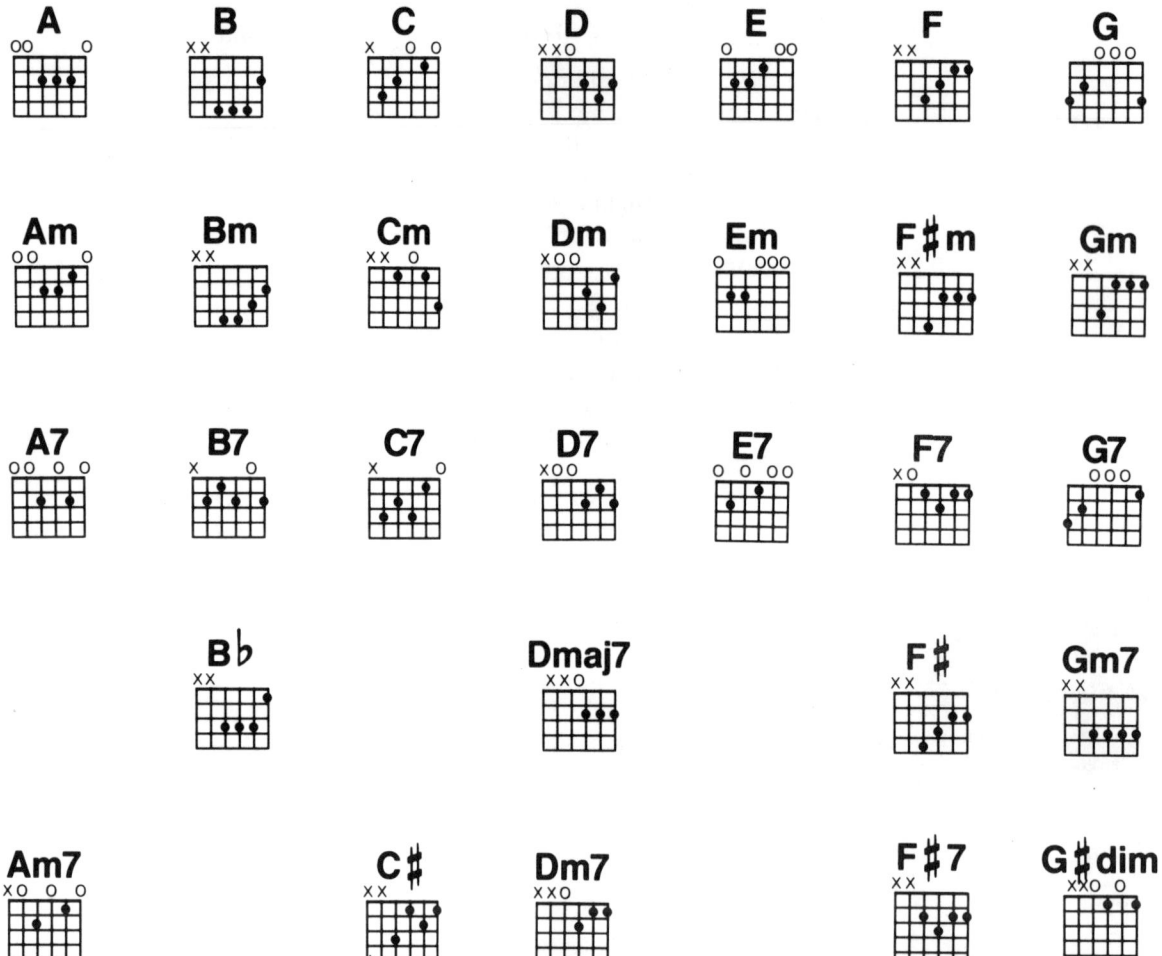

PROVENANCE

MORETON BAY   p 1

In 1952 John Manifold published his version of this song in *Bandicoot Ballads* (Ram's Skull Press, Ferntree Gully, 1951, 53,55, with Ron Edwards). It became widely known and was reprinted in *The Penguin Australian Song Book* (1964). In his *Who Wrote the Ballads*? (Australasian Book Society, Sydney, 1964 p.31) Manifold explained that his was an editor's version of the verses, a text assembled with the help of Warren Bowden and Bill Scott, using their recollections and some of the lines from the version of the self-styled 'last of the bushrangers', Jack Bradshaw, which was included in his 1911 *True History of the Australian Bushrangers* (Syd. ed, of 1924 pub. by W.J. Anderson and of 1930 (?) by the Workers' Trustees) and reprinted in his *Twenty Years of Prison Life in the Gaols of NSW* 1924 where it was sub-titled *On Poor Old Frank MacNamara*. In 1916 J.R. Scott discovered manuscript verses along very similar lines in Queensland. In 1944 Will Lawson published the Scott manuscript in *Australian Bush Songs and Ballads*.

Manifold claimed his version of all these verses formed a 'singer's text', (*Penguin Australian Song Book* p.27) and that the 'original', i.e. Bradshaw and Scott's versions, were probably meant to be recited, not sung. A version that differs very little from Bradshaw's appears in Ingleton's *True Patriots All* (Halstead Press, Sydney, 1952) and in Stewart and Keesing's *Old Bush Songs* (Angus and Robertson, Sydney, 1957, reissued 1976) under the title *A Convict's Lament on the Death of Captain Logan*, collected in Queensland in 1916, according to *Australian Tradition* No.5, November 1964.

Manifold's version has entered the realm of popular usage, but there is another authenticated, though lesser known, one. It was recorded by the Folklore Society of Victoria from the singing of Simon McDonald of Creswick, Victoria, who learnt it from his uncle, Jack McDonald, a ganger in the Victorian Railways, who was born about 1850. Both words and tune differ from the Manifold version. They appear in full in *Australian Tradition* No.5, November 1964. Manifold refers to the McDonald verses in his *Penguin Australian Song Book* notes to 'Moreton Bay' and discusses where they overlap or diverge. Where Manifold's version appears to have smoothed out the awkwardnesses of the original, to fit what he sees as a singers simpler needs, McDonald seems to have favoured an intact transmission of literary inconsistencies and the florid style which was the mark of much of the Gaelic-Irish balladry tradition.

Manifold's tune is that used for the Irish 'Youghal Harbour', which appears in George Petrie's *Ancient Music of Ireland* (Boosey and Co., London, 1902-5). You can also find it in Colm O Lachlainn's *Irish Street Ballads*, (Pan Books, London, 1978). 'Youghal Harbour' has spawned a family of related tunes, including 'The Foot and Mouth Disease' (written by the Irish patriot Joseph Plunckett). Songs related to 'Moreton Bay', or with parallel verse forms, can be found as far back as 'Father Murphy', otherwise known as 'Boulavogue', the tale of a priest executed for his part in the 1798 uprising. Descendants include 'The Galway Shawl' and Brendan Behan's 'The Ould Triangle' from *The Hostage*. Simon McDonald's tune is also related to 'Youghal Harbour', elaborating on the original melodic line and rhythm, though retaining its structure, so that it becomes something more than a variant.

For me there was always something potently evocative about Moreton Bay that wasn't explained by the verses or the deceptive serenity of its tune. For one thing its words held echoes of Ned Kelly's Jerilderie letter. My background is Irish and part of my family was from Mansfield in Kelly country. One used to have to take a stance on these matters and we were pro-Kelly, anti-authoritarian, and therefore anti-English. This song haunted me.

John Meredith and Rex Whalan, conscious of the same evocations, set out to resolve the matter. They published their results in *Rebels and Radicals* (ed. Eric Fry, George Allen and Unwin, Sydney, 1983) in an article on 'A Poet in Revolt: Francis McNamara', alias Frank the Poet. McNamara was an Irish convict born in 1811, a native of Wicklow in Kilkenny, who arrived at Sydney Cove in the *Eliza II* on 6 September 1832. His crime was stealing a plaid, for which he was sentenced to seven years transportation. Meredith and Whalan believe the real reason for his arrest was membership of the White Boys' Association, one of the illegal Ribbon Lodges, dedicated to an Ireland for the Irish.

McNamara was incapable of accepting the sentence and all subsequent attempts to break his spirit failed. Subjected to every brutality of the convict system - long periods of solitary confinement and on the treadmill, a total of 650 lashes, hard labour in irons - he remained an independent spirit, pouring out his bitter and defiant poetry. He absconded five times, the last time in rebellion at being sent down the coal mines at Newcastle on the Australian Agricultural Company's lands where he was part of the slave labour force used by absentee English landlords. In 1842 he was sentenced to another seven years which he served at Port Arthur, concurrently with John 'Red' Kelly, father of the legendary Ned. It is almost certainly here that Kelly learnt McNamara's 'The Convict's Arrival', alias 'Moreton Bay', written to celebrate Frank the Poet's arrival in Sydney and commemorating yet another colonial rebel, Jack Donahoe and the events surrounding his death in 1830. And *that* explains how Ned came to paraphrase the words of this song in his Jerilderie testament. McNamara served out his total of 15½ years of imprisonment and disappeared from the official records, never to surface again. Legend has pursued him ever since.

THE CATALPA p 2

This tribute to Irish cunning and American know-how describes the escape of six Fenian prisioners from Fremantle gaol in April 1876. It was thought to be part of a much larger plot by the Irish to break the Empire ties. The Irish in America sent the whaling ship *Catalpa* to aid in this extraordinary adventure, but after the prisoners were taken on board, the SS *Georgette* was sent in pursuit. The *Catalpa* raised the American flag. The *Georgette* hove to, aware that to fire on the whaler was tantamount to Australia declaring war on America (which would also involve the reluctant British). The six Fenians sailed off to safety. The words of the song are associated with several tunes, including derivations of 'Botany Bay', 'Judges and Juries' and 'The Dying Stockman', in the version similar to 'The Tarpaulin Jacket'. This tune is very close to that of the Irish 'Rosin the Beau' (see Peter Kennedy, *Folksongs of Britain and Ireland*).

John White, in *Australian Tradition*, September 1967, wrote that the *Catalpa* incident was not the first time a Fenian escape from Western Australia to the United States had been recorded. John Boyle O'Reilly (b. Ireland 1844), sentenced to transportation for life for treason while serving in the 10th Hussars, arrived in WA in January 1868. In February 1869 he escaped and boarded an American whaler homeward bound, settling in Boston where he became a poet, novelist and lecturer. He is sometimes referred to as the first poet whose work records references to Western Australia.

BEN HALL p 3

One of Sally Sloane's songs, this modal version was learnt from her mother, collected by John Meredith at Lithgow, NSW, and published in *Folksongs of Australia* by John Meredith and Hugh Anderson, (Ure Smith, Sydney, 1968). Ben Hall's sister-in-law assisted at Sally's birth at Parkes in 1894 and the friendship that developed between the women provided Sally with a repertoire of Hall stories.

There are several Ben Hall ballads, most of them using the come-all-ye tunes like this one, which is easily the shapeliest of all the bushranger ballads. In *Who Wrote the Ballads?* Manifold says: 'Bushranging has passed through the same developmental curve as other arts. The primitives are Donahue and his mates; classicism comes in with Hall, the Kellys are the romantics of the art'. Certainly the Ben Hall ballads are the most consistently interesting songs. Manifold also believed that the bushranger ballads show, for the first time, a distinctively Australian language, but it is also a form reliant on the style of Irish sung ballad making, though that reliance is less obvious in the Kelly examples.

IN A RAMSHACKLE HUT p 5

Tex Morton claimed authorship of this song, but John Meredith and Bill Scott say its origins can be traced to the area round Darwin at the turn of the century. (Meredith and Scott's *Ned Kelly*, Lansdowne Press, Sydney, 1980.) They give a compilation of verses from oral sources but provide no details. Their version of words and music is given here as the first song. The second is the Morton one with the yodel at the end.

Morton, who died in 1983, was responsible for popularising and commercialising an original Australian style of country music in the 1940s; a mix of Australian folk and American hill-billy, which still remains the basis of the form. He was a popular recording artist from 1936 to 1941 when, for unknown reasons, the discs cease. There was a single session in 1943, but no more until 1949, when he produced singles for the Tasman label, many of them with his sister Dorrie. There are only four singles for 1954, but in 1960 he was recording regularly again, though he never regained the standing he had in the 1940s. During the 1950s he spent much of his time overseas as a showman, sharpshooter, hypnotist, singer and Hollywood character actor.

The 1940 edition of 'The Ned Kelly Song' (Morton's title for 'Ned Kelly was Born In A Ramshackle Hut') published by Nicholson's Pty Ltd, Sydney, in *Tex Morton's Wild West and Rodeo Song Album No.5*, gives the recording of the song as: Regal Record No. G 24031. But in Eric Watson's *Country Music in Australia* (Rodeo Publications, Sydney, 1975), this number is reserved in the discography for 13/5/1940 for the titles 'Old Boko And Me' and 'The Stockman's Last Bed'. Watson gives 'The Ned Kelly Song' as recorded on Regal Zonophone G 23895, made on 20/11/1939 at Columbia Studios, Homebush, Sydney.

THE WILD COLONIAL BOY p 6

This is by far the most popular ballad of the bushranging days. No historical trace has been found of an outlaw called Jack Doolan or Donovan, Dowling, Duggan, Dolan, Donahoe, Donahue, Dollard or Davis as the dozens of versions of the verses give. There are as many tunes as there are ballads, all of them claimed as the oldest or the most authentic or the one sung in the Glenrowan pub the night before Ned and company were captured in 1880. Just to name a few: 'From Abroad', an extract from 'The Beggar's Opera'; 'The Wearin' of the Green' (the best-known version of which is by Dion Boucicault - the song 'Shaun the Post' in the play *Arrah na Pogue*) and Irish come-all-ye's of various relationships. Irish outlaw heroes abound too. In Australia — Billy Lees' (b 1878) tune, collected by Ron Edwards 23 August 1966, Thomas Meehan's (b. 1893) collected at Charters Towers 11 October 1966, Bill Harney's collected 1957 at Ferntree Gully, Victoria, Frank Evans' (b. 1892) collected at Mareeba, Queensland 3 September 1966, all in Edwards; *The Big Book of Australian Folk Song*. Then there is this version, which Edwards collected in 1960 from Thursday Islander Fred Ware. John Lahey uses it too in *Great Australian Folk Songs*. There are American cousins to the verses as well as the tunes. One of my favourites is the Irish-style version used in the Australian Ned Kelly film as sung by Englishman Mick Jagger, but the present tune, popularised in Dublin by Irish comedians, is the version in Waltons *132 Best Irish Songs and Ballads* c. 1900 (see A.L. Lloyd's sleeve notes to 'Her Mantle so Green', Topic Record 12 T 123, 1965).

The parody, 'A Mild Colonial Boy', was written by a builder's labourer in the mid 1970s when R.J. Hawke was still with the ACTU. At the time his political style was more extroverted than the style he adopted after becoming Prime Minister.

CLICK GO THE SHEARS p 8
The tune is based on 'Ring the Bell Watchman', a drawing room song by Henry Clay Work composed in 1865. Other songs of his include 'Come Home Father' (1864), 'Marching Through Georgia' (1865), 'The Ship That Never Returned' and 'Grandfather's Clock' (1876). (See Warren Craig's *Sweet and Lowdown*, New Jersey, 1978.) 'Ring the Bell Watchman' is often presumed to be a much older song than it actually is, but the internal evidence is against this. There is a strong stylistic similarity to other Work compositions as far as the words are concerned, and the tune is structurally similar to 'Marching Through Georgia' and 'Grandfather's Clock', in that it consists of contrasting phrases with a chorus that uses the second half of the verse for its second half.

The melody is also used for the revivalist hymn 'Pull for the Shore' and the temperance hymn 'Sign the Pledge Brother'. (See A.L. Lloyd's sleeve notes to *Across the Western Plains,* Wattle Recordings.) Although fragments have been collected from the 1920s in various parts of Australia, the well known version's recent dissemination in print must be credited to Dr Percy Jones's *Burl Ives Folio of Australian Folksongs* (1953).

A similar song called 'Click, Click, That's How the Shears Go' was collected from Jack Luscombe by John Meredith at Ryde in 1953 and published in Meredith and Anderson's *Folk Songs of Australia* (1967), but though the form used for the words concurs with the version given here, the tune is quite different. Still, Meredith also collected an extra verse from Sally Sloane:
'Now Mr Newchum, for to begin,
In number seven paddock bring all the sheep in,
Don't leave none behind, whatever you do,
And then you'll be fit for a jackeroo.'

THE SPRINGTIME IT BRINGS ON THE SHEARING p 10
In 1865 the *Creswick and Clunes Advertiser* published part of E.J. Overbury's poem *On The Wallaby Track* under the title *Bush Poems*. Fragments passed into the oral tradition, emerging, much altered, in the folksong repertoire, attached to a variety of tunes.

In 1953 Dr Percy Jones published a version of these fragments in his *Burl Ives Folio of Australian Folk Songs*. He does not name his source for either the tune he uses or for the words. In 1954, John Meredith began collecting songs from the legendary Sally Sloane and, somewhat later, from Bill Coughlin, both of whom gave him incomplete and differing versions of a song they also called 'Springtime it Brings on the Shearing'. Meredith published these with Hugh Anderson in *Folk Songs of Australia* in 1967.

The Jones song won the day, passing into general use, while the Sloane and Coughlin songs are rarely heard. All three are so short that singers often go back to the Overbury verses to flesh out the text. The original poem is included here in case singers wish to create something of their own without straying too far from 'The Wallaby Track'.

For the record, the Jones 1953 edition has only three verses of four lines each, the first and second corresponding to the first four lines of each of the third and second verses of 'The Wallaby Track', arranged in that order. The final verse has no equivalent in Overbury. In recent years the Bushwackers have popularised the Jones song using his second verse as a chorus and adding a version of the second half of Overbury's second verse before the final Jones verse. I have used the Jones words and melody but with the added verse from the Bushwackers and the chorus marked as they give it.

THE BANKS OF THE CONDAMINE p 11
The first of the two versions given here is from *The Queensland Centenary Pocket Songbook* (Federation of Bush Music clubs, Brisbane 1959). The melody is a variant of the widely used 'Irish Molly Oh' tune, but collectors in the 1950s also found the verses attached to a number of other melodies, including the come-all-ye's 'Tramps and Hawkers', 'Willy Reilly' and 'Paddy Sheehan'. Ron Edwards (see: *The Big Book of Australian Folk Song*) found an Australian horsebreaking version which he thinks may be the original, but Edgar Waters (see: *Australian Tradition* October 1966) believes all the tunes have a common ancestor in the English ballad 'The Banks Of The Nile', an early nineteenth century broadside about a girl and her soldier lover going off to fight the French in Egypt. Dialogue ballads of this sort, between sailors or soldiers going to war and the girls they left behind them, are common in Irish, Scottish and English broadsheets as far back as the seventeenth century. 'On The Banks Of The Condamine' then, may have a very extensive family tree.

The second tune, wayward and modal, was collected by John Meredith from Ron Manton at Erskineville in 1958. (See: *Folk Songs of Australia*.) Manton's memory failed him at the time, which is why the verses are incomplete.

FLASH JACK FROM GUNDAGAI p 13
Another of the tunes collected in the late 1920s by the English folk song authority A.L. Lloyd. John Manifold used it for *The Penguin Australian Song Book* in 1964, citing the Queensland Folklore Society as his source, not Lloyd. The melody is, in fact, based on the popular nineteenth century song 'The Son of a Gambolier'. (See: Sigmund Speath's *Read 'Em And Weep,* Doubleday Page and Co., NY, 1926.) It was frequently used for parodies and has been collected in Australia under other titles including 'I'm a Rambling Rake of Poverty' and 'Rambling Rake'.

'Flash Jack' also bears a striking resemblance to a seaman's song, the forebitter 'According to the Act' but it isn't alone in this. 'All Among the Wool Boys' (which supplied Glen Tomasetti with her tune for 'Don't Be Too Polite Girls') and 'The Cockies of Bungaree' both show signs of having undergone the same sea change.

The words are from Banjo Paterson's *Old Bush Songs* but Paterson's chorus length has been adjusted to fit the tune. Manifold thought this might indicate that another tune was once used. Indeed another tune *was* used by Vance Palmer in his *Old Australian Bush Ballads* (1950) but the music is by composer Margaret Sutherland and labelled 'restored'. It is doubtful that the tune comes from the folk tradition at all, let alone predates Lloyd or the tune from the Queensland Folklore Society.

Forebitter: a foc'sle shanty, a leisure song

LAZY HARRY'S p 14
The first of the two versions given was collected by Ron Edwards from Jack Parveez at Charters Towers in 1966 when the singer was seventy six. (See: *The Big Book Of Australian Folk Songs*.) Ted Egan uses a related tune in *The Shearers Songbook*, (Greenhouse, Melbourne, 1984). The words are from Banjo Paterson's *Old Bush Songs*, which were first published in 1924, though they were collected by the poet in 1905. 'Lazy Harry's' uses the complete set of Paterson verses, but omits his chorus.

The second tune is the more popular one. Ron Edwards adapted it from the one 'restored' by composer Margaret Sutherland in Vance Palmer's *Old Australian Bush Ballads* (Allan and Co, 1950).

Roto is a station north of Hillston in southern NSW
Whips and whips of rhino - a large sum of money i.e. lashings
To knock about - spend wildly
Three spot cheque - three hundred pounds
Pizen - poison i.e. adulterated liquor

ACROSS THE WESTERN PLAINS OR ALL FOR ME GROG p 16
English folk song authority A.L. Lloyd collected this song in Australia in the early 1930s. His recording of it in 1968 under the title 'Across The Western Plains' (Wattle Recordings) reintroduced it to the folk song repertoire. Ron Edwards published it under the Lloyd title, coupling it with 'This Old Hat Of Mine' since both tunes were evolved from 'Across The Western Ocean', also known as 'All For Me Grog'. (See: *The Overlander Song Book,* Ram's Skull Press, Ferntree Gully, 1956.) This sailors' song refers to the North Atlantic as the Western Ocean. In Australia the Western Ocean became the Western Plains.
To 'lamb down' was to keep a bushworker on a spree until his wages were spent, usually helped along by the publican arranging to have his grog (drink) adulterated. The drugged victim would wake to be told that though he couldn't remember it, he has 'shouted the bar' and had nothing left.

AUSTRALIA'S HAPPY LAND OR COME AND JOIN THE UNION p 18
This song has two titles but as 'Australia's Happy Land' it appears in *Tibbs Popular Song Book* (1887) where the present tune is cited as 'Ehren on the Rhine'. A year later Tibbs retitled it 'Australia's Sunny Land' in *Tibbs' Popular Australian Songs and Poems*. John Lahey in *Great Australian Folk Songs* gives a shortened version to a different tune supplied by a singer from the Murrumbidgee river area, Joseph Patrick Bourke. The song itself is a true union ballad, aggressive, bitter, defiant. As the penultimate verse shows, not everyone agreed with the continuing use of Kanaka slave labour in Queensland.

TRAVELLING DOWN THE CASTLEREAGH p 20
There are at least seven collected versions of this tune, all of them related to the nineteenth century Irish comic song 'Pat From Mullingar'. (See: Colm O Lachlainn's *Irish Street Ballads*, Pan, London, 1978.) John Meredith collected this adaptation from Joe Cashmere of Booligal (b.circa 1875), a bushworker, singer, fiddle player and friend of Hoopiron Lee of 'Widgeegowera Joe' fame. Cashmere was widely read and contributed stories and verses to various newspapers, including the *Albury Banner*, the *Bulletin* and the *Worker*, but in spite of this and his professed love of the poetry of Banjo Paterson, he seems to have been unaware that the verses he sang for 'Travelling Down The Castlereagh' had their origin in Paterson's *A Bushman's Song*. Cashmere thought the words were older than Paterson and indeed it is possible that Banjo published reshaped verses already circulating in the oral tradition of bushworkers, a tradition Cashmere had inherited. (See: Russel Ward's *Australian Folk-Ballads and Singers* in *Meanjin* No.3, 1954.)

THE FLASH STOCKMAN p 22
The English folklorist A.L. Lloyd claimed to have collected this song in Australia around 1930. (There are two well known Lloyd recordings and booklets of words. One dating from c.1956, *Australian Bush Songs* a USA Riverside Record, the other from 1958, *Across the Western Plains*, a Wattle Record.) The tune he uses is the one also used for 'The Drover's Dream' and 'The Wooloomooloo Lair'. All of them derive from the Irish comic cong 'The Day They Taught Them French at Killaloo'. In related guises the words appear in Ben Boyang (A.V. Vennard, in *Bush Recitations*, 6 booklets, 1932-40.) in the 2nd booklet c. 1933, and in Douglas Stewart and Nancy Keesing's *Old Bush Songs* (Angus and Robertson, 1957).

LADIES OF BRISBANE OR AUGATHELLA STATION p 24
There are two versions of this song currently in vogue in Australia, one in a major key and this one in the minor. Both derive their tunes directly from 'The Spanish Ladies', first published by Chappell, London, in 1840. It appears in later English folksong collections in both major and minor versions. The minor tune was collected during the 1930s in Australia by A.L. Lloyd, the English authority on English and European folkmusic, who edited *The Penguin Book of English Folksong* with Ralph Vaughan Williams (1959). The original verses appeared on broadsheets of the Catnach period. Cecil Sharp gives a version in *English Folk Songs* vol II (Novello, London, 1920), saying it is a capstan shanty also known in the Royal Navy as a song,

shanties not being officially permitted. The *Boomerang* of 28 February 1891 first published this parody whose author was probably S. Mendelsohn of Nanango (d. 1897). The Queensland Folklore Society derived the minor key version published in *The Queensland Centenary Pocket Songbook* from Lloyd's sung version on disc.

THE MARANOA DROVER OR THE SANDY MARANOA   p 25

Transmitted by Pat Murphy to collector Ron Edwards at Mt Kooyong in North Queensland in the mid-1950s. Murphy had it from an itinerant worker travelling between Mareeba and the mining hamlet of Minnie Moxam in the 1920s. Murphy's words were incomplete. Edwards has added to them from those in the Hurd Collection (c.1894-1900) in the Oxley Library, Brisbane. This is also the probable source of the version used by Banjo Paterson in *Old Bush Songs* (various editions 1905-1931,) where the words are attributed to A.W. Davis (b.1870) of Urangan, Queensland. Stewart and Keesing (*Old Bush Songs*, 1957) say R.C. Lethbridge, brother of Davis's late employer, also claimed authorship for Davis. The tune is derived from 'The Little Log Cabin in the Lane', published in 1871 as the work of W.S. Hays. There is a whole family of related tunes used in Australia which draws on this combined with older sources, e.g. 'Maggie May' (see: Radic, p.3. for the convict origins of 1830 and the minstrel connection via 'Darling Nellie Gray', *Treasury of Favourite Australian Songs*, Currey O'Neil Ross, Melbourne, 1983) and 'Eumerella Shore'.

The Maranoa river enters the Balonne near St George in Queensland. Gunedah is in NSW.

WHERE THE BRUMBIES COME TO WATER   p 27

Ron Edwards based the verses for this song on a ballad by Will Ogilvie. Edwards does not claim the melody as one he composed but attributes it to Jack Parveez, of Charters Towers, who heard it around 1908 while working in the Julia Creek area of North Queensland. Parveez used a very basic tune Edwards reports as similar to a version he used for 'The Wild Colonial Boy', but does not include it in *The Overlanders Song Book* (Rigby, Adelaide, 1971) or in *The Big Book of Australian Folk Song* (Rigby, Adelaide, 1976).

THE QUEENSLAND DROVER OR THE OVERLANDER   p 28

There are three distinct songs of this name, all on the same theme, but words and tunes differ. The tune used here was collected in Australia by John Manifold who learnt it from his father. Manifold dates his father's reception of the song as around 1900. There is a close similarity between this tune and that used for the early nineteenth century 'Thou Bonnie Wood o 'Craigielea' by James Barr to words of the Paisley poet Robert Tannahill. It became a popular drawing room 'Scotch song', and though one may not derive from the other they are certainly of the same family. James Barr's air is to be found in *The Miniature Museum of Scotch Songs* (1818). This is the tune sometimes cited as the source of 'Waltzing Matilda'.

THE DYING STOCKMAN   p 29

This song appears in dozens of guises and has been collected by many people in many places. It is basically a parody of the mid-nineteenth century drawing room song by Charles Coote (music) and C.J. Whyte Melville (words). 'The Tarpaulin Jacket' which begins: 'A tall stalwart lancer lay dying'. 'The Tarpaulin Jacket' song owes much to 'Rosin the Beau' an Irish jig tune used for quadrilles and country dances and, at times, more slowly as an old-fashioned waltz (see *Folksongs of Britain and Ireland*, edited by Peter Kennedy). In Australia the tune from 'The Tarpaulin Jacket' was used for the words now in use. It was written at Galton, Queensland in 1882 by Horace Flower and Walton Kent, then the manager at Rosewood station in the Lockyer district. It was printed in the *Portland Mirror*, 8 July 1885. Other details on the origins of the words are *Australian Tradition*, September issue 1968.

Other 'dying' songs to the same tune as 'The Dying Stockman' include 'The Dying Bagman' and 'The Dying Sleeper Cutter'. 'The Dying Fettler' was collected by Ron Edwards (see: *Big Book of Australian Folk Song*) from Vic Leonard at Lappa Junction, north Queensland on 21 August 1966. Leonard said he learnt it from Frank Stock of Koorboora, a now vanished mining centre. It appears in the *National Office News* of the Australian Railways Union (Winter, 1984) along with 'The Dying Bagman' and 'The Dying Sleeper Cutter'. 'The Fettler' and 'The Cutter' appear in *Navvy on the Line*, produced by Larrikin Records. A bagman was a single man who collected the dole by train jumping, town to town, often harassed on the way by railway police.

'The Dying Sleeper Cutter', also known as 'Cant-hook and Wedges', was collected by John Meredith in the mid 1950s in the Gulgong area, NSW, from two sources: Herb Tattersall and Norman Rowland (see *Folk Songs of Australia*). Neither remembered an intact set of verses. Rowland said he 'made up' his version in 1932 when he was 14. Tattersall denied this, saying Rowland began the verses but never completed them. The popularised version of the song seems to be an amalgamation of both. Meredith collected 'The Dying Bagman' (see *Folk Songs of Australia*) in North Sydney from Bill Foster, to whom he was introduced by Joy Durst, the Sydney folksinger and folklorist who established the Victorian Bush Music Club, Foster learnt the song 'on the track' during the 1930s depression.

Other versions appear in *Freedom Songs* (published by the Eureka Youth League, c.1954) and in *The Singabout Songster* (published by the Sydney Bush Music Club, 1968.) Edwards notes that there are other verses to the same tune: The 'Dying Digger' and 'The Dying Bargehand', to name only two. 'The Dying Shearer' is an entirely different song. 'The Dying Aviator' is usually attached to the tune of 'Botany Bay' Both 'Charlotte' (alias 'The Dying Harlot') and her associate, 'Lady Monroe', are considered too disreputable to print.

CANE KILLED ABEL   p 30

Based on a sea shanty model with words by ex-seaman, poet and husband of Dorothy Hewett, Merv Lilley (b.1920).

Music by Chris Kempster, who has been involved in the NSW folk revival since the 1950s and is an active performer.

THE CANE CUTTERS LAMENT p 31

Collected by Stan Arthur in 1958 in the sugar town of Childers in Queensland from cane cutters Norm Barnes and Arnie Warren. (See: Bill Scott's *Second Penguin Australian Songbook,* 1980.)

The tune is derived from the hymn *Here We Suffer Grief And Pain* by Thomas Bilby (b.1794). It was first published in 1831 and was a favourite Sunday School hymn around the turn of the century. (See: *A Dictionary of Hymnology,* second edition, edited by John Julien and published by John Murray, London, 1907.) The hymn itself can be found in *The Free Church Hymnbook* published by J. and R. Parlane, Paisley, Scotland, 1882.

There is some dispute about who was the first of the folk song revival collectors to 'discover; 'The Cane Cutter's Lament'. This may be due to a widespread knowledge both of the song and of the hymn from which it sprang. Several other versions collected by Ron Edwards appear in *The Big Book of Australian Folk Song.*

THE CANE GANG p 32

The tune is based on 'Villikins And His Dinah', the mid-nineteenth century burlesque version of a serious English ballad, 'William and Diana', itself a descendant of the much older traditional ballad 'William Taylor'. There is some evidence to suggest that there is a general 'Villikins' family of tunes dating from the early seventeenth century, but the many Australian songs which use variants of the tune stem from the version popularised by Frederick Robson in London at the Grecian Saloon and the Olympic around 1839. The popular entertainer Sam Cowell took up this 'Villikins And His Dinah' and, after using it in his shows, published it in *Sam Cowell's 120 Comic Songs* (Davidson, London, c.1850). The warehouse lists of the music sellers show that the book had strong sales in Australia.

The words were written in the 1920s by a Cairns cane cutter, Stan Dean. He explained to Ron Edwards, who collected the song thirty years later, that 'main toe' translates as ptomaine poisoning, a 'key and chain' was the roller-tightened chain used to clamp together a load of sugar cane, and that a 'd-eleven' was a long, straggling variety of cane. The last verse describes the custom that marked the end of a season when the last truck out was decorated with the dirty clothes of the cutters.

MY TRAPS ARE ALL A-JANGLE OR THE RABBIT TRAPPER'S SONG p 33

Wendy Lowenstein and Dave de Hugard collected this song from Basil Cosgrove at Armidale NSW (n.d.). It was published in *Tradition* 31:17 (1973). Cosgrove worked as a ringbarker in the New England district most of his life. He thought the words were by a woman and published in the *Women's Weekly* about 'fifty years ago' adding that 'we put a tune to it'. The *Women's Weekly* was first published in 1933. Wendy Lowenstein was uncertain about the line 'I'm a .... rabbit trapper'. It was sometimes sung as 'spurting' but sounded to her like 'snowpole' or 'smokehole'. 'Whistle' in the following line is her addition.

The tune has been collected in Australia associated with 'Travelling Down the Castlereagh' (See p.00). Singer Arthur Wood (b.1883), formerly of Winton, Queensland, transmitted a version of it to Ron Edwards on 17 September 1966 at Mt Molloy in Northern Queensland (see: *Big Book of Australian Folk Song*). It is a tune also found in Ireland. One well known text set to it is 'The Rosscrea Cows', a County Clare song with a nostalgic and rebellious bent that is perculiarly Irish. (Recorded on *The Russell Family of Doolin, County Clare* (Topic 12 TS 25).)

THE BUYER ON OUR RUN p 34

Collected by Wendy Lowenstein and Werner Lowenstein at Madura in 1969. The music was supplied by Fai Hockley, the wife of a rabbit trapper working on the Nullarbor Plain. Her delivery was described by the collectors as 'country and western style with overtones of yodelling'. Mrs Hockley said the words she used were by an 'old trapper mate'. The song was published in *Tradition 31* (1973) and described by C.L. in that edition as 'a contemporary working song'. C.L. points out the importance of the buyer to the trapper's way of life since his isolation meant he had to rely on the buyer for food, mail and money.

BULLOCKY-O p 36

Collected from Cyril Duncan of Nerang by the Queensland Folklore Society and published in 1959 in the *Queensland Centenary Pocket Songbook*. (Federation of Bush Music Groups, Brisbane, published by Edwards and Shaw, Sydney.) This tallies with the Manifold/Penguin version of 1964 but differs from Duncan's own performance of 1973, which can be heard on the LP *Bush Traditions* (Larrikin 007). This recorded version illustrates a common feature of an older generation of singers - to simplify the tunes of later verses after giving a complex performance of the first verse, possibly because of a text-centred approach. Singers of the revival don't usually do this, possibly because they are public singers and therefore not confined to the intimate approach from which this practice stems.

THE GREAT NORTHERN LINE p 37

Collected in the late 1950s by John Meredith and the verses printed alone in *Folk Songs of Australia* with the tune named as that used for 'The Knickerbocker Line', collected from Sally Sloane [b.1894], whose history he gives in that book. Her repertoire was extensive and largely Irish. The tune has also been used for 'Fowler's Bay' and, in a variant, 'The Station Cook'. This appears in *The Penguin Australian Song Book* in 2/4 time. John Manifold gives it as collected by Dr Percy Jones, Melbourne but the tune is from *Singabout*, vol 2, No.2. Ron Edwards gives a 4/4 version of it in *The Big Book of Australian Folk Song* where he adds that the English folklorist A.L. Lloyd says 'The Station Cook' was sung to the Scottish 'Musselburgh Fair' the tune known in America as 'The Cruise of the Bigler' (see sleeve notes to *Across the Western Plains,* Wattle Recordings, 1958). The same tune was used for 'Lachlan Tigers'. For the extraordinary effect of A.L. Lloyd on traditional Australian song see *Northern Folk* September 1966, No.6, an article on Lloyd by R.G. Edwards. The present tune is close to the Meredith version of The 'Knickerbocker Line'. It also appears in *Australian Tradition* and in John Lahey's *Great Australian Folk Songs* where he gives his source as *Singabout* vol 4, No.4, 1962.

Cecil Sharp the English collector, came across 'The Knickerbocker Line' at Shipton, outside Cheltenham, in Gloucestershire in 1911.

THE COCKIES OF BUNGAREE p 39

Collected by A.L. Lloyd in the 1930s in Albury and recorded for his 1957 LP *The Banks Of The Condamine*. The version given here is somewhat later and comes from the singing of Simon McDonald of Creswick. It was collected by Norm O'Connor and Mary Jean Officer of the Victorian Folk Lore Society in 1960. John Manifold, in *The Penguin Australian Song Book* reports that McDonald repeated the chorus at irregular intervals and he believed the song could be treated as a 'solo', using the chorus merely as the second verse. The singer of another version, (also collected by Norm O'Connor, but with Bob Michell,) Mr P.H. Bellchambers of Brunswick, Melbourne, remembered learning the song around 1899, so its Australian appearance dates back at least ninety years.

The tune is related to the forebitter 'The Lime-juice Ship', alternatively titled 'According To The Act', which satirised the 1794 Merchant Shipping Act and the mode of issuing rations, particularly the lime juice which earned British crews the nickname Limies. The tune is also heard in Nova Scotia, with verses about the sauerkraut and bully rations. (See: Stan Hugill's *Shanties From the Seven Seas*.)

The town of Bungaree is about sixteen kilometres east of Ballarat in Victoria. It achieved a public notoriety in the nineteenth century as a place of mean spirited farmers. Its residents were also called the 'savages of Bungaree' often in contrast with 'the gentlemen of Ballarat'. Bungaree was one of the intensely Irish areas of Victoria. Ballarat prided itself on its Anglo-Saxon majority.

THE CONSERVATIONIST p 40

By Michael Flanagan, an Irish emigrant from East Galway who has worked in the mines from Broken Hill to Kalgoorlie during the mining boom of the late 1960s. It appears on the record *Seventh Australian Folk Festival* (Klarion SF 263) recorded in 1973, sung by The Ramblers.

The tune is based on the Irish 'Cruiskeen Lawn' (see: *Irish Street Ballads*) by Colm O Lachlainn, Three Candles, Dublin, 1939.), which is a member of a family of such ritual tunes found right across Europe. (See: A.L. Lloyd's *Folksong in England* pp.71-84 and Lucy Broadwood's notes to tunes in the *Journal of the Folk Song Society* Vol.3, 1908, England.) Flanagan may also have been influenced in his choice of tune by the song 'We Gets Up in the Morn', which was popularised in Australia and British folk clubs at the time when 'The Conservationist' was written, having appeared on the influential Watersons album *Frost and Fire* (Topic 12T 136).

LOOK OUT BELOW p 42

The goldfields entertainer Charles Thatcher is responsible for the verses of this song but his tune, based on 'The Smuggler King', seems to have disappeared. The tune given here is a slight variant of the one John Meredith collected from Sally Sloane and Gladys Scrivener, which also used the Thatcher verses. (See: *Folk Songs of Australia*.) The Sloane-Scrivener tune was associated with the ballad 'The Three Butchers'. (See: *Marrowbones*, ed. by Frank Purlow. E.F.D.S. Publications, London, 1965.)

THE MINER p 43

A song collected from Tony Davis of Fruitgrove, Queensland on 11 April 1970 by Ron Edwards. (See: *The Big Book Of Australian Folk Song*.) The tune is based on the English music hall song 'Follow The Band'. Though there are several versions collected in Australia with differing tunes and verses – some earlier than this one – they all show evidence of a common subject origin, verse shapes and melodic structure. 'The Miner' is one of the few songs from the later period of gold mining. Its verses refer, not to the alluvial techniques common to the songs of the 1850s gold rush, but to deep-shaft techniques.

THE CHINAMAN p 44

A song from the Bendigo goldfields by Charles Thatcher. Hugh Anderson, the Thatcher scholar, song collector and folklorist, has reconstructed much of Thatcher's output and published it in *The Goldrush Songster* (Ram's Skull Press, Melbourne, 1958) and in *Studies in Australian Folklore, Vol. I: When First I Landed Here*. (Red Rooster Press, Melbourne 1980.)

Charles Thatcher, (1831-1878), known as the Colonial Minstrel, was a popular and controversial entertainer on the Australian and New Zealand goldfields, noted for his comic parodies (called paradoes) of popular tunes, the words frequently reflecting the working life of the diggers. Thatcher migrated to Australia in 1853 and after a highly successful career here, returned to England where he became a curio seller. He died of cholera in Shanghai 1878 on one of his trading missions. (See: *The Colonial Minstrel*, Hugh Anderson, F.W. Cheshire Melbourne 1960.) Contrary to popular belief, the Chinese were in Australia *before* the gold rush, working as shepherds in NSW. By 1861 Australia had at least 38 000 Chinese living here, most of them from South China and nearly all male. Possibly one in every nine in Australia was Chinese. Concentrated on the goldfields in the 1850s, they scattered thereafter, working as laundrymen, hotel cooks, fishmongers, furniture makers, pastoral workers and market gardeners. (See: *The Diggers From China* by Jean Gittens Quartet Books, Melbourne, 1981.)

The Chinese arrived in large numbers during the mid 1850s at a time when alluvial mining was petering out and large companies were investing in deep mining using unskilled labour. The Chinese, in debt to headmen, worked for less than Europeans and were resented both for this and for their ability to eke out a living from the discarded shafts and mullock heaps of the Europeans. Prejudice made scapegoats of the Chinese and mine owners and politicians alike were quick to encourage it. The press followed suit. There were riots and massacres, the worst at Lambing Flat near Young in NSW on 30 June 1861. By 1900 this ill feeling began to wane and what was then condoned (the Europeans at Lambing Flat were acquitted) is now condemned. Thatcher's songs about the Chinese stand in direct contrast to the feelings expressed by the majority; his call for tolerance was ignored.

MAN OF THE EARTH   p 46

Phyl Lobl wrote this song in 1975 using the verses of Jock Graham. She is a well known singer and composer of the second Australian folk revival movement and has been a member of the Music Board of the Australia Council.

Jock Graham was thirteen when he first went down the mines. He later served in destroyers and submarines during World War 1, returning to work as a miner and as a haulage driver in coal mines. He lost a leg in a pit accident in 1928 but continued as a driver. In 1945 he became secretary of the Kurri Kurri sub-branch of the Federated Engine Drivers' and Firemen's Association and later a delegate to the Local Coal Board and a Communist member of Kearsly Shire Council. A collection of his poetry, *Blood On The Coal*, was published by Current Book Distributors, Sydney in 1946. His work was recorded by Warren Fahey in 1974 and included in his Australian Folklore Unit tape collection.

GIVE US OUR TWO PENCE BACK   p 48

In July 1911 a miners' delegate was sacked by the owner of the Lithgow Steel Works and Colliery in New South Wales. His 'crime' was that he attended union meetings. The miners went on strike when his reinstatement was refused. In retaliation the owner dropped their wages by twopence a ton. Between five and six hundred men stayed out on strike for nine months, supported by the unions. When the state Labor government sent in the police to protect scab labour and prevent miners rioting, the miners stormed the mine, burning the free labourers' belongings along with the owner's car. The Labor government introduced an Ironworks' Bill under which it could take over any steel works in New South Wales, but the Act remained a dead letter because of pressure from employers. The Lithgow strike ended with the reinstatement of all those originally sacked. The 'hewing' rate was reestablished at two shillings and four pence per ton. (See: *The Builders' Labourers' Songbook*, The Australian Building Construction Employees' and Builders' Labourers' Federation, Melbourne, 1975.)

The tune given here is Graeme Smith's adaptation of 'When the Harvest Days Are Over Jessie Dear', composed by Harry Von Tilzer with words by Howard Graham, and published in 1900. (See: Julius Mattfield's *Variety Music Cavalcade* third edition, Prentice-Hall, Englewood, New Jersey, USA, 1962.) The original tune has vanished but the shape of the chorus of 'Give Us Our Twopence Back' suggests it may be a parody of 'Jessie Dear'.

THE UNION BOY   p 50

John Meredith collected this song from Bill Coughlin in the Centennial Hotel at Gulgong in 1956. (See: *Folk Songs of Australia*.) Coughlin picked it up as a sixteen year old during the 1902 shearers' strike at Cassilis in New South Wales.

The melody is a cut down version of the come-all-ye 'Johnny Harte'. The words are related to those of a whole family of Irish songs and their colonial derivatives, including 'The Roving Journeyman' (see: S. Baring Gould's and H. Fleetwood Sheppard's series *Songs And Ballads Of The West*,) 'The Roving Irishman', (sometimes called 'The Rambling Irishman',) and 'Ye Maids of Orleans'. (See: *Folk Songs of Canada* edited by Edith Fowke and Richard Johnston, Waterloo, Ontario, 1954.)

John Lahey (see: *Great Australian Folk Songs*) uses similar words but a different tune for his 'Union Boy', which he collected from eighty two year old Joseph Patrick Bourke in the Punt Hotel, Darlington Point, New South Wales, in 1959. Folksingers seem to favour the song Meredith collected.

THE BALLAD OF 1891   p 51

After I published this song in *A Treasury of Favourite Australian Songs* (Currey O'Neil Ross, 1983) its composer, Doreen Jacobs Bridges, wrote to me (21 June 1983) to tell me that '1891' and 'The Ballad of Eureka' were both written to words provided by Helen G. Palmer in 1951 when Dr Bridges (then Doreen Jacobs) was conducting a Sydney singing group, the Unity Singers whose members once included John Meredith, Alex Hand and Chris Kempster. The original version of '1891' was in three parts, 'Eureka' in unison with piano accompaniment. Copies found their way to Melbourne and to Dick Diamond, who was then, she believes, secretary of the New Theatre there. Diamond included 'Eureka' and '1891' in the stage play *Reedy River*, which also included a number of other songs from other sources. I had mistakenly thought both Bridges' songs had been written for the show. In the first production in Melbourne, in March 1953, both songs were given in a unison version but for the Sydney production of December that year '1891' was restored to its three part arrangement, since members of the Unity Singers were in the cast and already knew the song. The play was very successful and toured extensively.

The Diaphon Company brought out an LP with the Sydney cast and the newly-formed Bushwackers Band (not the more recent one). A book of the songs was issued. Mine, the third edition, is dated May 1966 and John Meredith is among those named who helped prepare it. The show used genuine traditional songs, but it also included the Palmer-Bridges (Jacobs) song, music by Louis Lavater and Chris Kempster and music 'restored' by Margaret Sutherland.

The fourth edition of 1971 was edited by Doreen Bridges and David Milliss. Doreen Bridges studied with Alan Bush in England and had been involved with the Workers Music Association there. When she returned to Australia in the early 1950s she became one of the earliest to apply the thinking of the British Left, epitomised by the WMA in England, to the study of workers folk music in Australia.

AFTER THE STRIKE   p 52
Collected by Ron Edwards and Allan Jenkins at Charters Towers, 13 October 1966, from Dan Nicholson, (b.1893), who said he learnt it from his father who had been in the big strikers' camp at Winton during the historic shearers' strike of 1891. The song describes events that followed. The tune is 'After the Ball' by Charles K. Harris who also wrote the original verses which 'After the Strike' imitates. First published in 1892 when Harris was 25, 'After the Ball' sold over half a million sheet music copies. Its composer began a music publishing firm from the profits and went on to write many more popular songs including 'Break the News to Mother' (1897) and 'Hello Central, Give Me Heaven' (1901). (See: *Sweet and Lowdown* by Warren Craig, pp.45-46., New Jersey, USA, 1978.) Winton, Queensland, is also the area that produced 'Waltzing Matilda'. Some recent writers take the view that 'Matilda' is a protest song, linked to the great shearers' strike. Certainly the strike spawned a number of such songs but 'Matilda' seems to have considerably older origins. (See: *Matilda My Darling*, a novel by Nigel Kraus published by Allen & Unwin, Sydney, 1983.)

STRUGGLE IN THE WEST   p 54
The song was published in the Brisbane *Worker* (then edited by the radical reformist William Lane of Paraguay fame) on 18 April 1891 at the height of the trouble between the shearers and their employers. John Lahey in *Great Australian Folk Songs* gives it as collected by Len Fox, nephew of the artist E. Phillips Fox. The tune is as for 'The Catalpa', in other words, 'Rosin the Beau'.

The reference to Price is Colonel Tom Price, whose notorious order to his troops at a union demonstration in Melbourne in September 1890 to 'fire low, and lay them out', has gone down in Australian history as the epitome of callousness.

'Struggle in the West' is based on 'The Men of the West', an Irish rebel song by William Rooney, whose *Poems and Ballads* was published in Dublin in 1902. Its style resembles nationalist songs published in the pre-Fenian newspaper *The Nation* (1842-91).

HOGAN'S FLAT   p 56
Collected from Mrs Bowen by composer Clive Douglas (n.d.) and included in his collection in the State Library of Victoria. George Dreyfus based the main theme of the music he composed for the Australian television series *Waterfront* (1983) on this song. When George heard I was compiling this book he kindly sent me the music and words as they stand here. (Dreyfus to Radic 27 October 1984)

In 1925 a seamen's strike paralysed Australian waterfronts at a time when the government of the day under Stanley Bruce (later Lord Bruce) apparently believed that a number of key unions were in the hands of revolutionary agitators who had little interest in national prosperity. To counter the strike the government used the Navigation Act and amended the Immigration Act to enlarge its powers of deportation. The New South Wales Labor premier, J.T. Lang, refused to permit state police to serve the Commonwealth summonses. Bruce introduced legislation to create the Commonwealth Police.

The Waterside Workers' Federation struck again in 1927. The government proposed a peace conference and tried to work out the problems with the new Australian Council of Trade Unions. The Council tried to bargain and demanded the withdrawal of the legislation to amend the Arbitration Act. The government refused and withdrew from the conference. In 1928 the Arbitration Act was amended to contain penal provisions against unions and union leaders who were inciting industrial unrest. (See: Gordon Greenwood's *Australia: A Social and Political History*, Angus and Robertson, Sydney, 1955.)

Ted Hogan (Edmond John Hogan) was Victorian State Premier from 12 December 1929 to 19 May 1932.

FREEDOM'S ON THE WALLABY   p 57
'Freedom's on the Wallaby' is also known as 'Australia's on the Wallaby' and 'On the Wallaby'. Henry Lawson published the words in 1891. It can be found in *The Men Who Made Australia*. It has been collected and published many times in many places, usually with the tune given, though a different one appears in *Singabout*, vol 1, No.2 (1956). John Manifold has it that the tune 'came drifting down from the Townsville area after the war'. So far no antique model for the tune has been found, though there are close variants. Ron Edwards' 'Song Index' in *The Big Book of Australian Folk Song* lists the published appearances as in A.B. Paterson's *Old Bush Songs* in the Stewart and Keesing edition, where the verses are given as by Anon but quoted from *Old Bush Recitations* and collected by 'Bill Bowyang' in 1932. The *Singabout* version mentioned above is reprinted in John Lahey's *Great Australian Folk Songs*. John Meredith collected the present tune and published it in *Folk Songs of Australia* for 'Australia's on the Wallaby' (collected from Noah Warren at Wallerawang near Lithgow) and 'Mazlim's Mill' (collected from Jim Bourke of Surry Hills), both slight variants.

THE BALLAD OF EUREKA   p 58
A song by Doreen Jacobs Bridges, words by Helen G. Palmer, composed in 1951. It has been used by Film Australia and the ABC. It has been published in *The Builders Labourers Songbook* as a traditional or anonymous work. Doctor Bridges has asked me to print a new ending for the song because this is the way groups tend to alter it themselves.

SHORES OF BOTANY BAY   p 59
Another of the Duke Tritton songs.   Duke learnt the tune in the 1890s when he was busking with Danny Clements in Sydney. He told John Meredith that he had heard 'The Shores of Americay' sung to the same tune. Those verses, however, are more often sung to the tune of 'The Star of the County Down', a tune referred to by English folk song scholars as 'Dives and Lazarus'. Duke

Tritton's tune bears no resemblance to this. The Bushwackers in their *Australian Song Book* (Anne O'Donovan, Melbourne, 1978) add an extra verse, which is given here.

TO DR MANNIX   p 61
In 1921 Melbourne's Catholic Archbishop, Dr Daniel Mannix [b. 1864, d.1963], returned to Ireland to visit his mother. Off Cork a British destroyer intercepted the vessel on which he was travelling and arrested him as an anti-British agitator. He was refused permission to land in Ireland. Mannix's mother died before a reunion could be negotiated, a denial of human feeling that embittered his supporters and became a major element in the legends that sprang up around this austere figure. The verses refer to this event and to the archbishop's successful anti-conscription campaign in World War 1. Mannix was a cult figure and rallying point for the then underprivileged, indeed often persecuted, Irish in Australia. Denied education, forbidden to speak their native tongue or practise their religion in Ireland, the Irish in Australia found themselves still underdogs to the British.

Their resentment of the authority of the establishment has shaped much of the character of Australians and underscored rebellions from Logan to Kelly, Lalor to Gallagher. As in Ireland, songs of protest became highly effective weapons in those rebellions. In this case the tune is a simplified version of the traditional air arranged by John Stevenson for the verses of Thomas Moore known as 'Let Erin Remember', first published in 1807 in Moore's *Irish Melodies*. Moore's nostalgic, sentimental drawingroom songs ('The Last Rose of Summer' and 'The Minstrel Boy' are examples) remained popular in Australia until the 1960s, though Irish nationalists have always found his historical perspective unacceptable.

LAST WORK WE GO HOME   p 62
Like the peoples of Polynesia, Melanesia and Micronesia, Thursday Islanders have adopted musical models from European music. Their 'island dance songs' are not indigenous but frequently use tonal harmonic polyphony, a style traceable to the influence of Samoan missionaries working in the Torres Strait islands in the late nineteenth century. Continued contact with peoples from the New Hebrides and the Solomon Islands and elsewhere, particularly on the pearl fishing boats, gradually introduced other outside songs which were later used as models for local song composition. 'Last Work We Go Home' is a fine example of this composite music. (See: Wolfgang Laade's *Neue Musik in Afrika, Asien und Ozeanien*, Heidelberg, West Germany, 1971.)

Ron Edwards collected this trochus shell trade song in the mid-1950s from Mat Savage, who learnt it while working as a shell diver. (See: *The Big Book of Australian Folk Song*.) The words refer to the end of the season when the luggers make their final trip before turning north on the run home to Thursday Island before the monsoon.

QUEENSLAND WHALERS   p 63
By Scottish ship's engineer Harry Robertson who worked on whalers in the Antarctic fleet in the 1960s and wrote many songs about the life. (See: *Ship Repairing Men* p.00) He has also been a railway worker and in recent times has held a series of workshops on songwriting sponsored by the Australian Railways Union. He can be heard on *Whale Chasing Man* (Larrikin LRF 049).

COCK OF THE MORNING OR SAILOR HOME FROM THE SEA   p 65
Also known as 'Sailor Home from the Sea'. The words are by playwright and poet Dorothy Hewett, the music by Bill Berry. It first appeared in *Australian Tradition* in March 1964, with an additional two verses printed later in July.

WE BUILT SOME GREAT SHIPS   p 66
Ray Sowerby, a Whyalla shipyard worker, wrote the words of this song for the 1978 documentary film produced by Peter Green, *We Built Some Great Ships*, which dealt with the closure of the Whyalla shipyards. The song begins with a reference to the British shipbuilding industry and it should be noted that the influence of British migrants on Adelaide and the industrial towns of South Australia was stronger than elsewhere in the country. The brutal manner of the closures of the shipyards in Britain was repeated in Whyalla. The tune is from 'The Pub With No Beer' the Slim Dusty hit which he recorded in 1957 as the B side of his 'Saddle Boy'. The original poem for 'Pub With No Beer' was by North Queensland balladist Dan Sheehan, which country singer Gordon Parsons set to a variant of Stephen Foster's 'Beautiful Dreamer' i.e. the tune used here, which is now associated with Dusty.

SHIP REPAIRING MEN   p 67
Words and music by Harry Robertson. [See also: 'Queensland Whaler'] Robertson grew up in Glasgow in the 1930s depression, the son of a sea-going engineer. Both parents were amateur musicians, his mother a pianist, his father a fiddle player. Robertson, himself a ship's engineer, acquired a repertoire of songs and Bobby Burns poetry from his extended family, one section of which worked in the mines. Robertson writes from this Scottish background but frequently with an Australian context. His songs are deeply concerned with questions of social justice, the dignity of working life and the role of the common man in society. 'Ship Repairing Men' first appeared in *Australian Tradition* in May 1970.

THE ANTI-FOULING ROLL   p 69
Words by poet and waterside worker Merv Lilley and music by Bill Berry, 'The Anti-fouling Roll' first appeared in *Australian Tradition*, September 1967. Bill Berry was a member of the Queensland Union Singers in the late 1960s.

THE LAUNCESTON AND DELORAINE RAILWAY   p 70
From *The Railway Songster*, a Tasmanian publication of the last century, reprinted in Patsy Adam-Smith's *Romance of Australian Railways* (1973). The tune is 'Marching Through Georgia', by Henry Clay Work, first published in 1865.

BILLY SHEEHAN   p 72
A song originating with railway workers in Hughenden just before World War 2 and set to the tune 'Steamboat Bill', a Mississippi riverboat melody which is also the source of the American railway song 'Casey Jones'. Dave Scott, a member of the Moreton Bay Bushwackers and a railway loco driver at Bundaberg, learnt it in Queensland, It was recorded on Wattle C 9, *Folk Songs from Queensland*, issued for the Queensland Centenary Year in 1959 by the Moreton Bay Bushwackers and the Bandicoots.
Spirit of P — the *Spirit of Progress*, a loco put into service in 1937 between Melbourne and Albury.
The C16 a type of light steam locomotive.
Strict QT with extreme secrecy.

THE GRANVILLE RAIL DISASTER   p 74
A song by Tom Bridges, written shortly after the accident near Sydney on 18 January 1977. It was published in the December 1983-January 1984 edition of *National Office News* for the Australian Railways Union as part of a drive by the Bush Music Club of Sydney and Matilda's Mob Bush Band to collect Australian railway songs and music. The accident was given national news coverage and provoked public debate on the safety standards of rail travel and the working conditions associated with it.

THE POISON TRAIN   p 75
A song by Michael O'Rourke, an important singer and songwriter of the Australian folk revival. O'Rourke was brought up on the Atherton tableland, which seems to have supplied the central image of the song. The train he refers to is the defoliant special used in tropic northern Queensland to keep the tracks clear of weeds. O'Rourke equates it with the ruthlessness of economic forces against which the rural community feels powerless.

THE HUNGRY MILE   p 77
The words are by the radical poet of the 1930s, Ernest Anthony, and the music is a setting by Peter Parkhill of 'The Rufford Park Poachers' a folksong collected by the composer Percy Grainger from the folksinger Joseph Taylor at Brigg in Lincolnshire, England, in 1906.
    Peter Parkhill is a respected singer in the folk revival and a scholar in traditional music in Australia.

WALTZING MATILDA (TWO VERSIONS)   p 78
There seems to be no doubt that A.B. (Banjo) Paterson wrote the words of 'Waltzing Matilda' in 1894 to a tune supplied by Miss Christina Macpherson at Dagworth homestead near Winton in Queensland. Paterson, by the way, is said to have been tone-deaf. The tune Miss Macpherson gave Banjo was one she had heard at the Warrnambool races on 24 April 1894. That tune is thought to have been 'Thou Bonnie Wood o' Craigielea'. music by James Barr (b. Tarbolton 1781, d. 1860) and words by Robert Tannahill. It was first published in *The Miniature Museum of Scotch Songs* (1818), but, according to Magoffin, composed in 1805. Military bands (woodwind and brass are indicated by this title, not the occupation of the players) were a regular feature at Victorian race meetings. Later traditional singers claimed they knew the tune long before Paterson and Macpherson collaborated. Since Barr's tune is sometimes claimed as a traditional Scottish tune this is quite likely to be true.

Mrs Marie Cowan set a slightly altered version of Paterson's words. It was published by James Inglis and Co. as a hand-out with 'Billy-tea' in 1903. It, too, is derived from 'Craigielea', as an overlay of the two tunes reveals, particularly when placed over the band version of 'Craigielea' supplied by Pearce in *On the Origins of Waltzing Matilda* (1971). Marie Cowan seems to have selected her notation from the older tune quite consciously, as any composer would. It is obviously not a simple recalled, imperfect version, but a controlled stress point removal of essential material to fit her musical needs. Over the years other theories on the origins of the tune have been put forward. One source is said to be 'The Bold Fusilier', allegedly an English folk song from the Marlborough wars. It has not been collected in Britain as far as I know. Late reportings of it in Australia after 1903 cannot be accepted as evidence for its existence before that date, though such reports do exist. Verse shape similarities suggested by John Meredith in *Folk Songs of Australia* do not conclusively prove musical similarity, as the example of the exchangeable tunes of come-all-ye's shows.

The controversy has inspired at least five books: Oscar Mendelsohn's *A Waltz With Matilda (1966);* Sydney May's *The Story of Waltzing Matilda* (1955); Harry H. Pearce's *On the Origins of Waltzing Matilda* (1971); and Richard Magoffin's *Fair Dinkum Matilda* (1973); and Nigel Krauth's *'Matilda My Darling'* (Allen and Unwin, Sydney, 1983).

The Queensland version of 'Waltzing Matilda, sometimes called the Buderim or the O'Neill version, was collected by John Manifold from John O'Neill of Buderim, Queensland. It keeps to the Paterson text. The tune has also been independently collected to the Irish song, 'The Bonny Green Tree'. Yet another theory has it that Paterson may have written his verses on the model of the verses of the Irish tune and that later they were set to the 'Craigielea' tune supplied by Miss Macpherson. 'The Overlanders' is also sung to a tune derived from 'Craigielea' which may point to its popularity in Queensland and probably throughout Australia. Paterson's verses are thought by some writers, to have older antecedents again than 'Craigielea'; to be by some other bush balladist or to be a composite.

Richard Magoffin adds a fascinating postscript to his book containing what he claims are photographs of the Christina Macpherson manuscript given to the Bartlam family and in the present possession of Mrs Barbara Roulston. There are handwriting comparisons and samples and the ownership is authenticated. The tune of the manuscript is an intermediary stage between 'Craigielea' and Cowan.

Recent musicological analysis of the relationship between the Buderim version and the Irish song 'The Bonny Green Tree' supports the suggestion that the text of 'Waltzing Matilda' predates the Macpherson 'Craigielea' setting *and* Paterson. The textual similarities between 'Waltzing Matilda' and 'The Bonny Green Tree' indicate the possibility that the Irish song was used as a poetic basis for 'Waltzing Matilda', which would therefore have been sung to this tune, i.e. 'The Bonny Green Tree'. It may also have been recited i.e. performed without a tune. Paterson may have collected them in this form, *then* given the verses to Macpherson to set.

According to folklorist Richard Magoffin the girl's name Mathilde was given to a tradesman's pack in the mediaeval German states. The same name was given to the women picked up along the way by young journeyman apprentices as they travelled from town to town, looking for work. Early printers referred to these probationary wanderings as 'auf der waltz' - going on the waltz. During the Thirty Year War (1618-1648) German-speaking soldiers called camp followers Matildas, a euphemism possibly picked up by the allied armies, including the British, during the war of the Spanish Succession (1701-1714) when it was applied to the blanket and greatcoat roll that substituted for the Matildas on cold nights. It doesn't appear in Australia until the 1850s however. Magoffin also suggests 'Waltzing Matilda' is a song born of the colonial class war that culminated in the shearers' strikes of the early 1890s. Squatter and shearer were in opposite camps. The swagman is the out of work itinerant shearer denied social justice. The Labor Party was born of those strikes and of a demand for justice for the underdog that has been a major unifying factor in an Australia largely populated by, or descended from, migrant peoples in search of a new deal and a fair go. In this, if in little else, they are at one with the native inhabitants. The ghost of the swaggie lives on, Magoffin says, calling us to remember where we came from, and on those in authority to honour the rights of the individual that are paramount in the democratic way of life for which our ancestors fought.

THE SANDY HOLLOW LINE p 81
The words are by Duke Tritton. (See: 'Shearing in a Bar'.) The first tune supplied here is one usually associated with 'The Great Northern Line', 'The Lachlan Tigers', 'The Knickerbocker Line' and 'The Shearer's Cook', among others. The common source seems to be 'Musselburgh Fair'. This first tune is in common use, but I have also given a second tune, the air of 'Dunlaven Green', which is used by John Dengate for his performances of 'The Sandy Hollow Line'. He uses it unaccompanied. (See: John Meredith's *Duke Of The Outback*, Red Rooster Press, Melbourne, 1983.)

The Sandy Hollow line was a projected railway link between Sandy Hollow and Maryvale, which was to join the northern and western rail systems and provide a direct link to Newcastle for primary producers of the north west of New South Wales. Construction of the line commenced in 1936 to provide employment in the depression-struck state. Tritton worked on it from 1936 to 1938. Most of the navvies had unemployment relief tickets and worked from 7.30 am to 5 pm. Conditions were particularly hard. The song tells of an episode which occurred when Duke Tritton was working on the line as a powder monkey. The line was never completed, and the project abandoned in 1951. As a newspaper report put it: 'The line remains as an undisguised affront to the efforts of the men sent to build it.' (Meredith op. cit.)

SOUP OR MY BONNIE LIES OVER THE SEA p 83
Sung to the tune of 'My Bonnie Lies Over The Ocean', traditional Scottish air often erroneously attributed to H.J. Fulmer (Charles E. Pratt) this is one of dozens of parodies set to the same air. This version dates from the 1930s Depression, originating in the American Wobbly movement but gaining popularity in Australia when, in August 1931, in Sydney alone, a million loaves of bread were given out each week to the unemployed. As is noted in 'The Battler's Ballad', a third of the Australian workforce was without a wage at the time.

BATTLER'S BALLAD p 84
The original tune and text were collected by Alan Scott and published in *A Collector's Songbook* by the Bush Music Club in 1970. The verses are by Jack Wright of Coogee, New South Wales. The tune given here is the one used by the Bushwackers' Band.

The 'battler' of this depression song has taken to the roads, 'humping his bluey' town to town in search of work at a time when a third of the Australian workforce was unemployed. The battlers developed an unwritten code of conduct based on working class ethics: never inform, never rat, and never steal from your mates.

WEEVILS IN THE FLOUR p 87
Dorothy Hewett, whose poem is set here by Michael Leyden, was born in Perth in 1923, the daughter of a Wickepin wheat farmer. She moved to Sydney in 1948 and worked in a variety of jobs in the factory area of Alexandria, returning to Perth in 1960, where her early plays were produced. She has since become one of the country's leading playwrights and poets. The title of this poem has also been used for Wendy Lowenstein's book of oral history of the 1930s Depression in Australia. (See: *Weevils in the Flour* by Wendy Lowenstein, Hyland House, Melbourne, 1978.)

MANDRAKE p 88
Recorded by Tex Morton (See: *Ned Kelly was Born in a Ramshackle Hut*,) on 28 May 1941 on G 24345 and now available on EMI TC-FA 157009.

LES DARCY p 90
Set to the tune of 'Way Down in Tennessee' by Walter Donaldson, with words by 'Percy the Poet' (P.F. Collins), this song was recorded by Ron Edwards on 24 April 1965 at Mt Kooyong in northern Queensland from the singing of Pat Murphy (b.1902). Murphy said he learnt it shortly after Darcy's death. (See: *Big Book of Australian Folk Song*.) Les Darcy was the Irish-Australian blacksmith who became a legendary middle weight boxer. Only 1.7m (5ft 7inches) but with a 1.85m (73½inch) reach, he had forty odd fights in six years and lost only four. He was at the height of his career during World War I when conscription became a major political issue, with the Catholic Arch-

bishop of Melbourne leading the anti-conscription movement. Darcy's Irish origins alone made him a target for those opposed to Mannix.

In September 1916 Darcy beat George Chip, a prestigious American fighter, at the Sydney Stadium. Shortly afterwards he left Australia as a stowaway in the *Hattie Luckenbach*, bound for America. He was branded a cur and a coward for trying to avoid the call-up. Conscription for overseas service was not brought in by the Australian government during World War I but the debate was extensive and divisive. Darcy himself said the British army could well do without him for a few months while he earned enough to support his family for the time he would be at the front. He offered the Australian government a thousand pounds to release him for six months but the money was refused. It is thought that his Australian opponents — those outside the ring — used their influence to prevent him getting bouts in America. He was finally matched with middleweight Len Rowlands at Memphis, Tennessee but, on 24 May 1917, Darcy died at the Gartly-Ramsey Hospital, Memphis. He had a neglected tooth infection. Pneumonia set in. It was rumoured that Americans had murdered him by administering 'dope'. Darcy was 21. Back home, later generations of Australians refused to think ill of him.

KEEP YOUR TAIL UP KANGAROO   p 91
By Neil McBeath (for his 'I'm Going Back Again to Yarrawonga') in England during which the English unveiled their bodyline tactics. The 'brick like that' refers to Harold Larwood, the English fast bowler and prime mover for this offensive. Australians regarded the English tactics as outrageously unfair and unsporting, hence this homespun support song.

UP THERE CAZALY   p 93
The composer of this football hymn is Mike Brady, television producer and jingle writer. Three hundred thousand copies of the record, in its extended version, were sold by the end of 1979 (see *Sydney Morning Herald*, 27 December 1979), making it the biggest selling single in Australian record history, to that date. It was originally written as a one minute jingle by Brady and his arranger Peter Sullivan, with Brady singing. When Ron Tudor, managing director of Fable Records, realised its potential, he had Brady and Sullivan expand the song to two minutes. Slim Dusty's version of 'The Pub With No Beer' sold more than 500 000 (recorded) copies worldwide, but fewer than 200 000 in Australia (see Melbourne *Herald*, 10 September 1979). Brady's success led to demands for jingles from London Weekend Television and several soccer clubs. He used the Cazaly tune for a soccer jingle, 'Put It Away'. He is also known for his ABC jingle for cricket commentator Alan McGilvray, 'The Game Is Not the Same Without McGilvray', and for the solo album *Invisible Man*, an attempt to be taken more seriously as a song writer.

Brady sang the Cazaly song at the 1979 Grand Final at the Melbourne Cricket Ground before more than 100 000 fans. The song is also recorded as part of an album. *Songs of Football's Greatest Songs*, put out by Full Moon Records with a sixty-member choir formed by the Melbourne Singers. He attributes his musical talent to his Irish heritage. 'I discovered that the melodies I was putting down were parts of Irish folk-songs — Irish keens, actually' (*Sydney Morning Herald*, 27 December 1979). His Irish ancestors seem to have been keen on 'Click Go the Shears' and 'Just a Wee Dock and Dorris'.

THE TAB PUNTERS' SONG   p 95
Words by John Dengate (see other Dengate songs in this book) set to the tune of 'Seamus O'Brien', an 'Irish' comic song by W.S Hays (1837-1907), the late 19th century American songwriter who also gave us 'The Little Log Cabin in the Lane'. He is estimated by P. Havlice in his Song Index (Scarecrow Press Mutuchen, NJ 1975) to be the third most popular American songwriter before the Tin Pan Alley era.

THE LAND WHERE THE CROW FLIES BACKWARDS   p 97
Composer Dougie Young has both Aboriginal and European ancestry. He was born near Cunnamulla, south-central Queensland, about 1935 or 1937. He carried his swag as a boy, but eventually married and settled outside a hamlet on the Darling River in western NSW. Dougie Young recorded this and five other songs on Wattle 19/3, made from a field tape collected at Wilcannia Aboriginal camp NSW by Dr Jeremy Beckett, an anthropologist working at Monash University, 1963-1964. Musical influences in such music are not tribal, but country and western and, more recently, reggae. Australian Aboriginals have adopted the country and western forms and styles and made them their own. Laconic and often sardonic, the words, allied to the ironically gentle style of the music, make a powerful comment on Australian life that whites here would be well advised to note.

The reference in the chorus to the land 'where the pelican builds his nest' is to a popular 19th century Australian ballad, 'Where The Pelican Builds Her Nest', by Mary Hannay Foott (1846-1918). Young has altered the sex of Foott's bird. This legendary land of promise existed beyond the furthest western cattle runs, a land which lured pioneers to their deaths. (See: *The Penguin Book of Australian Ballads* ed. by Russel Ward, 1964.)

PRISON'S NOTHING SPECIAL   p 99
The tune of 'Prison's Nothing Special' is based on 'Camoweal Races', which is also used for 'Bill the Bullocky' (See John Manifold's *Penguin Australian Songbook*). Cherie Watkins sings it on *The First Australians, songs by Aboriginals and Torres Strait Islanders*, AAA 004 (Aboriginal Arts Agency.) Manifold gives his tune as collected by Geoff Wills but gives no details. The song uses the classic come-all-ye opening and verse form. It is common in Australian ballad style to sing the opening verses in full but to simplify the music as the verses go on.

VICTOR PODHAM'S RUSTY HUT p 101
By Dougie Young (See: 'The Land Where the Crow Flies Backwards')

Three sharp turns — the triangular shaped bottle of methylated spirits, sometimes called goom.

GURINDJI BLUES p 103
The composer of this song, Ted Egan went to live and work in the Northern Territory when he was seventeen. He now lives at Alice Springs where he has conducted Aboriginal studies courses for urbanised Aboriginal children at the high school. He speaks two dialects and holds his BA from the Australian National University majoring in Australian studies and politics. He writes, sings and records his own songs, which are featured in the Ted Egan Outback Show in Alice Springs. He is currently producing a series of recording albums with companion books, *Faces of Australia Series* (Greenhouse Publications, Melbourne). Egan was a welfare officer in the Northern Territory during the period in the 60s when the Gurindji Aboriginals of Wave Hill reclaimed their ancestral land from the meat-packing multi-national Vestey Corporation. The men of Gurindji worked as stockmen for Vesteys but they were paid one tenth of the wages of whites doing the same work. In 1967 the Gurindji went on strike for equal pay. They remained on strike for a year, eventually winning their case. The tribe left the Wave Hill station and camped at Wattie Creek nearby. On 12 May 1986 the land was made over to them by the Australian Government. Wave Hill station is now Daguragu.

THE HOUSEWIFE'S LAMENT p 105
The verses, called 'The Housekeeper's Lament' are in the diary of Mrs Sara A. Price of Ottawa, Illinois, USA, mother of seven children all of whom predeceased her. Some of her sons were killed in the Civil War. The song occurs in 19th century songsters and has been collected only once — from a traditional singer in Florida. (It appears in *Sing Out* Vol. 16, No.4. See: Fowke and Glazer's *Songs of Work and Protest*.) It has been recorded by Walt Robertson for Folkways records. The air is sometimes referred to as having an Irish flavour, though it is likely to have originated in the United States. The title is sometimes given as 'Life is a Toil'. It regained circulation during the first, and again in the second wave, of the feminist movement. My mother, a housewife and former countrywoman from the Riverina, living in an industrial suburb, also sang it, having learnt it from my grandmother before World War 1.

'The Housewife's Lament' continues, in the New World, a British tradition of songs about housework dating from the 17th century. (See: *My Song Is My Own*, by Kathy Henderson with Frankie Armstrong and Sandra Kerr, Pluto Press, London, 1979.) *All Our Lives*, an American women's songbook cited in Henderson, gives this alternative last verse, written by thirteen year old Lydia Snow:
'But when I awoke I found it was over
I threw down my broom and I ran towards the door.
Reaching outside, I cast off my apron
And swore I would never clean house anymore!'

Recorded on *The Female Frolic*, Argo ZDA 82. Also by Peggy Seger on *Penelope Isn't Waiting Any More* BR 1050.

THE OLD MAN AND HIS WIFE p 107
A song from my grandmother's and my mother's repertoire. The song is found in Britain and America but was sung in Australia with the place name of the first verse localised. My grandmother, Jessie MacIntyre de Mamiel Wise, learnt the song in the Howlong district of the Riverina in the late 1870s.

WALLABY STEW p 108
A.L.Lloyd recorded a version of this song on 'Across the Western Plains' (Wattle Recordings, 1958), claiming to have heard it while working on the Lachlan around 1930. His text was not complete: additions have been made from *Old Bush Songs*. The sleeve notes say the tune was widely known among seamen to the words of 'According to the Act'. There are other versions using the *Queensland Centenary Songbook* tune. The present one is an arrangement by Peter Evans from John Lahey's collection *Great Australian Folk Songs* (Hill of Content, Melbourne, 1965).

GENTLE ANNIE p 109
In his notes to *Traditional Singers and Musicians of Victoria* (Wattle Archives Series 2, Page 12) Edgar Waters says:

'Tom Newbound learnt this song from Lame Jack Cousens of Springhurst a small town in northern Victoria, a few miles from Rutherglen. Cousens had travelled around farms in both northern Victoria and the Riverina with a steam threshing machine. These travelling threshing machines played an important part in the wheat harvesting, and the workers who travelled with them probably played quite an important part in spreading songs around the wheat farming districts. Jack Cousens said that he had written the words of the song himself, about a girl named Annie Waits, who lived on a farm at Moorwatha on which he had worked a threshing machine.

'Gentle Annie' is a parody of the song of the same name by Stephen Foster, published in 1856. Many popular songs from the American stage and concert platform were well known in Australia in the latter half of the nineteenth century, and were frequently adapted by bush song-makers to their own ends. Such songs reached Australia in a number of ways. From the time of the gold rushes of the 1850s onwards, they were often introduced to Australia by touring American entertainers belonging to black-face minstrel or variety shows, and — in the case of songs which had caught the popular taste in England — through touring English entertainers also. On the criteria commonly used for the definition of folk song in English-speaking countries, this parody of 'Gentle Annie' is not a folk song. Leaving this question of definition aside, it exemplifies one source of tunes and texts used by bush songmakers in the latter part of the nineteenth century. Its gentle, rather playful tone casts a somewhat unexpected light on the manners of the bush workers.'
NOTE: Mr Newbound pointed out that the first two lines of the second verse are a hint that the mutton had been

smuggled across the border from Victoria: the song dates from the period before the federation of the Australian colonies in 1901. The Riverina grows sheep for wool; northern Victoria also grows fat lambs for meat.

Foster's 'Gentle Annie' appears in a number of the extant Australian songsters of the nineteenth century, amongst them the *Australian Melodist*, no. 2, pp 30–1, Cf. Spaeth, *A History of Popular Music in America*, p. 117.

It is not easy to document briefly the widespread knowledge of American popular songs in the Australian bush during the latter part of the nineteenth century, but reference may be made to Lawson's account of the songs sung on the New South Wales goldfields in *The Songs They Used to Sing*, to Anderson's *The Colonial Minstrel*, for mention of English and American entertainers on the Victorian goldfields, and to Disher, *Victorian Song*, and Spaeth, *A History of Popular Music in America*, for the ready acceptance of American songs into the repertory of the English popular stage, and vice versa, during the nineteenth century. Most of the extant Australian songsters of the nineteenth century, such as the *Australian Melodist*, reprint the texts of numerous American, as well as British, popular songs.

THE REBEL GIRL p 110

A song with words by Joe Hill c.13 February 1915. Though Hill claimed the tune as his it is in fact a parody of 'She is more to be pitied than censured' (See: *Read 'em and Weep* by Sigmund Spaeth pp209-210, Doubleday, Page and Co. NY, 1926) by William B. Gray, who copyrighted it in 1898. It was a moralising tearjerker. In 1916 the Hill song was copyrighted to Bill Hayward. Joe Hill was the thirty-three year old Wobbly writer who was executed by firing squad at the Utah State Penitentiary on 19 November 1915 for shooting a Salt Lake City grocer on 10 January 1914. His guilt is still a matter of dispute. Money for his defence was raised by sales of a special Joe Hill edition of the IWW song book which included his own songs. He remains a hero of the left. (See: *Rebel Voices* ed. J.L. Kornbluh, Ann Arbor, the University of Michigan Press, 1964, for a biography.)

BREAD AND ROSES p 112

In 1912 in the woollen centre of Lawrence, Massachusetts, 20 000 workers went on strike against a pay cut. Under the impressive leadership of the IWW the workers won important concessions for the 250 000 textile workers of New England. During one of the workers' parades, girls carried a banner reading 'We want bread and roses too'. This was the inspiration for James Oppenheim's poem, set to music by Caroline Kohlsaat. There is also an Italian song 'Pan e Rose' written by Arturo Giovannitti, used by the Italian Dressmaker's Local 89 of the International Ladies' Garment Workers' Union. (See: Fowke and Glazer *Songs of Work and Protest*.) The song has long been associated with feminist movements, in the USA and England, as well as in Australia.

WIFE TO A COCKIE FARMER p 113

By Richard Keam and based on his experience working as a research assistant to a poverty commission investigating dairy farmers in northern NSW. The song has its origins in two tunes - the first phrase from 'The Valley of Knocknanure' and the second phrase from 'The Star of the County Down' which the English folk song scholars used to call 'Dives and Lazarus', after one ballad text which was sometimes sung to it. This 'Dives and Lazarus' tune group extends right through the British Isles. (See: Lloyd, 1967.)

The chords should be applied with restraint, as with many of the songs here. Better to let the sense of each verse dominate the phrasing rather than allow a regular rhythm to do so.

HUSH LITTLE BABY p 114

Words written in May 1985 by Pam Collier of Mount Newman, who describes herself as housewife/mother/courier/soda-stream agent. A bitter lullaby to a traditional tune used for lullabies, it commemorates the lot of the modern miner's wife. First published in Roger Montgomery's *Pilbara Connection* (See: 'Weekend Warrior') Montgomery recorded the songs, poems and stories of the iron-ore-workers and their families living in Western Australia's north-west Pilbara region as part of an Art and Working Life Project funded by the Music and Community Arts Boards of the Australia Council via the Australian Folk Trust. It was published in 1985 by Roger Limpid Productions, Belmont, Western Australia.

DONT BE TOO POLITE GIRLS p 115

With words by Glen Tomasetti set to the tune of 'All Among the Wool Boys' alias 'Flash Jack From Gundagai', this is a song on the equal pay cases which began in June 1969. It was published in 1970 by R.A. Hulme and M.G. Dugan, Melbourne, in *Song From a Seat in the Carriage*, a set of eight Tomasetti songs. Glen Tomasetti is a well known folksinger, song writer and political activist. She is also a highly regarded novelist and poet.

This song has been widely used for demonstrations, films and as a theme song for women's radio. It has also entered the folk process, existing anonymously and in various versions. It was first sung in 1969 on Channel 7 in the current affairs programme *This Week*.

Equal pay passed into law, if not into practice, in 1972 and there are A grade journalists today.

THE PINEAPPLE TRIMMERS p 117
THE BASIC WAGE DREAM p 119
A FIRST CLASS BOILER MAKER p 120
ISA p 121

Don Henderson is well known as a writer of protest songs, epitomised by his Mt Isa strike-related talking blues 'I Can Whisper'. I have included four of his songs here: 'Isa' 'The Pineapple Trimmers', 'The Basic Wage Dream' and 'A First Class Boiler Maker'. These songs were first published by

Horwitz Grahame in *I Can Sing* (1970). He is, by profession, a guitar maker.

Wendy Lowenstein in *Australian Tradition* (December 1967) called Henderson the most prolific of our contemporary songwriters and described his songs as rough hewn and sometimes sentimental but original, witty and devastatingly honest: 'Through them he hits at human pretensions and also at the things which rob men of their humanity'. She adds: 'Don Henderson feels strongly that an artist must maintain his independence at all costs and that Government interference or support is fatal to artistic honesty, (he) does not feel it is the songwriters business to get other people to sing his songs, although his are probably more widely known than those of any other protest songwriter specially in Queensland trade union circles and among the younger folk singers'.

THE BONING ROOM LADIES   p 118

A song commemorating cold in a tropic climate, 1960s tight matador pants worn for protection against it, sexual harrassment, and exhaustion. Boning was done in low temperature chambers to preserve the meat, not the workers, on whom it had the opposite effect.

The words are by Des Byers, a boner at the Queera meat works near Cairns. Ron Edwards collected the song from him in Edmonton on 28 August 1966. (See: *The Big Book Of Australian Folk Song*.)

The tune is that of 'The House Of The Rising Sun', a blues classic popular with New Orleans jazz bands before World War 1. The now widely used version here was collected by Alan Lomax from a miner's daughter in Kentucky in 1937 and popularised through the recording of the black singer Josh White (Brunswick 03749). It was revived in the 1960s through a recording made by the Geordie rhythm and blues singer Eric Burdon (and the *Animals* his group).

SONG OF THE SHEET-METAL WORKER   p 123

By Sydney songwriter John Dengate, whose 'Trifecta Song' is also included in this collection. Dengate is known for his political satire and his skill in fitting his verses to traditional Irish tunes. In this instance he has chosen the tune 'The Valley Of Knocknanure', a rebel song of the War of Independence. (See: Colm O Lachlainn's *More Irish Street Ballads*, Pan Books, London, 1978, first published 1965.) Dengate published 'Song Of The Sheet Metal Worker' in the *New City Songster* (an English periodical c. 1968 on, ed. by Ewan MacColl and Peggy Seger,) and recorded it on *Rebel Chorus* (Larrikin LRF 2053). It is dedicated to his father, Norman William Dengate, who was born at Carlingford in 1908, which explains the references of the verses.

PETER THE CABBY   p 124

The Adelaide group *Redgum* wrote this tribute to the hard life and times of taxi drivers in the late 1970s. The group consisted of Michael Atkinson, John Schumann, Verity Truman and Chris Timms. Beginning life on the campus circuit, the quartet developed a recording and concert life with the addition of Chris Gunn, Tom Stehlik and Dave Flett. The music they produce is idiosyncratic, based on regional awareness and the nuances of the Australian accent. Their political stance is overtly nationalistic. Working life is central to their repertoire. (see: *The Redgum Songbook: Stubborn Words, Flagrant Vices*, Tombala Publishing, Sydney, n.d. circa 1982.)

JOURNEYIN'   p 126

Words and music by Chris Landon and published in *Lyrebirds, Coots and Cockatoos*, an anthology of songs by the people in the Canberra region, with a preface by Col Webb, May 1980.

PICKIN' UP SPUDS   p 127

Words by Col Webb to the tune of 'Rosin the Bow' (see: *The Catalpa*) published in *Lyrebirds, Coots and Cockatoos*, an anthology of songs by people in the Canberra area, May 1980, with a preface by Col Webb:

'This song is based, with some exaggeration, on personal experience picking up spuds for my uncle in the hilly red-soil country near Robertson, an area famed for its potatoes. Everyone connected with getting the spuds to market worked very hard — the farmers, the pickers-up, the truck drivers. Men, women and kids would spend the summer days picking up after the tractor with the digger, on steep paddocks which seem somehow to follow the sun's path from dawn to dusk. Green potatoes are ones which have been left uncovered in the sun — they are reputedly poisonous. Chats are small spuds, for which the farmer gets a higher price, so they must be picked up separately. Most of the farms around Robbo have turned to mechanical pickers — so ends a way of life for many people in the summer months, albeit a hard one. My uncle died on his tractor, in the spud paddock, a few years ago. I don't think he would have minded my song too much'.

THE SOUTHERN CROSS IS CALLING ME   p 129

A song by Joe Paolacci, who was born in a southern Italian village in 1950 and whose parents migrated to Melbourne two years later. As a child, he says, he was 'surrounded' by Italian folkmusic; he has been singing for as long as he can remember. He has been associated with a number of bands, including *The Colonials* and *Captain Moonlight*.

'The Southern Cross is Calling Me' is based on his father's experiences as a migrant in the early 1950s which were, as he writes: 'the days of full employment and when pubs used to close at 6pm'. Of his father he says: 'When he arrived he really did share a house with four families. This was not unusual at the time. I went to school with some Egyptian boys whose families did the same in one room!'

THE WESTGATE BRIDGE DISASTER   p 130

A song written by Ken Mansell as a response to the disastrous collapse of the Westgate Bridge while under construction. The subsequent inquiry left doubts about the construction and design companies involved and the role of the state government in pushing through an unexpectedly complex and problematical construction job for the political kudos of completing a spectacular landmark.

The tune used by Mansell is 'The Blantyre Explosion', a Scottish coalmining disaster ballad included in Ewan McColl's collection *Scotland Sings* (Oak, New York, 1965) and is related to the tunes used for 'The Unfortunate Rake' ballad group, of which the best known is 'The Streets of Laredo'. The tune included here, however, is one written by Graeme Smith and is based on 'The Young Trooper Cut Down In His Prime'.

THE WEEKEND WARRIOR p 133
The melody is by Roger Montgomery (see: 'Hush Little Baby') with words by Barbara Brandt of Paraburdoo. Published in Montgomery's *Pilbara Connection* (Roger Limpid Productions, Belmont, 1985) as part of an Art and Working Life project of the Australia Council.

FREIHEIT p 135
On 16 February 1936 a liberal-democratic government under Emanuel Anzana won a decisive electoral victory over its fascist and monarchist opponents. On 18 July 1936, five months later, civil war broke out as organised fascist forces crossed the Straits of Gibralter to invade southern Spain. In Australia the response of the left was to deepen anti-fascist feeling towards Germany, Italy and Japan. 57 Australians served in the famous International Brigade (the 15th Brigade of the Republican Army). To this day the Australian political left retains an attitude of militant support for the Spanish left. *Freiheit* is a song by Peter Daniel, with words by Karl Ernst. The Thaelman Battalion was the German section of the International Brigade and was noted for its fine and varied singing. Freiheit means freedom, Thaelman was the name of the leader of the German communists. According to Stephen Murray-Smith and Edgar Waters he died in a Nazi concentration camp during the war. (See: *Rebel Songs*, Australian Student Labour Federation, 1947.)

During the 1930s and 1940s many new songs spread through the labour and anti-fascist movements throughout the world. One of the major sources of songs for the left, during this period, was the Spanish Civil War. Although only a handful of Australians volunteered and fought alongside the Spanish republican forces, the inspiration of the International Brigades gave a new significance to the songs of the socialist movements of many countries. Right up to the 1950s songs such as 'Freiheit', from the German International Brigade, 'The United Front Song' (Brecht/Eisler), 'The Peat Bog Soldiers', and the Spanish song 'The Four Generals', were popular as a confirmation that the Australian labour movement was not isolated.

I'M GOING BACK AGAIN TO YARRAWONGA p 136
By Neil McBeath, arranged by Claude McGlynn and copyrighted to Francis Day and Hunter Ltd., London, 1919, released locally by Albert and Son, Sydney. A song obviously written on the 'It's a Long Way to Tipperary' model, with a modification of the formal melodic design towards the AABA pattern favoured by the classic 32-bar ballad which was becoming standard in popular songs of this period.

GO TO THE WAR, TOILER p 138
The words are by K.N. Pepper, the pen name of William Robert Winspear, (see: *The Mightier Pen* by Verity Burgmann in *Rebels and Radicals* ed. Eric Fry, George Allen and Unwin, Sydney, 1983), the socialist newspaper editor who first produced the *Radical* in 1887, a paper whose extreme views attracted the attention of the police as well as the newly formed Labor Party and the Australian Socialist Party. Winspear's first contribution to the latter party's paper the *International Socialist* appeared in December 1910. He was later its editor until 1916. The tune to 'Go to the War, Toiler' is 'Ring the Bell Watchman', (slightly adjusted), by Henry Clay Work (1832-1884). See: 'Click Go the Shears'. The song is included in *Socialist Songs* (Socialist Labor Party of Australia, 1927, in the State Library of Victoria.)

THE PEATBOG SOLDIERS p 139
The air for this was a favourite marching song of the International Brigades during the Spanish Civil War. It was collected by the composer Hanns Eisler and disseminated widely thereafter, but its origins seem to be older than that suggests, since the song as a whole is believed to have come out of the Borgermoor concentration camp in 1933. However, Pierre Martinot, who was a prisoner in Dachau in 1944-5, claims that the old prisoners there said it was created at Dachau and then smuggled into Borgermoor. It commemorates the prisoners who were marched, day after day, to the bog to dig peat. As they marched, shovels on shoulders, they sang this subversive song, risking death should the guards realise the meaning of the words. It was eventually forbidden, not for its meaning, but for the gusto with which it was sung. (See Fowke and Glazer *Songs of Work and Protest*.) There are some Australians who remember the song, the work, the two wars and the camps.

KEVIN CONWAY p 140
The first Australian soldier to die in the Vietnam War was warrant officer Kevin Conway. He was killed in July 1966. The words and music are by Clem Parkinson, a member of the New Theatre Drama Group and of the Victorian Folk Music Club.

THE FIXIN' TO DIE RAG p 141
'The Fixin' to Die Rag' was written by Joseph McDonald (b. 1 January 1942, El Monte, California, named for Joe Stalin by his leftist parents). McDonald was lead vocalist and rhythm guitar for the 1960s political rock group *Country Joe and the Fish*. In 1965, after moving to Berkeley, McDonald met Barry (the Fish) Melton (lead guitar, b. 1949, Brooklyn, NY) on the local folk circuit, and with three friends — Bruce Barthol (bass, b. 1949, Berkeley, California), David Cohen (lead guitar and keyboards, b. 1944, NY City) and Chicken Hirsch (drums, b. 1942) the act became *Country Mao and the Fish* (the name derived from a Chairman Mao quotation.) The group gained its

original reputation by appearances at the Berkeley student demonstrations, where their 'Fixin' to Die Rag' and 'Fish Cheer' became protest anthems, In late 1966 they signed on with Vanguard to record as *Country Joe and the Fish*. Their first album of protest songs, *Electric Music for the Mind and Body* appeared in mid 1967. Their fame was at its height when they appeared at the Woodstock Festival in 1969 and in the subsequent film. (See *Rock On* by Norm.N. Nile Vol II, NY, Thomas Y. Cornwell, 1978.)

The song was well known in Australia where it was adopted by the generation eligible for conscription and service in Vietnam. Ragtime is a synthesis of military marches, Euro-American dances (Polka, Quadrille, Schottische), popular music and saloon music. The uniting link is syncopated rhythm, also found in African, Caribbean and Afro-American music. The synthesis goes back to the travelling black pianists of the American midwest, but the first printed rag — January 1897 — was composed by a white bandmaster, William H. Krell — 'Mississippi Rag'. Two years later black composers' rags began to find their way into print. The ragtime craze reached a climax in 1910 then began to fade, though elements survive in jazz and other popular forms. Probably the most famous name among its originators is that of pianist-composer Scott Joplin (b. Texas 1868), whose 'Maple Leaf Rag', published 1891, became the model for later versions of the form.

CANAKKALE ICINDE — AT GALLIPOLI   p 143

A Turkish song about the encounter at Gallipoli when Australians were the enemy, from *Kriva Reka: A Rich Celebration of Balkan Life*, by Linda Dawson and Hatice Basarin (The Boite, Melbourne, 1985). No composer or poet is named but the song is given as originating in Thrace, the eastern section of the Balkan Peninsula, bounded on the north by the Danube and on the south by the Aegean. The Gallipoli Peninsula was once part of Thrace. At various times Thrace has been colonised by the Greeks, the Persians, the Bulgarians and the Turks.

The usual accompanying instrument for such Thracian songs is the saz, a long necked lute with three courses each of two strings. The bowl is carved from a single piece of wood. The melody is played on the top course of strings and the other strings provide a drone, nearly always as open strings. The table of the bowl is struck with the fingers of the right hand to provide rhythmic additions. The neck is fretted with wrap around wires. These are spaced, not according to the Western tempered scale as with the guitar, but according to the principles of Turkish and Arabic classical music theory. I have suggested an open D tuning as given in the body of the song merely as a reasonable substitute, nothing more.

EL PUEBLO UNIDO   p 144

A Chilean song from the left wing 'new song movement' founded on the work of the song collector and writer Violetta Parra (1918–67). In the 1960s, popular political song movements sprang up all over South America, revitalising traditional music everywhere and providing a vehicle for political protest. In Chile the movement spread through the penas (the left wing music clubs) and through the work of the recording company founded to popularise it, Discoteca del Cantar Populat, eventually finding its way to Australia through the Chilean migrant communities where it remains a cultural force.

'El Pueblo Unido' was written by Sergio Ortega in 1972. It has been popularised outside Chile by exiled music groups, notably by Quilapayun. Quilapayun and Illimani were touring Europe at the time of the coup and both groups have chosen to remain in exile.

BELLA CIAO   p 146
SEBBEN CHE SIAMO DONNE   p 147

From the repertoire of Bella Ciao, the performance group created in 1977 and allied to the Italian Federation of Migrant Workers and Their Families (FILEF) in Sydney. The group is concerned at the absence of traditional music in the Australian-Italian community. Its ambition is: 'to retrieve songs from the Italian popular tradition, particularly the songs from the workers' movement, the Resistance, women's songs, work songs, children's songs and the songs of migration'... 'Our aim is not only to keep alive popular Italian music in the Australian community but also to consciously contribute to the development of a more open and progressive Italo-Australian culture'. (Sleevenotes. Cassette of Bella Ciao songs released by FILEF, Leichhardt, 1982.)

'Bella Ciao' a traditional women's work song from the northern rice fields supplied the tune for words created by the Italian resistance movement during World War 2. 'Bella Ciao' (Farewell, beautiful), is a partisan invention, not a historical figure.

'Sebben che siamo donne' is a song from the 1870-90 agricultural depression in the Po valley. It describes the rise of worker and peasant movements at that time. It passed into oral tradition and survives in many forms. The last verse is a mobile strophe or 'floater', a device found in many Italian songs. The musical style is typical of northern Italian idioms, with a solo and choral response. The tune is constructed with the possibility of harmonising in parallel thirds in mind.

The song regained popularity during the Italian folk festivals of the 1960s. It was featured in the Bella Ciao show of the 1964 Spoleto Festival. In the 1970s it was adopted by the Italian feminist movement.

BALLAD OF THE SUNWORSHIPPERS   p 149

The words are by Nazim Hikmet, written in 1925. The music is by Yeni Dunya (Members of the New World Chorus). Nazim Hikmet was a dissident Turkish poet born in Istanbul in 1902. He died in Moscow in 1963. In 1950 he was awarded the World Peace Prize at a time when an international committee of writers, artists and intellectuals was campaigning for his release from prison where he was serving a 28 year sentence for inciting revolt. He was released under a general amnesty the same year but was obliged to leave Turkey for Russia to avoid being drafted into the Turkish army - at the age of 48. Much of his poetry was written in jail and smuggled out. His writings in Turkish are highly regarded and his name honoured.

BIR MAYIS p 151
Words and music by Timur Selcuk, a popular performer in Turkey. Composed in the late 1970s, 'Bir Mayis' commemorates the May Day worker's anti-government demonstrations in Istanbul, first celebrated in 1976, using the annual spring festival events for political protest. The 1977 demonstrations ended in violence as military police were called on to intervene. Banned in Istanbul in 1978-9, May Day was nonetheless celebrated in smaller towns. In 1980 it was forbidden everywhere. Left wing Turkish workers in Australia take May Day very seriously because of these associations.

BELLOGIANNIS LIVES p 153
Nikos Bellogiannis was a Greek communist party member who was exiled to eastern Europe after the defeat of the Greek leftist forces in the Greek civil war. He returned to Greece and was arrested in 1952 for having entered the country illegally. He was tried with twenty-eight others for spying. Bellogiannis was accused of being the ring leader and eventually, with seven of the others, sentenced to death. Four were executed in March 1952. International protests were made.

Though this is a later song, it follows some of the stylistic features of the *andartika* or rebel songs of the resistance movement which fought a persistent guerilla campaign against German occupation, and subsequently against the right wing government forces which were established, supported by the western allied powers, after the liberation of Greece.

Many of these partisan songs are similar to the *klephtic* songs about the heroic bandit figures who fought against Turkish occupation, and in the song about Bellogiannis the same heroic mood is evoked.

Andartika songs were banned for over thirty years. It was only in 1974 that the bans were lifted. (See: *Greek Music From Ancient Times to the Modern Period*, The Boite, Melbourne, c.1979.)

AUSTRALIAN STEELWORKS (STILVORK AUSTRALISKI) p 155
Vaska Ilieva, the composer of this song, is regarded as a legend in Yugoslavia. Born in the village of Drachevo in the district of Skopsko Pole, she made her first public appearance in 1950 with the national Macedonian Folk Ensemble and rose rapidly to become a national figure. Since 1954 she has been associated with Radio Skopje, but has also travelled extensively wherever Macedonians have migrated. She is, in effect, a travelling ambassador for her people. During one of her Australian tours she was taken to see the steelworks in Woollongong where she met Macedonian workers. She wrote this song the following day. She has recorded over 500 songs for radio but there are six commercial LPs and several singles available. She has written some 70 songs in that repertoire. *Stilvork Australiski* appears in the album: *Orkestarot na goce ristevski*. The instruments used for the recording are bass guitar, two piano accordions, guitar, tarabuka and clarinet.

THE COMMONWEALTH OF TOIL p 157
One of the great labour anthems, with words by Ralph Chaplin (see also 'Solidarity Forever') and set to the tune of 'Darling Nellie Gray', an anti-slavery song popular with the northern forces in the American Civil War, and composed by B.R. Hanby.

In 1905 the Industrial Workers of the World (IWW), nicknamed the Wobblies, was inaugurated in Chicago to organise unskilled industrial and farm workers rejected by the American Federation of Labor, the main trade union body. The Wobblies used music and poetry to spread their message. In 1908-9 they published the first edition of the long lived *Little Red Song Book* using songs by T-bone Smith, Harry McClintock, Richard Brazier, Joe Hill and Ralph Chaplin. The cover of the book read: 'IWW Songs — To Fan the Flames of Discontent'. The Wobblies motto was 'Sing and Fight'.

On the recording cited the song is attributed to D. Hatzi and D. Penti

TODAY, BLACK IS THE SKY p 159
A song composed and written by Kostas Tsourdalakis, a Cretan poet, musician and activist in the Cretan community and the ALP who now lives in Broadmeadows, Melbourne. He is a noted player of the laouto (the upright bowed fiddle used in Crete for dance music and song accompaniment) and is a prolific composer of songs and poems, often drawing on the poetic tradition of Cretan verse and musical forms.

The song describes the sacking of the Whitlam government and the installation of Fraser as caretaker prime minister. Tsourdalakis wrote the song in the brief period of political confusion which took place before the subsequent election of the Fraser government.

The music is taken from a Cretan seventeenth century heroic romance, the *Erotokitos*. Along with the textual style, the choice of music demonstrates a great seriousness towards the subject matter. In *Meanjin* No. I, 1983 (pp. 120-139) musicologist Peter Parkhill goes into considerable detail about music and text. The song may be heard on *Cretan Traditional Music in Australia*, Kostas and George Tsourdalakis, TAR 010 (Traditional Australian Records, Melbourne).

THE MARSEILLAISE p 162
'The Marseillaise' words and music by Rouget de Lisle (1760–1836). The French national anthem and the international song of revolution though the young French captain who wrote it was loyal to his king and did not conceive the song in terms of revolt or revolution. He was a talented musician and was asked to write this song in April 1792 while he was stationed at Strasbourg — an official request. News had come that France had declared war on Prussia and Hungary. Inscribed 'Chant de guerre pour l'armee du Rhin', it was published in Strasbourg and Paris and was sung at a banquet in Marseilles as volunteers were leaving for Paris. This battalion sang it along the route and at the storming of the Tuilleries. The Paris mob took it up

and it was renamed 'The Marseillaise' in honour of the volunteers. The composer had fired off at German princes and Prussian soldiers but the mob reaimed the song at France's rulers. De Lisle was discharged from the army for his royalist leanings and jailed but escaped the guillotine and in 1794 reenlisted in the army of the French Republic. On 15 July 1795 the song became the official national anthem and a symbol of the revolution, the rights of man, liberty, equality and fraternity. European rebellions and revolutions since then have used it for the same purpose.

THE INTERNATIONALE p 164
An international proletarian hymn, the party hymn of the Communist Party of the Soviet Union and other communist parties, it has been sung widely in Australia by left wing workers, students and intellectuals. The text is by Eugene Pottier (1871, published 1887) and the music by Pierre Degeyter (1888). It was first performed 23 June 1888 by the Lille workers' choir of the Workers Lyre Choral Society at a festival of newspaper vendors and published that year in Lille by M.Boldoduc. In 1894 the French socialist A. Gosselin was sentenced to jail for writing the second edition of the music of the song. It was first translated from the French in the 1890s and spread worldwide wherever socialism was espoused. (See: *Great Soviet Encyclopaedia*, Macmillan, NY, 1974.)

THE RED FLAG p 166
'The Red Flag' was written by Jim Connell in 1889. He was an Irish journalist who used to say: 'I was educated under a hedge for a few weeks'. He sent 'The Red Flag's' verses to a weekly paper called *Justice*; it appeared in the Christmas issue, and within a week it was being sung in Liverpool and Glasgow. (See *Songs of Work and Protest* compiled by Edith Fowke and Joe Glazer. Dover Press. NY, 1973. p.191.)

According to Fowke and Glazer the use of the tune 'Maryland' (or 'Tannenbaum') derives from Adolphe Smith Headingley. These writers also give an account of the singing of 'The Red Flag' in the House of Commons on the postwar election of the Labour government, which gives an indication of the importance of this song for the British labour movement.

Connell's original verses are often shortened these days but I have given the full eight verses as they appear in *Socialist Songs* (Published by the Victorian Socialist Party, c. 1910).

According to *The Builders Labourers Songbook* (The Australian Building Construction Employees' and Builders Labourers' Federation, Melbourne, 1975), Connell was inspired by the London dock strike of 1889, the work of the Irish Land League, and the hanging of the Chicago workers in 1887.

Socialist Songs has 'The Red Flag' verses sung to the tune known as 'The White Cockade'. Since the Socialist party of Victoria was musically quite active at the time, with a newspaper which regularly featured poems and songs and supported a choir, orchestra and brass band, I am inclined to think the attribution of an associated air is authentic. A.L. Lloyd says of the two tunes: 'Jim Connell...meant it to be sung to...'The White Cockade'. Staider counsel in the Social Democratic Federation threw out the folk tune in favour of the pedestrian German melody of 'Tannenbaum', a tune which as Connell scornfully said, is 'calculated to remind people of their sins and frighten them into repentance'. (Lloyd, 1967, pp.379-80.)

'The White Cockade' is a march tune, probably of 18th century Scottish origin. It was used frequently as the vehicle of texts in the 19th century, and in Ireland was associated with the Jacobite cause and hence with the cause of Irish Catholicism and national independence. It was one of the tunes described by a Select Committee on the Orange Lodges (c.1835) as 'obnoxious to the Protestant'. No doubt Connell the Irishman had its significance as a tune of rebellion in mind when he chose it for his internationalist text.

SOLIDARITY FOREVER p 168
Words by Ralph Chaplin to the tune of the American Civil War song 'John Brown's Body'. Originally there were six verses as given here, but three are all that are in present use. 'Solidarity Forever' became the most popular union song in North America. Chaplin was a famous poet, artist, writer and organiser for the Industrial Workers of the World. He wrote his text on 17 January 1915, inspired by the earlier coal mining strike in the Kanawha Valley. The tune, 'John Brown's Body', also carries the text for 'The Battle Hymn of the Republic'. It began life as a camp meeting hymn 'Say Brothers Will You Meet Us' by a southerner composer, William Steffe, written in the mid-1850s. It was taken up by the 12th Massachusetts Regiment stationed at Warren in Boston Harbour. The parody is said to have originated there.

In 1859 the northern hero John Brown was hanged for an armed attempt to free slaves at Harper's Ferry. In December 1861, Julia Ward Howe saw and heard marching soldiers passing her Washington hotel singing 'John Brown's Body'; the Union campfires were visible from her window. Inspired by the sight, she subsequently wrote the verses of 'The Battle Hymn of the Republic', which were published early in 1862 in the *Atlantic Monthly*. *The Labour Song Book* (c. 1910, published Melbourne, possible by the *Tocsin* newspaper: in Merrifield Collection, State Library of Victoria) gives William Morris's verses 'The March of the Workers' to the same tune.

SELECT BIBLIOGRAPHY

A Collection of Australian Folk Songs and Traditional Ballads. Folk Lore Council of Australia, 1967.
Anderson, Hugh McDonald, *The Dying Stockman, A Ballad.* Ram's Skull Press, Ferntree Gully, 1954.
— *Goldrush Songster.* Ram's Skull Press, Ferntree Gully, 1958.
— *Songs of Billy Barlow.* Ram's Skull Press, Ferntree Gully, 1956.
— *Time Out of Mind.* National Press, Melbourne, 1974.
— *The Colonial Minstrel.* F.W. Cheshire, Melbourne, 1960.
— *The Story of Australian Folksong.* Hill of Content, Melbourne, 1970.
Australian Folk-Ballads and Singers. Russel Ward. Meanjin, No. 3, Vol. B, 1954.
Australian Folk Songs of the Land and its People. Compiled by the Folk Lore Council of Australia. Lowden Publishing Co., Kilmore, Victoria, 1974.
Australian Tradition. Folklore Society of Victoria and the Victorian Folk Music Club, 1964 1974
Bagot, Alec. *Coppin the Great.* Melbourne University Press, 1965.
Bunting, Edward. *The Ancient Music of Ireland.* Waltons, Dublin, 1969; and incorporating *A General Collection of Ancient Irish Music*, Power, Dublin, 1796. *A General Collection of the Ancient Music of Ireland,* Clementi, London, 1809, and *A Collection of the Ancient Music of Ireland*, University Press, Dublin, 1840.
Bushwacker Songs, Old and New. Bush Music Club, Sydney, 1954-1955.
Chappell, William. *Popular Music of the Olden Time.* Chappell, London, 1855. Re-issue by Dover, New York, 1965.
Costello, Eileen. *Amhrain Mhuighe Seola.* Traditional Folk Songs from Galway and May. Three Candle Press, Dublin, 1919.
Country Music in Australia. Eric Watson Rodeo Publications and Eric Watson, Sydney, 1975.
Coxon's Comic Songster. W.M. Brown, Ballarat, 1858-1859
Craig, Warren. *Sweet and Lowdown.* New Jersey, 1978.
Curwen, J. Spencer. *Folk Songs of Many Lands.* J. Curwen and Sons London, 1911.
Davison, Peter. *Songs of the British Music Hall.* Oak, New York, 1971.
Edwards, Ronald George. *The Overlander Songbook.* Ram's Skull Press, Ferntree Gully, 1956.
— *A Quartpot of Songs.* Ram's Skull Press, Ferntree Gully, 1966.
— *Australian Bawdy Ballads.* Ram's Skull Press, Ferntree Gully, 1972.
— [ed.] *Northern Folk.* Later *National Folk.* Cairns Folk Club, n.d.
The Big Book of Australian Folk Song. Ridby, Adelaide, 1976.
Eureka, the Songs That Made Australia. Compiled by Warren Fahey, Omnibus Press, Sydney, 1984.
Flashes of Merriment: A Century of Humorous Songs in America 1805-1905. Uni. of Oklahoma Press, Norman, Oklahoma, 1971.
Folk Songs of Canada. Edited by Edith Fowke and Richard Johnston, Ontario, 1954.
Game, Peter. *The Music Sellers.* The Hawthorn Press, Melbourne, 1976.
Hood, Alex. *Australian Folk Songs Songster.* J.Albert and Son, Sydney, 1964.
Hugill, Stan. *Shanties from the Seven Seas.* Routledge & Kegan Paul, London, 1961.
— *Shanties and Sailors' Songs.* Herbert Jenkins, London, 1969.
— *Songs of the Sea.* McGraw-Hill CBook Co., New York., 1977.
Hurd Collection. Cutting Book. c.1894-1900, as cited by Ron Edwards in *The Big Book of Australian Folk Song.*
Ingleton, Geoffrey. *True Patriots All.* Halstead Press, Sydney, 1952.
Jenkins, Graham. *Songs of the Great Australian Balladists.* Rigby, Adelaide, 1978.
Jones, Percy. *Burl Ives Folio of Australian Folk Songs.* Southern Music Publishing Co., Sydney, 1953.
Journal of the Folk Song Society. Vols 1-8 Nos 1-35). London, 1889-1931. *(From 1932 this became English Folk Dance and Song Society Journal,* London, 1932-1965, after which it is known as *Folk Music Journal*, London, 1965- .)
Journal of the Irish Folk Song Society. London, 1903-1939. Republished by Dawson, London, 1967
Joyce, Patrick Weston. *Old Irish Folk Music and Song.* Dublin, 1909.
Joy Durst Collection. Victorian Folk Music Club, Melbourne, c.1971.
Kennedy, Peter. *Folksongs of Britain and Ireland.* Cassell, London, 1975.
Kidson, Frank. *Traditional Tunes.* Charles Taphouse and Son, Oxford 1891. Republished by S.R. Publishers, Menston, 1970.
Laade, Wolfgang. Neue Musik in Afrika, Asien und Ozeanien. Heidelberg, 1971.
Korson, George. *Minitrels of the Mine Patch.* Folklore Associates, Hatboro, 1964.
Lahey, John. *Great Australian Folk Songs.* Hill of Content, Melbourne, 1965.
Lavater, Louis. (ed.) *Swagman's Treasure.* Allan and Co., Melbourne, 1938.

Lawrence, Vera Brodsky. *Music for Patriots, Politicians and Presidents.* Macmillan, NY, 1975.

Lloyd, Albert Lancaster. *Banks of the Condamine* (record notes to record of same title). Wattle Records, 1957.

— *Across the Western Plains.* Wattle Recording D.I., 1958.

— *Her Mantle So Green* (record notes to 12T 123). Topic Records, London, c.1965.

— *Folk Song in England*, Lawrence and Wishart, London, 1967. Republished by Panther, London, 1969.

— *The Folksongs of Britain* (notes to the series of LP recordings). Topic Records, London, 1968.

— *Australian Bush Songs* (record notes to same title). Riverside Records, USA, n.d.

Long, Lionel and Jenkins, Graham. *(Favourite Australian Bush Songs*, Rigby, Adelaide, 1964.

Magoffin, Richard. *Fair Dinkum Matilda.* Mimosa Press, Charters Towers, 1973.

Manifold, John. *The Penguin Australian Song Book.* Penguin Books, Australia Ltd, Melbourne, 1964.

— *Who Wrote the Ballads.* Australasian Book Society, Sydney, 1964.

Manifold, John and Edwards, Ron. *Bandicoot Ballads.* Ram's Skull Press, Ferntree Gully, 1951, 1953, 1955.

Mendelsohn, Oscar. *A Waltz with Matilda.* Lansdowne Press, Melbourne.

Meredith, John. *Duke of the Outback.* Red Rooster Press, Melbourne, 1983: Studies in Australian folklore No. 5.

Meredith, John and Anderson, Hugh. *Folk Songs of Australia.* Ure Smith, Sydney, 1967.

Meredith, John and Scott, Alan *Authentic Australian Bush Ballads. Southern Music Publishing Co.,* 1960.

Meredith, John and Scott, Bill. *Ned Kelly.* Lansdowne, Sydney, 1980.

Moffat, Alfred. *The Minstrelsy of Ireland.* Augner and Co., London, 1897.

Nathan, Hans. *Dan Emmett and the Rise of Early Negro Minstrelsy.* Norman, Oklahoma University Press, Oklahoma, 1962.

Nettle, Reginald. *Seven Centuries of Popular Song.* Phoenix House, London, 1956.

O Lachlainn, Colm. *Irish Street Ballads.* Three Candles, Dublin, 1939. Republished by Pan Books, London, 1978.

— *More Irish Street Ballads.* Three Candles, Dublin, 1965. Republished by Pan Books, London, 1978.

O'Neill's Music of Ireland. Edited by Francis O'Neill and arranged by James O'Neill. First published 1903 and 1907 out of the 1890-1900 Chicago Music Club, and reissued by Daniel Michael Collins, New York, 1979.

O'Sullivan, Donal J. (ed.). 'The Bunting Collection of Irish Folk Music and Song' in *Journal of the Irish Folk Song Society.* Vols XXII-XXIII. London, 1927-1939.

Page, Martin, *Kiss Me Goodnight Sergeant Major.* Hart-Davis MacGibbon, 1973.

Passing the Time in Ballymenone: Culture and History of an Ulster Community. Henry Glassie University of Pennsylvania Press, Philadelphia, USA 1982.

Pearce, Harry Hastings. *On the Origins of Waltzing Matilda.* The Hawthorn Press, Melbourne, 1971.

Pearsall, Ronald. *Edwardian Popular Song.* David and Charles, London, 1975.

Petrie, George. *The Petrie Collection of the Ancient Music of Ireland.* Boosey and Co., London, 1902-1905.

Purslow, Frank (ed.). *Marrow Bones, English Folk Songs from the Hammond and Gardiner MSS.* E.F.D.S. Publications, 1965

Radic, Thérèse. A Treasury of Favourite Australian Songs. Viking, Melbourne, 1988.

Rebel Voices. Edited by J.L. Kornbluh. Ann Arbor: The Uni. of Michigan Press, 1964.

Reedy River Song Book. Songs from Reedy River by Dick Diamond. Prepared by David E.Milliss and John Meredith. New Theatre, Sydney, May 1966.

Scotland Sings: Folksongs and Ballads of Scotland. Oak, 1965.

Scott, Bill. *The Second Penguin Australian Songbook.* Penguin Books, Australia Ltd., Melbourne, 1980.

Sears, Minnie Earl [ed.]. *Song Index.* H.W. Wilson, New York, 1926.

— *Song Index Supplement.* H.W. Wilson, New York, 1934.

Seeger, Peggy and McColl, Ewan. *The Singing Island.* Mills Music, London, 1960.

Seeger, Pete. *American Favourite Ballads.* Oak Publications, New York, 1961.

Seghers, Jean Clouzet. *La Nouvelle Chanson Chillienne.* Paris 1975.

Sharp, Cecil J. [ed.]. *English Folk Songs.* Vols I-II. Novello, London, 1920. Reprinted as one book, 1959.

— *English County Songs.* Novello, London, 1961.

Simpson, Claude M. *The British Broadside Ballad and its Music.* Rutgers University Press, New Brunswick, 1966.

Singabout. Bush Music Club, Sydney.

Smith, James T. and Maxfield, W.H. (eds.). *One Hundred Gems of Scottish Song.* Bayley and Ferguson, London, n.d.

Smith, Laura. *The Music of the Waters.* Kegan Paul, Trench and Co., London, 1888.

Songs of the Kelly Country. Bush Music Club, Sydney, 1955.

Songs of the Redcoats 1642-1902. Lewis Winstock. Leo Cooper Ltd, London, 1970.

Speath, Sigmund. *Read 'em and Weep.* Doubleday, Page & Co, NY, 1926.

Stand Together: a new songbook. edited and published by the Hackney and Islington Music Workshop, London 1978.

Stewart, Douglas and Keesing, Nancy. *Australian Bush Ballads.* Angus and Robertson, Sydney, 1955.

— *Old Bush Songs.* Angus and Robertson, Sydney, 1976.

Thatcher, Charles. *Thatcher's Colonial Songs.* Facsimile edition, South Australian Library Council, 1964.

The Anzacs. Compiled by Ted Egan, text by Peter Forrest. Greenhouse Publications, Melbourne, 1986.

The Bushwackers, Australian Song Book. Anne O'Donovan, Melbourne, 1978.

The Best of Bawdry. Don Laycock. Angus and Robertson, Sydney, 1982.

The Folk Songs of North America. Alan Lomax. Cassell, London, 1960.

The Great Song Thesaurus. Roger Lox and Frederick Smith,

editors. NY; OUP; 1984.

The Melbourne University Students' Songbook. Edited by Niall Brennan. Students' Representative Council, University of Melbourne, 1946.

The Overlanders. Compiled by Ted Egan, text by Peter Forrest. Greenhouse Publications, Melbourne, 1984.

The Queensland Centenary Pocket Songbook. Foreword by Dr Robert Dalley-Scarlett. Edwards and Shaw, Sydney, n.d.

The Redgum Songbook: Stubborn Words, Flagrant Vices. Tombala Publishing, Sydney, n.d. circa 1982.

The Roche Collection of Traditional Irish Music. Ossian Publication, Cork, Ireland, 1982.

The Second Bushwackers Australian Song Book. Compiled by Dobe Newton, music by Roger Corbett. Anne O'Donovan, Melbourne, 1983.

The Shearers. Compiled by Ted Egan, text by Peter Forrest. Greenhouse Publications, Melbourne, 1984.

Thorp, N. Howard ('Jack'). *Songs of the Cowboys.* Expanded by E. Austin and Alta S. Fife. Bramhall House, New York, 1966.

Tibbs Popular Song Book. Sydney, 1887.

Vaughan Williams, Ralph. *Folk Songs of the Four Seasons.* Oxford University Press, 1950.

Vaughan Williams, Ralph and Lloyd, A.L. *The Penguin Book of English Folksong.* Penguin, Harmondsworth, Middlesex, 1959. Reprinted 1968.

Vennard, A.V. ('Bill Bowyang'). *Bush Recitations.* Six booklets. 1932-1940.

Wannan, Bill. *The Folklore of the Irish in Australia.* Currey O'Neil, Melbourne, 1980.

Waters, Edgar. *Convicts and Currency Lads* (record notes to title of the same name). Wattle Records, 1957.

Watson, Eric. *Country Music in Australia.* Second edition. Rodeo Publications, Eastlake, N.S.W., 1975.

Zimmerman, George Denis. *Songs of Irish Rebellion: political street ballads and rebel songs.* 1780-1900. Folklore Associates, Hatboro, Pennsylvania, 1967.

— *Irish Poliical Street Ballads and Rebel Songs 1780-1900.* Genève Imprimerie la Sirène, 1966.

Index of First Lines

A noble whale ship and commander   2
A strapping young stockman lay dying   29
A young man left his native town   42
As we come marching, marching in the beauty of the day   112
Arise ye sons of France to glory!   162
Arise ye workers from your slumbers   164
Australia's a big country   57

By profession and birth I'm a man of the earth   46

Come, all you young Australians, and everyone besides   3
Come listen all you Nungas, come listen to my tale   99

Each Saturday morning I crawl out of bed   95

Far and wide as the eye can wander   139
Farewell and adieu to you, sweet Brisbane ladies   24
From the workshops off we go   67

Given that we are women   147

Hark, hark, the dogs are barking   12
He hasn't had a break you know for twenty seven years   129
How we suffered grief and pain   31
Hush little baby, don't say a word   114
I am the one that has carried the can   113
I draw for Speckle's Mill, bullocky-O   36
I dreamed a doctor told a judge   119
I heard a week before Christmas   127
I left school when I could have stayed   120
I was a cane cutter, but now I'm at sea   30
I went out, I fought for my country   83
I'm a stockman to my trade   22
I'm on me way down to the quay   59
I'm travelling down the Castlereagh   20
In the gloom of mighty cities   157
It is only oppression that the days bring   151
It is strike time in the dear old Lithgow valley   48
I've sailed the North Atlantic   63
I've shore at Burrabogie, and I've shore at Toganmain   13

Kevin Conway was a soldier who left his native shore   140

My love he is a teamster, and a handsome man he is   37

Ned Kelly was born in a ramshackle hut   5
Now, all you blokes take my advice   39
Now Digger was a soldier, and he sailed across the sea   136

O cock of the morning   65

O hark the dogs are barking, love   11
Oh, hear the railway whistle boys   70
Oh, my traps are all a-jangle   33
Oh Peter's a cabbie on Adelaide's roads   124
Oh time is a power that's precious and golden   131
Oh, there once was a swagman camped by a billabong   80
Oh, when I was a boy in Carlingford   123
Oh you steelworks, steelworks of Australia   155
On an island in a river   87
On the forty pound rails steamed a C-16   72
Once a jolly swagman camp'd by a billabong   78
Once a little maiden climbed an old man's knee   52
One day I was walking, I heard a complaining   105
One morning I awoke   146
One Sunday morning as I went walking   1
Out across the Nullarbor, where roos and rabbits roam   34
Out on the board, the old shearer stands   8

Poor bugger me, Gurindji   103
Poor Dad, he got five years or more   108

Screw down the saddle, make 'er good and tight   88
Some men are pink or yellow   69
Soon we will capture the sun   149
Spanish heavens spread their brilliant star-light   135
Stand up and sing for victory will come   144

The bore wheel's a turnin'   126
The cocky complained that our cut was not clean   32
The early morning train from Mt Victoria   74
The fir trees and plane trees they know him   153
The job is hard, but hard or not   117
The miner he goes and he changes his clothes   43
The night is dark and stormy and the sky is clouded o'er   25
The people's flag is deepest red   166
The price of wool was falling in 1891   51
The shearing's nearly over, but with many, much I fear   18
The springtime it brings on the shearing   10
The sun was blazing in the sky and waves of shimmering heat   81
The Wilcannia boys are all down this year   101
The year was nineteen sixty four   40
There are women of many descriptions   110
There is a mirrored market at Gallipoli   143
There is a shed near Edmonton   118
There was a mild colonial boy   7
There was a Wild Colonial Boy   6
There was an old man who lived in the woods   107
There's a land that bears a well known name   44
There's a lonely grave half hidden   27
There's a struggle going on in the West, boys   54

There's a trade you all know well 28
They came from the Clyde 66
They tell of one Port Melbourne man 56
They tramp there in their legions 77
They're leaving ship and station 58
This old town has had its day 75
Today, black is the sky 159

War is in Europe, toiler, blasting the land 138
Way down in Tennessee 90
We been leaving Mackay 62
We started down from Reio (Roto) 14
We welcome you back, and we greet you with love 61

Well come on all of you big strong men 141
Well I am a rambling lad me story it is sad 16
Well I was born in the scrub of the outback 97
Well you work to earn a living 93
We're really on the way, girls 115
We've got a little song to sing 91
When I first arrived in Quirindi 50
When the harvest time comes, Gentle Annie 109
When the Union's inspiration 168
Where a giant copper mine feeds a hungry railway line 121
Working until Friday night on city council rounds 133

You are just a lonely battler 84